Scribe Publications
THE WAY OF THE KNIFE

THE WAY OF THE KNIFE

THE CIA, A SECRET ARMY, AND
A WAR AT THE ENDS OF THE EARTH

MARK MAZZETTI

SCRIBE
Melbourne • London

Scribe Publications Pty Ltd
18–20 Edward St, Brunswick, Victoria 3056, Australia
50A Kingsway Place, Sans Walk, London, EC1R 0LU, United Kingdom

Published by Scribe 2013

This edition published by arrangement with the Penguin Group,
Penguin Group (USA) Inc., New York.

Text design by Nicole LaRoche
Printed and bound by CPI Group (UK) Ltd, Croydon, CR0 4YY

National Library of Australia
Cataloguing-in-Publication data   356.160973

Mazzetti, Mark, author.

The Way of the Knife: the CIA, a secret army, and a war at the ends
of the Earth / Mark Mazzetti.

9781922070661 (paperback)
9781922247063 (hardback)
9781922072573 (e-book)

1. United States. Central Intelligence Agency. 2. United States. Department
of Defense. 3. National security–United States–Decision making.
4. Interagency coordination–United States. 5. United States–Military policy–Decision
making.

356.160973

scribepublications.com.au
scribepublications.co.uk

B000 000 010 3369

FOR LINDSAY AND MAX

CONTENTS

PRINCIPAL CHARACTERS

THE CENTRAL INTELLIGENCE AGENCY (CIA)

Charles Allen, Assistant Director, Collection, 1998–2005

J. Cofer Black, Director, Counterterrorist Center (CTC), 1999–2002

Dennis Blair, Associate Director, Military Support, 1995–1996; Director of National Intelligence, 2009–2010

Richard Blee, Chief, Alec Station (bin Laden Unit of Counterterrorist Center), 1999–2001

William Casey, Director, 1981–1987

Duane "Dewey" Clarridge, operations officer and founder of the Counterterrorist Center

Raymond Davis, CIA contractor, arrested in Pakistan in 2011

Porter Goss, Director, 2004–2006

Robert Grenier, Chief of Station, Islamabad, 1999–2002; Director, Counterterrorism Center, 2004–2006*

Michael Hayden, Director, 2006–2009

Stephen Kappes, Deputy Director, 2006–2010

Art Keller, operations officer in Pakistan, 2006

Mike, Director, Counterterrorism Center, 2006–

---

* Name of CTC was changed from Counterterrorist Center to Counterterrorism Center in 2005

Ross Newland, operations officer in Latin America and Eastern Europe; later, top official at CIA headquarters

Leon Panetta, Director, 2009–2011

James Pavitt, Deputy Director, Operations, 1999–2004

David Petraeus, Director, 2011–2012; Commander, United States Central Command, 2008–2010

Enrique Prado, operations officer working the Counterterrorist Center and later a Blackwater employee

Jose Rodriguez, Director, Counterterrorist Center, 2002–2004; Deputy Director, Operations, 2004–2007

George Tenet, Director, 1997–2004

DEPARTMENT OF DEFENSE

Robert Andrews, Acting Assistant Secretary of Defense for Special Operations and Low-Intensity Conflict, 2001–2002

Stephen Cambone, Under Secretary of Defense for Intelligence, 2003–2007

Michael Furlong, Defense Department official involved in information operations who eventually oversaw private spying operation

Robert Gates, Secretary of Defense, 2006–2011

General Stanley McChrystal, Commander, Joint Special Operations Command (JSOC), 2003–2008

Admiral William McRaven, Commander, Joint Special Operations Command (JSOC), 2008–2011

Admiral Michael Mullen, Chairman, Joint Chiefs of Staff, 2007–2011

Thomas O'Connell, Assistant Secretary of Defense for Special Operations and Low-Intensity Conflict, 2003–2006

Leon Panetta, Secretary of Defense, 2011–2013

Donald Rumsfeld, Secretary of Defense, 2001–2006

THE WHITE HOUSE

John Brennan, Assistant to the President for Homeland Security and Counterterrorism, 2009–2013

Richard Clarke, Counterterrorism Coordinator, 1998–2001

PAKISTAN

Shakil Afridi, Pakistani physician hired to spy for the CIA

Lt. General Mahmud Ahmed, Director-General, Inter-Services Intelligence (ISI), 1999–2001

Lt. General Ali Jan Aurakzai, Pakistani military commander responsible for operations in Federally Administered Tribal Areas (FATA)

Raymond Davis, CIA contractor arrested in Lahore in 2011

Lt. General Ehsan ul Haq, Director-General, Inter-Services Intelligence, 2001–2004

Jalaluddin Haqqani, leader of criminal network based in Pakistani tribal areas who has carried out attacks against American troops in Afghanistan

General Ashfaq Parvez Kayani, Director-General, Inter-Services Intelligence, 2004–2007; Chief of Army Staff, 2007–

Baitullah Mehsud, Pakistani Taliban leader after the death of Nek Muhammad Wazir

Brigadier-General Asad Munir, ISI station chief in Peshawar, 2001–2003

Cameron Munter, United States Ambassador in Islamabad, 2010–2012

Lt. General Ahmad Shuja Pasha, Director-General, Inter-Services Intelligence, 2008–2012

Hafiz Muhammad Saeed, head of Lashkar-e-Taiba ("Army of the Pure")

Nek Muhammad Wazir, Pakistani Taliban leader in tribal areas

YEMEN

Ibrahim al-Asiri, master bomb maker for al Qaeda in the Arabian
  Peninsula (AQAP)

Abdulrahman al-Awlaki, son of Anwar al-Awlaki

Anwar al-Awlaki, radical preacher and member of AQAP who was an
  American citizen

Ali Abdullah Saleh, President, 1990–2012

SOMALIA

Aden Hashi Farah Ayro, early leader of al Shabaab

Sheikh Hassan Dahir Aweys, leader of Islamic Courts Union

Michele "Amira" Ballarin, American businesswoman and government
  contractor

Saleh Ali Saleh Nabhan, Kenyan member of al Qaeda's East Africa cell
  killed in 2009

Alliance for the Restoration of Peace and Counter-Terrorism (ARPCT),
  collection of CIA-funded Somali warlords

Al Shabaab ("The Youth"), armed wing of Islamic Courts Union

THE WAY
OF THE KNIFE

PROLOGUE:
THE WAR BEYOND

"Good intelligence work, Control had always preached, was gradual and rested on a kind of gentleness. The scalphunters were the exception to his own rule. They weren't gradual and they weren't gentle either. . . ."

—*John le Carré*, Tinker, Tailor, Soldier, Spy

Escorted by Pakistani policemen, the burly American spy was brought into a crowded interrogation room. Amid a clatter of ringing mobile phones and cross talk among the cops speaking a mishmash of Urdu, Punjabi, and English, the investigator tried to decipher the facts of the case.

"America, you from America?"

"Yes."

"You're from America and you belong to the American embassy?"

"Yes," the anxious American voice boomed above the chatter. "My passport—at the site I showed the police officer . . . It's somewhere. It's lost."

On the jumpy video footage of the interrogation, he reached beneath his checkered flannel shirt and produced a jumble of identification badges from a lanyard around his neck. It was one of the few things he had managed to hold on to after the chaotic scene at the traffic circle.

"This is an old badge. This is Islamabad." He showed the badge to the man across the desk and then flipped to a more recent badge proving his employment in the American consulate in Lahore.

A telephone rang, and one of the officers in the crowded room dispatched with the call quickly. "We arrested an embassy man. I will call you back." The interrogation resumed.

"You are working at the consulate general in Lahore?"

"Yes."

"As a . . . ?"

"I, I just work as a consultant there."

"Consultant?" The man behind the desk was skeptical. He paused for a moment and then shot a question in Urdu to another policeman. "And what's the name?"

"Raymond Davis," the officer responded.

"Raymond Davis," the American confirmed. "Can I sit down?"

"Please do. Give you water?" the officer asked.

"Do you have a bottle? A bottle of water?" Davis asked.

Another officer in the room laughed. "You want water?" he asked. "No money, no water."

Behind the chair where Davis had taken a seat, another policeman walked into the room and asked for an update.

"Is he understanding everything? And he just killed two men?"

Raymond Allen Davis—a former high school football and wrestling star from western Virginia, a retired Army Green Beret and onetime private soldier for Blackwater USA, and now a clandestine CIA operative in Pakistan—had hours earlier been navigating dense traffic in Lahore, his thick frame wedged into the driver's seat of a white Honda Civic. A city once ruled by Mughals, Sikhs, and the British, Lahore is Pakistan's cultural and intellectual capital, and for nearly a decade had been on the fringes of America's secret war in Pakistan.

But by 2011, the map of Islamic militancy inside Pakistan had been redrawn, and factions that once had little contact with each other had cemented new alliances to survive the CIA's drone campaign in the western mountains. Groups that had focused most of their energies dreaming up bloody attacks against India had begun aligning themselves closer to al Qaeda and other organizations with a thirst for global jihad. Some of these groups had deep roots in Lahore, which was the very reason why Raymond Davis and a CIA team had set up operations from a safe house in the city.

But now Davis was sitting in a Lahore police station, having shot two young men who had approached his car with guns drawn, while riding a black motorcycle, at a traffic circle congested with cars, bicycles, and rickshaws. Davis had taken his semiautomatic Glock pistol and blown a handful of bullets through the windshield, shattering the glass and hitting one of the men in the stomach, arm, and elsewhere on his body. As the other man fled, Davis got out of his Honda and shot several rounds into his back.

He radioed the American consulate for help, and within minutes a Toyota Land Cruiser was in sight, careering in the wrong direction down a one-way street. But the car struck and killed a young Pakistani motorcyclist and then left with Davis still standing in the middle of the road. An assortment of bizarre paraphernalia was scattered at the scene, including a black mask, approximately one hundred bullets, and a piece of cloth with an American flag. The cell phone inside Davis's car contained photos of Pakistani military installations, taken surreptitiously.

Within days of the debacle at the traffic circle, the CIA director would lie to Pakistan's spymaster during a phone call and private meeting, denying that Davis worked for the CIA. President Barack

Obama was vague during a press conference about Davis's role in the country, calling for the release of "our diplomat in Pakistan." The CIA's station chief in Islamabad, who had arrived in the country just days before the shootings, fought openly with the American ambassador there, insisting that the United States give no ground, and cut no deals, to secure Davis's release. The game in Pakistan had changed, he said, and the time of friendly relations between the CIA and Pakistan's spy service had passed.

From now on, things would be handled according to Moscow Rules—the unwritten, unforgiving ways of spycraft practiced between enemies during the Cold War.

In an instant, the bloody affair seemed to confirm all the conspiracies ginned up inside crowded bazaars and corridors of power in Pakistan: that the United States had sent a vast secret army to Pakistan, men who sowed chaos and violence as part of a covert American war in the country. The wife of one of Davis's victims, convinced that her husband's killer would never be brought to justice, swallowed a lethal amount of rat poison.

But the Davis affair also told a bigger story. The former Green Beret hired by the CIA for a manhunt in Pakistan was the face of an American spy agency that has been transformed after a decade of conflicts far from declared war zones. No longer a traditional espionage service devoted to stealing the secrets of foreign governments, the Central Intelligence Agency has become a killing machine, an organization consumed with man hunting.

And just as the CIA has come to take on tasks traditionally associated with the military, with spies turned into soldiers, so has the opposite occurred. The American military has been dispersed into the dark spaces of American foreign policy, with commando teams running spying missions that Washington would never have dreamed of approving in the years before 9/11. Prior to the attacks of September

11, the Pentagon did very little human spying, and the CIA was not officially permitted to kill. In the years since, each has done a great deal of both, and a military-intelligence complex has emerged to carry out the new American way of war.

The historical contours of the wars in Afghanistan and Iraq are by now well known. But for more than a decade a separate and parallel war has been waged, a dark reflection of the "big wars" that America began after the September 11 attacks. In a shadow war waged across the globe, America has pursued its enemies using killer robots and special-operations troops. It has paid privateers to set up clandestine spying networks and relied on mercurial dictators, unreliable foreign intelligence services, and ragtag proxy armies. In places where the United States couldn't send ground troops, fringe characters material-ized to play outsize roles, including a chain-smoking Pentagon official who teamed up with a CIA figure from the Iran–Contra scandal to run an off-the-books spying operation in Pakistan, and an heiress from the horse country of Virginia, who became obsessed with Soma-lia and convinced the Pentagon to hire her to hunt al Qaeda opera-tives there.

The war has stretched across multiple continents, from the moun-tains of Pakistan to the deserts of Yemen and North Africa, from the simmering clan wars of Somalia to the dense jungles of the Philip-pines. The foundations of the secret war were laid by a conservative Republican president and embraced by a liberal Democratic one who became enamored of what he had inherited. President Barack Obama came to see it as an alternative to the messy, costly wars that topple governments and require years of American occupation. In the words of John Brennan, one of President Obama's closest advisers whom Obama eventually tapped to run the CIA, instead of the "hammer" America now relies on the "scalpel."

The analogy suggests that this new kind of war is without costs or blunders—a surgery without complications. This isn't the case. The way of the knife has created enemies just as it has obliterated them. It has fomented resentment among former allies and at times contributed to instability even as it has attempted to bring order to chaos. It has short-circuited the normal mechanisms for how the United States as a nation goes to war, and turned the American president into the final arbiter of whether specific people in far-off lands live or die. This way of war has had many successes, including the eventual killing of Osama bin Laden and his most trusted followers. But it has also lowered the bar for waging war, and it is now easier for the United States to carry out killing operations at the ends of the earth than at any other time in its history. What follows is a story about an experiment that has lasted more than a decade, and what has emerged from the laboratory.

SIR RICHARD DEARLOVE SAW a glimpse of the future just weeks after the September 11 attacks. The head of the British Secret Intelligence Service, MI6, Dearlove came to the United States with other top British intelligence officials to show solidarity with the United Kingdom's closest ally. Dearlove arrived at CIA headquarters in Langley, Virginia, to deliver the message personally that British spies were opening up their books, giving the CIA rare access to all the MI6 files on members of al Qaeda.

The British had tutored the Americans in the dark arts during World War II but had long approached the spy game differently. In 1943, one member of Winston Churchill's Special Operations Executive complained that the "American temperament demands quick and spectacular results, while the British policy is generally speaking long-term and plodding." He pointed out the dangers of the strategy carried out by the Office of Strategic Services, the CIA's precursor, which relied on blowing up weapons depots, cutting telephone lines, and land-mining enemy supply lines. The Americans had more money than brains, he warned, and the OSS's "hankering after playing cowboys and red Indians" could only lead to trouble for the alliance.

Dearlove had grown up in the classic British spying tradition. He graduated from Queens' College at the University of Cambridge, a traditional recruiting ground for the British secret services, and had served in foreign postings in Africa, Europe, and Washington. Like his predecessors, as the head of MI6 he signed all internal memos with his code name, "C"—by tradition, always in green ink.

Shortly after his plane, carrying the call sign ASCOT-1, landed in Washington, Dearlove found himself inside the Counterterrorist Center at CIA headquarters. On a large screen, CIA officers were watching video of a white Mitsubishi truck driving along a road in Afghanistan. Dearlove had known that the United States had developed the ability to wage war by remote control, but he had never before watched the Predator drone in action.

Several minutes went by as the Mitsubishi was framed by the crosshairs at the center of the video monitor, until a missile blast washed the entire screen in white. Seconds later, the picture clarified to show the wreckage of the truck, twisted and burning.

Dearlove turned to a group of CIA officers, including Ross Newland, an agency veteran who months earlier had taken a job as part of a group overseeing the Predator program. He cracked a wry smile.

"It almost isn't sporting, is it?"

1: PERMISSION TO KILL

"You are there to kill terrorists, not make enemies."

*—Pakistani president Pervez Musharraf to U.S.
ambassador Wendy Chamberlin, September 14, 2001*

The lights in the White House Situation Room dimmed, and the CIA men began the slide show.

The pictures had been taken in haste and were grainy and out of focus. Some were of men getting into a car, or walking down the street. The scene in the darkened room resembled a mafia movie, where FBI officers sip coffee and scroll through photographs of mob kingpins. In this case, however, the images were of men who the Central Intelligence Agency was proposing to kill.

Gathered around the table were all the vice president's men, including legal adviser David Addington and chief of staff I. Lewis Libby, an old Washington hand known as "Scooter." At the head of the table, Vice President Dick Cheney watched the rogues gallery of slides with intense interest. It was a cold, late-fall day in 2001, just weeks after President George W. Bush had signed a secret order giving the CIA power it had lost in the 1970s, after a series of grisly and sometimes comic revelations about CIA assassination attempts had led the White House to ban the spy agency from exterminating America's enemies. On that day in the Situation Room, the CIA was reporting back to the White House on how it intended to use its newly acquired license to kill.

The two CIA officers leading the presentation, Jose Rodriguez and Enrique Prado, told the group that the Counterterrorist Center was recruiting CIA officers for a highly classified new program: a project to insert small teams of assassins into other countries to hunt down and kill the people that the Bush administration had marked for death. Among the photographs was one of Mamoun Darkazanli, a Syrian who the CIA believed had helped organize the September 11 attacks and was living in the open in Germany. There was also a picture of Dr. Abdul Qadeer Khan, a hero in Pakistan for his work developing its atomic bomb but a villain in the West for secretly transferring nuclear technology to Iran, Libya, and other pariah states. By shooting each photograph at close range, the CIA was making an eerie, unmistakable point: We can get close enough to take their pictures, so we can get close enough to kill.

But behind the bravado were unanswered questions. How would CIA hit squads slip unnoticed into Germany, Pakistan, and other countries? Could a group of American assassins really set up a net of surveillance and then, at the appointed time, manage to put a bullet into the head of their target? The agency had figured out none of the logistics, but Rodriguez and Prado had not come to the White House prepared to answer detailed questions about the operations. They were just looking for permission.

Cheney told them to get to work.

PRESIDENT GEORGE W. BUSH, the son of a former director of central intelligence* for whom the agency had renamed its headquarters in Langley, inherited a shrunken and dispirited spy service, a shade of

---

* Before 2005, the CIA director held the official title of director of central intelligence, or DCI.

what it had been during the Cold War. But in the final months of 2001, Bush had put the CIA in charge of a global manhunt, and its performance had buffed up the agency's image of itself as nimble and responsive to the demands of the commander-in-chief—the antithesis of the lumbering, bureaucratic Pentagon.

The CIA was now running a secret war at the direction of the White House, and the agency's once ignored Counterterrorist Center had become the war's frantic command post. The center had once been a backwater within the CIA, viewed by many at Langley as a collection of odd zealots who had ended up there after failing at more prestigious assignments. But after the September 11 attacks the Counterterrorist Center began the most dramatic expansion in its history, and over the course of a decade it would become the CIA's beating heart.

Hundreds of clandestine officers and analysts were taken off the Asia and Russia desks and reassigned to the maze of hastily built cubicles jammed inside the CTC's operations hub. The layout became so complex that people had difficulty finding their colleagues. Cardboard street signs were erected to help find cubicles located along "Usama Bin Lane" and "Zawahiri Way." A sign was eventually posted above the center's door—a constant, oppressive reminder that another terror attack could be days, or even minutes, away. The sign read, TODAY IS SEPTEMBER 12, 2001.

Directing the whirlwind in the war's early months was J. Cofer Black, a flamboyant officer who had been obsessed with hunting Osama bin Laden ever since he ran the CIA's station in Khartoum, the capital of Sudan, when bin Laden was living in exile in the country. Black had cultivated an image inside the CIA as something of a cross between a mad scientist and General George Patton. On September 11, when some feared that the final hijacked airplane might be headed toward Langley, Black refused to allow CTC officers to evacuate CIA headquarters along with the rest of agency personnel.

In the months that followed, CIA director George Tenet rarely went to the White House without Black at his side, and a mythology developed about Black's determination to kill off as many al Qaeda operatives as possible. During an Oval Office meeting two days after the attacks, Bush asked Black whether the CIA was up to handling its new assignment, which involved inserting paramilitary teams into Afghanistan to ally themselves with Afghan warlords and fight the Taliban. In ghoulish hyperbole, Black claimed that by the time the CIA was done with al Qaeda, bin Laden and his brethren would "have flies walking across their eyeballs." That was the kind of talk Bush wanted to hear, and he took an immediate liking to the bombastic counterterrorism chief. But some of the president's war cabinet cringed at the macho talk and began referring to Black as "the flies-on-the-eyeballs guy."

Black's exalted status with those who counted in the White House led to friction inside the CIA and constant battles with his boss, James Pavitt, whom he considered weak and unimaginative. Pavitt headed the Directorate of Operations, the branch of the agency responsible for all foreign espionage and covert action missions, and thought Black was a showboat and a cowboy. He believed that Black was far too eager to get the CIA involved in the kind of overseas exploits that had been a constant source of trouble for the agency, and in the years before the 9/11 attacks they had fought bitterly over whether the CIA should embrace the armed Predator to hunt and kill bin Laden in Afghanistan.

But the success of the CIA's initial strategy in Afghanistan in late 2001 was a victory for Black and the Counterterrorist Center, and it seemed to prove to the CIA's detractors that there were virtues to a small cadre of officers at the CIA running a campaign against a diffuse organization like al Qaeda. Teams of CIA paramilitary officers, later joined by Army Green Berets, had turned a ragged collection of Afghan militias into a conquering army. Riding on horses and in rusted Soviet-era armored vehicles, the Afghans had driven the Taliban from Kabul and Kandahar.

The strange new conflict had also upended how the United States waged war. The traditional wartime chain of command—passing from the White House to the secretary of defense to a four-star commander with a staff of hundreds to build and execute a war plan—had quietly been circumvented. The CIA director was now a military commander running a clandestine, global war with a skeleton staff and very little oversight. Tenet began pushing aggressively to bulk up the CIA's paramilitary teams in Afghanistan, and he sold the White House on a program to capture terrorists, hide them in secret jails, and subject them to an Orwellian regimen of brutal interrogation methods. Only Bush, Cheney, and a small group at the White House were overseeing decisions about who should be captured, who should be killed, and who should be spared.

This was an abrupt change for Tenet, who in the years before the September 11 attacks had liked to tell his bosses at the White House that CIA officers should stay removed from the process of making policy. He evoked an almost monastic image of the spies at Langley producing intelligence assessments, while those "across the river," at the White House and in Congress, made decisions based on these assessments. James Pavitt would later tell investigators from the 9/11 Commission that one lesson from the Iran–Contra scandal of the 1980s was that "we don't do policy from [Langley] . . . and you don't want us to."

If that idea had already been something of a useful myth, certainly by late 2001 the CIA could no longer claim that it stood apart from messy decisions about war and peace. Bush demanded that Tenet come to the Oval Office each day for the president's daily brief—it was the first time since the agency's founding that the CIA director, rather than a lower-level analyst, provided the regular morning briefing at the White House. Like his CIA predecessors, Tenet was eager for the access to the president, and every morning he and Cofer Black arrived at the White House with the catalogue of terrorist plots and plotters to tell a rapt audience about the steps that the CIA was taking to protect the country. The daily audiences with the president made Tenet and the CIA indispensable to the White House, which had an insatiable appetite for information about any threats.

But such high-level attention was also beginning to have a distorting effect on the analysis that the CIA was producing—making it narrower, more tactical. Hundreds of CIA analysts were now working on terrorism, which was understandable in the aftermath of an attack that killed nearly three thousand Americans. But it became immediately obvious to the analysts that the path to career advancement at the CIA was to start working on terrorism, with the goal of producing something that might be read to the president early one morning inside the Oval Office. And what the White House was most interested in were leads about the whereabouts of specific al Qaeda operators, not broader subjects like the level of support al Qaeda had in the Muslim world or the impact that American military and intelligence operations might have on radicalizing a new generation of militants. The CIA focused its efforts accordingly.

Even the language of spycraft was gradually changing. CIA case officers and analysts had once used the term "targeting" as they made decisions about which foreign government official should be targeted for information or which foreign national could be turned into a CIA informant. Eventually, "targeting" came to mean something quite different for the analysts who moved into the Counterterrorist Center. It meant tracking down someone deemed a threat to the United States, and capturing or killing him.

The fights between Cofer Black and James Pavitt intensified, and by early 2002 Black had decided to leave the clandestine service and take a job at the State Department. His replacement was Jose Rodriguez, who had been one of the Counterterrorist Center's top officers and the humble counterpoint to Black. Cofer Black had Middle East experience and was one of a handful of CIA officers with intimate knowledge about the terror network led by Osama bin Laden; Rodriguez had never served in the Muslim world and spoke no Arabic. But he was close to Pavitt, and some clandestine officers suspected that Rodriguez initially had been installed at the center so that Pavitt could keep tabs on Black. A native of Puerto Rico and the son of two teachers, Rodriguez had joined the intelligence agency in the midseventies after graduating from the University of Florida's law school. His undercover career had been spent mostly inside the Latin America division, the home of the CIA's adventures in Nicaragua, El Salvador, and Honduras during the 1980s. But at that time Rodriguez was still junior enough to avoid being enmeshed in the Iran–Contra investigations that would cripple the division for years. Rodriguez was well liked inside the clandestine service but had never distinguished himself as one of the best case officers in his CIA peer group. He served in a number of CIA stations in Latin America, including Bolivia and Mexico, and fostered an image as a maverick who liked to stick it to bureaucrats at Langley who he thought were micromanaging field operations. He was an avid horseback rider, and while he was station chief in Mexico City he named his favorite horse Business, instructing subordinates that if one of the bosses at Langley called to inquire about his whereabouts they should be told that Rodriguez was "out on Business."

When he took over the Latin America division, in 1995, it was once again in turmoil. John Deutch, President Clinton's second CIA director, had just fired a number of case officers for what the CIA euphemistically calls "close and continuing contacts with foreign nationals." In other words, the men down in Latin America were having illicit affairs, and there were concerns that their promiscuity could make them vulnerable to blackmail. Rodriguez soon found trouble of his own. When a childhood friend was arrested in the Dominican Republic on a drug charge, Rodriguez intervened to stop Dominican police from beating his friend while in prison. It was a clear conflict of interest for the head of the CIA's Latin America division to intervene with a foreign government on behalf of a friend, and the spy agency's inspector general reprimanded Rodriguez for showing "a remarkable lack of judgment." He was removed from the job.

But by 2001 his career had rebounded, and Rodriguez found himself among a number of Latin American hands—including his friend Enrique Prado—helping to run the CIA's new war. He became a regular at the daily 5 P.M. meetings around Tenet's conference table, where senior CIA officials received daily battlefield updates about operations in Afghanistan and elsewhere. It was during one of those sessions that Rodriguez made an offhand suggestion that would lead to one of the most fateful decisions of the Bush administration.

The question before the group was what to do with all the Taliban fighters that American troops and CIA officers were picking up in Afghanistan. Where could they be held over the long term? The meeting turned into a brainstorming session, with various CIA officers suggesting countries that might be willing to accept the detainees. One officer suggested the Ushuaia prison, on Argentina's Tierra del Fuego, a desolate facility at the bottom of the world. Another suggested the Corn Islands, two tiny specks in the Caribbean Sea off the Nicaraguan coast. But all of these suggestions were dismissed as unrealistic options. Finally, Rodriguez offered up an idea, almost in jest.

"Well, we could put them at Guantánamo Bay," he said.

Everyone around the table laughed, thinking about how much it would anger Fidel Castro if the United States were to jail the prisoners of its new war on the American military base in Cuba. But the more they thought about the prospect, the more everyone thought Guantánamo actually made sense. It was an American facility, and the fate of the prison would not be jeopardized there as it could be in another country if the government changed leadership and decided to kick the United States' prisoners out. And, the CIA officials figured, a prison at Guantánamo Bay would be outside the jurisdiction of American courts. A perfect location, it seemed.

Cuba became the CIA's top recommendation for the new American prison, and soon enough the agency would build its own secret jail in one corner of the Guantánamo Bay prison complex. A maximum-security facility, it was dubbed Strawberry Fields by CIA officers because the prisoners presumably would be there, as the Beatles sang, "forever."

ON A CHAOTIC BATTLEFIELD seven thousand miles away from Washington, the first war of the twenty-first century was turning out to be a far messier affair than it had first appeared inside the warren of cubicles at the CIA or in tidy PowerPoint presentations delivered in wood-paneled offices on the top floors of the Pentagon. By early 2002, Afghanistan was neither a daily shooting war nor a hopeful peace but a twilight conflict beset by competition and mistrust between soldiers and spies. American missions were often based on shards of intelligence from unreliable sources, as when dozens of Navy SEALs and Marines spent eight days digging up graves at a cave complex at Zhawar Kili, in eastern Afghanistan, based on intelligence that Osama bin Laden might have been killed in a recent airstrike on the base. They were hoping to exhume bin Laden's body and provide a reason to end the Afghan war after just three months. They dug up a handful of bodies but didn't find what they were looking for.

Sometimes, poor communication between the CIA and the military had deadly results. On January 23, a team of Army Green Berets launched a raid in the dark of night on two compounds at Hazar Qadam, a hundred miles northeast of Kandahar. The compounds consisted of several buildings perched on the side of a hill. As an AC-130 gunship circled overhead, two teams stormed the compounds simultaneously.

Staccato bursts of AK-47 gunfire erupted from the buildings as the teams blew a hole in the outer walls. The Americans returned fire and began moving from room to room as some fought hand to hand with the suspected Taliban gunmen. By mission's end, the Americans had killed more than forty people inside the compounds, and the AC-130 had reduced the structures to rubble.

But what the soldiers learned when they returned to their base was that, days earlier, the CIA had turned the men inside the two compounds away from the Taliban and convinced them to fight for the other side. Hanging in one of the buildings that night was the flag of the new government of Afghanistan, led by Hamid Karzai. The CIA had never told the special-operations task force that the dozens of Afghan men living in the compounds were now their allies.

The confusion in Afghanistan was partly the result of normal battlefield turmoil, but it also had its origins in the jockeying between the Pentagon and CIA for supremacy in the new American conflict. Secretary of Defense Donald Rumsfeld had felt stung that CIA paramilitary teams had been first into Afghanistan. It wasn't just a matter of logistics, though it was true that the platoons of Green Berets had been delayed by bad weather and problems getting access to bases around Afghanistan. It was that the invasion was, at its inception, conceived and led by the CIA with the U.S. military in a supporting role. The ability of the CIA to move more swiftly than the military with just a fraction of the Pentagon's budget and manpower gnawed at Rumsfeld. He began overhauling the Pentagon's bureaucracy to ensure it didn't happen again.

Rumsfeld had been struggling in his efforts to revamp a Defense Department he saw as hidebound and controlled too much by parochial military services consumed with protecting their prized weapons systems. A former defense secretary during the Ford administration, Rumsfeld had returned to the Pentagon after a successful turn in the business world. He had amassed a personal fortune at the pharmaceutical company G. D. Searle, where he rolled out hit products like NutraSweet and orange Metamucil, and when he took over the Pentagon he made his intentions clear: He wanted to apply the laws of the private sector to a bloated Defense Department.

At sixty-nine, Rumsfeld would soon become the oldest defense secretary in American history, and his frequent complaints about Defense Department waste sometimes had the flavor of a grandfather spinning tales of life during the Depression. His efforts to remake the Pentagon drew immediate comparisons to those of Robert McNamara, the defense secretary during the Kennedy and Johnson administrations who arrived from Ford Motor Company with his "Whiz Kids," determined to change the Pentagon's culture. Some generals, put off by Rumsfeld's approach, dubbed the group of aging businessmen that Rumsfeld had brought in to run the various military services the "Wheeze Kids." By the time that American Airlines Flight 77 slammed into the Pentagon's western façade on the morning of September 11, 2001, the military had already successfully thwarted many of Rumsfeld's more ambitious attempts to cancel expensive, Cold

War–era weapons. There was open speculation in Washington that Rumsfeld might be the first top member of the Bush administration to step down. But over the next year he soon turned into the most visible and popular member of President Bush's cabinet. The United States pushed the Taliban out of Afghanistan's cities by December 2001, using an innovative war plan for which Rumsfeld received public credit, and his blunt, high-profile press briefings made him the public face of the Bush administration's retaliation for the terrorist attacks that had killed nearly three thousand Americans. Rumsfeld didn't mince words or lapse into militaryspeak when talking about the aims of the war. He talked about "killing Taliban."

Rumsfeld also saw early on that much of the new war would be waged in dark corners of the world, away from declared war zones. It would look nothing like the infantry skirmishes of the nineteenth century, the trench warfare of the First World War, or the tank battles of World War II. The Pentagon needed to start sending soldiers into places where—by law and tradition—only spies had been allowed to go. For instance, the Pentagon at the time didn't have a dedicated counterterrorism cell like the CIA's Counterterrorist Center, but within weeks of the September 11 attacks, Rumsfeld proposed building one of his own. Only bigger. In a memorandum to CIA director Tenet, Rumsfeld wrote, "From everything I hear, CTC is too small to do a 24-7 job," and sent Tenet a proposal describing his plan for a Joint Intelligence Task Force for Combating Terrorism, an entirely new organization that might give the Pentagon control of the new war.

Four days after he sent the proposal to Tenet, Rumsfeld put his thoughts about the scope of the new war into a top-secret memorandum for President Bush. The war would be global, he said, and the United States needed to be up front about its ultimate goals. "If the war does not significantly change the world's political map," he wrote to the president, "the U.S. will not achieve its aim."

The Pentagon did not yet have the machinery in place to carry out such a war, and Rumsfeld knew it as well as anyone. There was much to do.

ON A CLEAR NIGHT in early February 2002, three Afghan men and a young boy jumped from a white truck and into the darkness, their clothes billowing around them as the rotors from an American military helicopter churned dust into the sky. They waved their hands wildly as a group of commandos approached them with gun barrels pointed forward.

Forty miles to the north, inside a makeshift operations center adjacent to Kandahar Airfield's bombed-out passenger terminal, special-operations troops watched the mission unfold on a video feed provided by a CIA drone. The special-operations commander, Navy captain Robert Harward, picked up a secure phone and called his bosses in Kuwait to tell them about the captives. Mullah Khairullah Khairkhwa, the Taliban leader everyone had been hunting, he said, was now in custody.

There was a long pause at the other end of the phone. Finally, Lt. General Paul Mikolashek, in Kuwait, spoke up.

"If they are not the right people," he asked, "will you be able to return them?"

Harward shot a puzzled look to the other officers inside the command center. Taking a breath to let his anger pass, he assured the general that the detainees who had just been handcuffed and shoved into a helicopter and were flying back to the Kandahar base could—if necessary—be returned to the place where they had been arrested.

What Mikolashek had just learned, but Harward still didn't know, was that it was not Mullah Khairkhwa and his aides inside the helicopter. Khairkhwa, the Taliban interior minister, was driving in a different white truck that had just crossed the border into Pakistan. And the CIA knew it.

It was the fourth month of the Afghan war, and American troops were pouring into the country in greater numbers. A new government had just been installed in Kabul, and Mullah Khairkhwa had spent days negotiating with the new Afghan president's half brother, Ahmed Wali Karzai, about surrendering and becoming a CIA informant. Ahmed Wali himself was on the CIA's payroll—an alliance that years later would be a source of tension between the CIA and the military in Kabul—and American spies relayed the message to Mullah Khairkhwa that he could avoid arrest and a long stint in the newly built prison at Guantánamo Bay.

But after several days of negotiations, Mullah Khairkhwa wasn't sure he could trust the Americans. He phoned another Taliban commander to tell him he was planning to escape to Pakistan; the call was intercepted by American military spies. The intelligence officers warned Mikolashek, who told Captain Harward, in Kandahar, to capture the Taliban minister before he made it over the border. The helicopters took off and headed south to grab Khairkhwa, with the CIA Predator that was tracking his white truck leading the way.

But the CIA had a different plan. The war in Afghanistan had forced the spy agency into a tight embrace with Pakistan's spy agency, the Directorate for Inter-Services Intelligence (ISI), and CIA officers thought they might be able to get Pakistani spies to capture Mullah Khairkhwa and encourage him to become an informant. Or, at least, a high-profile arrest of a Taliban leader in Pakistan might earn Islamabad some goodwill in Washington.

Shortly after the military helicopters lifted off from Kandahar, the CIA drone pulled off from tracking Khairkhwa's truck, leaving the troops in the helicopter blind about the location of their target. Intelligence officers inside the special-operations command post began screaming into their phones to resume the Predator surveillance. It was several minutes before a second CIA Predator arrived—and began tracking an entirely different white truck.

The CIA was now leading the commandos in the helicopter to the wrong target, while Mullah Khairkhwa and his entourage sped over the desert border at Spin Boldak and into Pakistan. Days later, after several more fruitless rounds of negotiation to turn Khairkhwa into an informant, Pakistani security forces closed in on the house where he was hiding, in the village of Chaman. Pakistani spies handed the Taliban leader over to CIA officers in Quetta, Pakistan, and Mullah Khairkhwa began his long journey to Guantánamo Bay, Cuba. He became one of the island prison's first inmates.

As for the three men and the young boy who had been arrested and brought to a detention facility in Kandahar, they were loaded back into helicopters and flown forty miles south, where their truck was in the same spot it had been before they'd been ambushed by the American helicopters. The Afghans were sent on their way with several boxes of military Meals Ready-to-Eat. Out of respect for the detainees' faith, the meals containing pork had been removed.

2: A MARRIAGE AMONG SPIES

"Pakistan has always seen such matters in black and white."

—*Lt. General Mahmud Ahmed, head of Pakistan's Directorate for Inter-Services Intelligence, September 12, 2001*

Generations of CIA officers have graduated from "The Farm," the agency's training facility in the Virginia tidewater, having learned the first lesson of spycraft: There is no such thing as a friendly intelligence service. The spy services of other nations are meant to be penetrated, their officers "turned" to work for the United States by spying on their own countries. Foreign intelligence services may be useful for joint operations but never fully trusted. The greater the reliance on liaison services for an operation, the greater the danger that the operation gets blown.

It was a philosophy that worked well enough during the Cold War, when the CIA's primary mission was stealing the secrets of the Soviet Union and its client states—traditional foreign espionage. Bosses at Langley knew that the Soviets were trying to do the exact same thing to the United States and knew that Moscow had planted its own spies in foreign intelligence services to position itself for greater access to

American secrets. The primary reason for getting close to foreign spies was for counterintelligence purposes: figuring out how deeply another foreign spy service had penetrated the CIA and catching the moles before they burrowed too deeply.

But the dictates of a new war quickly changed the rules of the spying game. The CIA's top priority was no longer gathering intelligence on foreign governments and their countries, but man hunting. The new mission put a premium on getting detailed intelligence about specific individuals, and it mattered little how that information was collected. As a result, the CIA immediately became more reliant on the foreign spy services that had spent years building dossiers on terror organizations. Desperate for information to stop the next attack, the CIA wasn't picky about choosing its friends. During the early years after the September 11 attacks, the CIA's relationship with spy services with unsavory histories of brutality—Egypt's Mukhabarat, Jordan's General Intelligence Directorate, even the intelligence service of Muammar Gaddafi's Libyan pariah state—grew much closer.

Some leaders of these countries relished the idea of lecturing the United States about the gritty business of terrorist hunting. Over dinner in Cairo in early October 2001, Egyptian president Hosni Mubarak advised Donald Rumsfeld that bombs would do little good in America's new war and that the United States should "put your money into buying allies on the ground in Afghanistan." Mubarak, a modern-day pharaoh who had consolidated his power partly by crushing Islamist movements in his country, no doubt saw he had much to gain from a muscular partnership with a United States that was groping for a new strategy against terrorists. With a rhetorical flourish, he told Rumsfeld that the fight against terrorism was necessary "to save the planet."

But for a CIA now at war, there was no relationship more important than that with Pakistan's Directorate for Inter-Services Intelligence. For years, it had had all the worst qualities of a failing marriage:

Both sides had long ago stopped trusting each other but couldn't imagine ever splitting up.

In this way, the rapport between the spy services was just the U.S.–Pakistani relationship in miniature. The close bonds between the CIA and ISI during the 1980s, when American and Pakistani spies ran guns into Afghanistan and trained mujahedeen to shoot down Soviet helicopters, had frayed during the 1990s. Washington had lost interest in post-Soviet Afghanistan and imposed harsh sanctions on Islamabad as punishment for the country's clandestine nuclear program. Pakistan began nurturing the Taliban, a group of semiliterate Pashtun tribesmen from the southern part of Afghanistan, as a counterweight to the factions that comprised the Northern Alliance, which had long received support from India.

The ISI had viewed the Taliban as Pashtun allies who, while strange and fanatical, could keep the Northern Alliance from taking over Afghanistan and setting up what Islamabad feared would be an Indian proxy state along its western border. Pakistani military officials also figured that for all they had done to expel the Soviet Union from Afghanistan, they had earned the right to hold the strings of the government in Kabul.

With Pakistani intelligence providing succor to the Taliban with both money and advice on military strategy, and with the spigot of money from Washington to Islamabad shut off, American officials stationed in Islamabad during the 1990s found they had no leverage with the ISI when they demanded that Pakistani spies push the Taliban government in Kabul to hand over Osama bin Laden. The United States turned up the pressure in late 1998, after al Qaeda simultaneously bombed the American embassies in Kenya and Tanzania, but Pakistan's spy service was unmoved. The Americans in Pakistan sent a string of cables to Washington detailing their frustrations. One State Department cable from Islamabad in December 1998 carried a

dry, understated subject heading: "Usama bin Ladin: Pakistan seems to be leaning against being helpful." When one American diplomat brought up bin Laden's name during a meeting with General Ehsan ul Haq, a future ISI chief, the Pakistani general grew testy.

"I cannot understand why you Americans are so concerned about Afghanistan," he snapped.

On the morning of September 11, 2001, General Mahmud Ahmed, the head of the ISI, happened to be in Washington meeting with lawmakers inside a secure chamber of the House Permanent Select Committee on Intelligence. A short, stocky man with a bushy white mustache extending across the middle of both cheeks, Ahmed had taken over the ISI after the 1999 military coup that installed General Pervez Musharraf as president, and he did little to hide his sympathies for the Taliban. He once scolded a Pakistan military analyst who had told President Musharraf that Pakistan's policy toward the Taliban was hurting its standing with other nations. "The Taliban," the ISI chief said, "is the future of Afghanistan."

On that morning on Capitol Hill, Ahmed was having a friendly exchange with Representative Porter Goss, the committee's top Republican, regaling the congressman with his knowledge of obscure facts about the American Civil War. Goss had wrapped a book about the Civil War to give to Ahmed as a gift, but the pleasantries were cut short when committee staffers raced into the meeting room to tell the lawmakers and the ISI chief that the second plane had just hit the World Trade Center. "Mahmud's face turned ashen," recalls Goss. The Pakistani spymaster quickly excused himself from the meeting and jumped into the embassy car waiting for him. The book, still wrapped, was left inside the room.

The following morning, General Ahmed was called to the office of Richard Armitage, the deputy secretary of state, who was in no mood for diplomatic correctness. President Bush had announced the night

before that the United States would treat both the terrorists and their patrons equally, and Armitage presented the ISI's dilemma in Manichean terms.

"Pakistan faces a stark choice; either it is with us or it is not," Armitage told the Pakistani spy chief, saying the decision was black and white, with no gray.

Insulted by Armitage's bluntness, Ahmed responded that although Pakistan had long been accused of "being in bed" with terrorists, nothing could be further from the truth. His country would back the United States without hesitation, he said, assuring Armitage that "Pakistan has always seen such matters in black and white." Armitage warned that the United States was preparing a laundry list of demands for Pakistan that were likely to cause "deep introspection" in Islamabad.

The terms of the CIA–ISI marriage were discussed the next day. Armitage told General Ahmed that the United States wanted unfettered access to Pakistani airspace and the ability to carry out military and intelligence operations inside Pakistan. America also wanted access to Pakistani ports, airstrips, and bases in the mountains along the border with Afghanistan. Finally, he insisted that the ISI hand over to the CIA all the intelligence it had about al Qaeda.

Ahmed assured Armitage he would pass the list of demands to Musharraf. But, he said, Pakistan wanted something in return: assurance that it would be reimbursed for its support in the campaign against al Qaeda. If Pakistan was going to turn against the Taliban and agree to a war on its western border, it would need to be rewarded for it.

The parameters of America's dysfunctional relationship with Pakistan in the post-9/11 era had been set: The United States insisted on the right to wage a secret war inside Pakistan, and Islamabad extracted money in return. President Musharraf had acceded to most, but not

all, of Washington's requirements. For instance, he put limits on where American planes could fly in Pakistani airspace, fearing that the United States might try to conduct surveillance flights over Pakistani nuclear sites. He also denied the United States access to most military bases, allowing the American military to station personnel at only two air bases: Shamsi, in the southwestern region of Balochistan, and Jacobabad, in the northern province of Sindh. In the end, Washington and Islamabad's renewal of their vows left both sides believing they had given up more than they were getting, creating recriminations and resentment that would boil over years later.

The rhetoric from Washington had been unambiguous, and Musharraf knew it. A man who had spent his career in the military, he considered his options as if this were a war game. He later wrote in his memoir that if he had chosen to protect the Taliban, the United States would consider Pakistan a terrorist state and, for all he knew, would attack Pakistan, eviscerate Pakistan's military, and seize the country's nuclear arsenal. India had already offered its bases for the Afghan war, and Musharraf figured that soon enough the United States could be flying combat missions from a base in Amritsar, in northwestern India. The bombers would streak over Pakistani territory on their way into Afghanistan, and back again after they had delivered their deadly payloads. Even worse, the Indians could seize the opportunity to open an offensive in Kashmir, with America's blessing. The strategic balance in South Asia, which had long aligned Pakistan with the United States against India and its historic ally Russia, would change permanently. Pakistan would be a crushed, impoverished outcast.

On the evening of September 19, Musharraf told the people of Pakistan how he had answered Washington's demands. He was dressed in a crisp military uniform, but his face was haggard and drawn, the toll of endless meetings with his generals, civilian politicians, religious

leaders, and American diplomats. His televised speech was not a denunciation of al Qaeda or the Taliban, and at no time did Musharraf condemn the attacks on the World Trade Center and the Pentagon. He instead framed his decision to help America in narrow, nationalistic terms. India had already pledged its full support to Washington, he said, and New Delhi was determined to ensure that "if and when the government in Afghanistan changes, it shall be an anti-Pakistan government." He said that Pakistan had four priorities: the security of its borders; the Kashmir cause; the revival of its economy; and, finally, the protection of its "strategic assets."

That final item on the list was not just a reference to the nuclear arsenal that Pakistan had built to destroy India. Pakistan's military had other "strategic assets" to consider. By 2001, groups like the Afghan Taliban and the militia network run by mujahedeen leader Jalaluddin Haqqani were considered critical elements of Pakistan's defenses, and Musharraf made it clear in the speech that night that he still regarded the Taliban as an important bulwark against India. Even as he was leaning on Mullah Omar to give up bin Laden, he told the country that the tactic was a way to emerge from the crisis "without any damage to Afghanistan and the Taliban."

Things weren't, in fact, black and white. One week after the September 11 attacks, and one night before President Bush in front of a joint session of Congress accused the Taliban of "aiding and abetting murder," Musharraf was still hoping that the Taliban could remain in power. Washington had been comforted by the belief that Musharraf had pushed all of his poker chips to the center of the table on a bet on the Bush administration. In fact, he adopted a far more nuanced strategy— a strategy that even after more than a decade of war in Afghanistan, many American officials would still have difficulty discerning.

The ISI was still hoping that another bloody Afghan war could be avoided, especially one that might replace the Taliban with the Tajiks

and Uzbeks of the Northern Alliance. After General Ahmed returned to Islamabad, he implored American ambassador Wendy Chamberlin not to start a war out of revenge. A true victory in Afghanistan, Ahmed said, would come only by negotiating. "If the Taliban are eliminated," he said, "Afghanistan will revert to warlordism."

To try to convince Taliban leader Mullah Mohammed Omar to give up bin Laden, General Ahmed flew to Kandahar on a plane loaned by the CIA. Omar, a former mujahedeen commander who had lost one eye during the Soviet war, mocked the Pakistani general as the Bush administration's errand boy and rejected the demands. He issued a stinging rebuke to his longtime ISI benefactor. "You want to please the Americans, and I want to please God," he said.

THE AFGHANISTAN STRATEGY had created divisions in the CIA from the beginning, with rifts opening between officers at Langley and those posted at the CIA station in Islamabad. Cofer Black, the CTC chief, pressed to immediately arm the Northern Alliance and begin a push south toward Kabul. But Robert Grenier, the Islamabad station chief, fought against the plan. He warned that any move to arm a militia backed by India and Russia could immediately destroy relations with Pakistan just as they were thawing after years of mistrust. These internal fights got a wider audience three weeks after the September 11 attacks, when CIA officers went to the Pentagon for a teleconference between Washington, Islamabad, and United States Central Command headquarters, in Tampa.

During the call, Grenier said that any ground offensive using the Northern Alliance ought to be put on hold to give the ISI more time to pressure the Taliban to release bin Laden. Backing the Northern Alliance could lead to another bloody Afghan civil war, Grenier said, adding that an air campaign could be enough for the time being to

bring the Taliban to negotiations. But Hank Crumpton, a CTC officer who had been designated by Cofer Black to run the CIA's war in Afghanistan, thought Grenier was being naive. He was merely reflecting the ISI's position, Crumpton thought, and was displaying a bad case of "clientitis." After the meeting, Crumpton told Rumsfeld he thought that Grenier was dead wrong.

Grenier may have been channeling the concerns of the ISI, but they were hardly unreasonable worries. For weeks, ISI officials had been whispering to their CIA counterparts in Islamabad that a war in Afghanistan could spin wildly out of control. It would upset a delicate balance in the region, they said, perhaps even leading India and Pakistan toward a full-blown proxy war inside Afghanistan.

As the negotiations dragged on and September turned to October, the CIA quietly began inserting paramilitary teams into Afghanistan to make contact with the warlord commanders who fought under the Northern Alliance banner. Meanwhile, a torrent of threat information continued to come into the agency's Counterterrorist Center from CIA stations in the Middle East and South Asia. On October 5, two days before the United States dropped the first bombs on Afghanistan, Armitage sent an eyes-only cable to Ambassador Chamberlin demanding that she meet immediately with General Ahmed. He wanted a simple message delivered to Mullah Omar, and he wanted Ahmed to deliver it. If another attack was traced back to Afghanistan, Armitage wrote, the American response would be devastating:

"Every pillar of the Taliban regime will be destroyed."

The day after America's war in Afghanistan began, Musharraf replaced General Ahmed at the ISI. CIA leaders in Washington had been pressing for General Ahmed to be sacked, and his replacement was an uncontroversial choice. General Ehsan ul Haq, an urbane commander who at the time was leading the army's corps in Peshawar, had been part of the cabal of military leaders who installed

Musharraf in power in 1999, and unlike Ahmed, he had no obvious loyalties to the Taliban. Within weeks he was sitting by Musharraf's side at the United Nations, where Musharraf and Bush met for the first time since the September 11 attacks to discuss America's plans in Afghanistan.

To prepare Bush for the meeting, Secretary of State Colin Powell wrote the president a memo that praised Musharraf and said unequivocally that Pakistan's government had "abandoned the Taliban." "President Musharraf's decision to fully cooperate with the United States in the wake of September 11, at considerable political risk, abruptly turned our stalled relationship around," the memo began. In hindsight, Powell's analysis was naive—it was what American officials wanted to believe and chose to hear. Musharraf hadn't fundamentally shifted Pakistan's foreign policy as much as he had reprised a deal that General Muhammad Zia-ul-Haq, Pakistan's former president, had struck with the Americans during the 1980s. Musharraf would help the United States get what it wanted in Afghanistan, and Pakistan would be paid handsomely.

Musharraf hadn't managed to prevent the war, but he wanted it to be short and for the United States to leave his neighborhood as quickly as possible. This is the message he brought to Bush at the United Nations: Do what you need to do to expel Osama bin Laden and his followers from Afghanistan, but the last thing the United States should do is stay in Afghanistan for years.

As it turned out, the Pakistanis had misread the Americans just as badly as the Americans had misread the Pakistanis. In the months after the September 11 attacks a string of intelligence cables from ISI headquarters went out to Pakistan's embassies in Washington and elsewhere. The spy service's analysts concluded that the United States had no plans for a long-term commitment to Afghanistan beyond the defeat of al Qaeda there, a conclusion that had been informed by the

knowledge that Washington had lost interest in Afghanistan after the last war as soon as the Soviets had withdrawn. This is how it appeared to Asad Durrani, a retired Pakistani lieutenant-general who had run the ISI during the 1990s. Durrani was serving as Pakistan's ambassador to Saudi Arabia in late 2001, when the ISI cables began arriving in the foreign embassies. America's new war in Afghanistan, Durrani said years later, "seemed as if it was going to be a very short-term affair."

Pakistani spies were still trying to ensure that it was, and in November and December 2001 they held a series of secret meetings with Afghan tribal leaders to determine how many outer layers of the Taliban's followers could be peeled away from the movement's fanatical core. During one of these meetings, General Ehsan ul Haq, the new ISI chief, sat down with Jalaluddin Haqqani in Islamabad. General ul Haq had called Haqqani to the capital to gauge the loyalties of the wizened militia leader. Haqqani had once been the CIA's greatest ally in Afghanistan, during the war against the Soviets, but in the years since had pledged loyalty to al Qaeda and had built up a sprawling criminal empire from his base in Miranshah, in North Waziristan.

It became clear during the meeting that Haqqani wasn't about to be turned. The American invasion of Afghanistan, Haqqani told General ul Haq, was no different from the Soviet war years earlier. With chilling prescience, he predicted that the new war would play out just as the last one had. Haqqani said that he could not stop American bombers, but eventually the United States would have to send in large numbers of ground troops. When that happened, Haqqani told the ISI chief, he would be on level ground with the Americans.

They can occupy all the cities, but they can't occupy all the mountains, the militia leader continued, as General ul Haq recalls the meeting. "So we will go to the mountains and we will resist. Just like we did against the Soviet Union."

News that the famous commander had been in Islamabad quickly spread to the American embassy, and CIA station chief Robert Grenier immediately visited General ul Haq to get more information. Not only had Haqqani been in the capital, ul Haq acknowledged, but he had met with him. He hadn't bothered to tell the CIA chief, he said, because nothing productive came from the meeting.

"I don't think he is going to be helpful," ul Haq said.

ALTHOUGH HE HAD INSTALLED a new general to lead the ISI, Musharraf's purge of Islamists inside the military went only so far. At the same time General ul Haq took over the military spy service, Musharraf appointed Lt. General Ali Jan Aurakzai, a close friend and longtime Taliban sympathizer, to take over the army's corps in Peshawar, the same job that ul Haq had just vacated.

Peshawar, a bustling market city, is the capital of Pakistan's North-West Frontier Province, a territory named by the British for its position at the outer edge of the "settled" lands.** The job in Peshawar also gave General Aurakzai oversight of the Federally Administered Tribal Areas, the harsh, mountainous lands ruled by wild men of the Wazir and Mehsud tribes and where the government's writ meant little.

The British had had little success taming the tribal lands that had been part of the British Raj, and eventually gave up. As a twenty-three-year-old journalist visiting India in 1897, Winston Churchill spent six weeks with Britain's Malakand Field Force and sent dispatches to *The Daily Telegraph* describing the snowcapped mountains where "range after range is seen as the long surges of an Atlantic swell,

---

** The Pakistani government would later change the name of the North-West Frontier Province to Khyber Pakhtunkhwa.

and in the distance some glittering snow peak suggests a white-crested roller, higher than the rest."

"The drenching rains which fall each year," Churchill continued, "have washed the soil from the sides of the hills until they have become strangely grooved by numberless water-courses, and the black primeval rock is everywhere exposed." Just as the lands had changed little since Churchill's time, the people of the tribal areas remained fiercely distrustful of outsiders. It is a place, Britain's future prime minister observed, where "every man's hand is against the other, and all against the stranger."

General Aurakzai had long ago proven his loyalty to Musharraf as another of the military conspirators behind the 1999 coup. According to some accounts it had been Aurakzai who showed up at former president Nawaz Sharif's house, pointed a gun in his face, and told him that the military was taking charge in Pakistan. He was a commanding figure who had been raised in the tribal areas and had spent enough time in the mountains to know that regular Pakistani troops were not trained for the mission they were about to undertake. He told Musharraf he doubted there were many foreign al Qaeda operatives fleeing across the border into Pakistan.

But CIA officers in Islamabad thought differently. Months after Pakistani soldiers moved into the tribal areas, CIA officers began feeding the ISI steady reports about the arrival of Arab fighters in the mountains, but General Aurakzai's military patrols turned up nothing. Grenier, the CIA's Islamabad station chief, said that Aurakzai and other Pakistani officials with whom he met worried that Pakistani troops rumbling through mountain villages could touch off a tribal uprising. The officials didn't want to believe that al Qaeda had established a new base in Pakistan, less than a hundred miles from the bases in Afghanistan where the group had planned the September 11 attacks. It was "an inconvenient fact," said Grenier.

Aurakzai held the Peshawar command until his retirement in 2004 and for years continued to deny the presence of Arab fighters in the tribal areas. In 2005, he told a reporter that the notion that Osama bin Laden might be hiding in Pakistan was purely conjecture, and he never saw any evidence that Arab fighters had set up operations in the tribal areas. The hunt for bin Laden and al Qaeda in Pakistan, he said, was pointless.

BUT OTHERS KNEW BETTER. Brigadier-General Asad Munir had just assumed his post as the ISI's chief of station in Peshawar when the September 11 attacks occurred, and it wasn't long before the Americans began arriving there. They came in small numbers at first, no more than a dozen, and set up at the fortified U.S. consulate inside the city. It was late 2001, and they had come to work with their Pakistani counterparts to hunt down al Qaeda operatives escaping the fighting in Afghanistan. They had come to work with Asad Munir.

"I had never met a CIA man," Munir recalled, taking long drags of a Benson & Hedges cigarette, the smoke sometimes obscuring a face with the rugged looks of an aging Bollywood leading man. His thoughts turned wistfully to the early years after the September 11 attacks when the spies of America and Pakistan seemed to be fighting the same enemy.

"We were just like friends."

The Americans, led by a CIA officer named Keith, were at first suspicious of Munir and most everyone else from the ISI. But after two weeks, Munir said, the suspicions had dissolved. Peshawar was the westernmost city in which the CIA could establish a large base, and by the middle of 2002 the agency had turned the American consulate there into a hub for espionage operations. Antennas were erected on the roof, new computers were installed, clandestine offi-

cers arrived using thin covers. It was, in effect, a spy station posing as a diplomatic outpost.

Munir also remembered the other men who arrived, the "technical people." Munir wouldn't have known, but the technical teams were part of a shadowy Pentagon unit called Gray Fox—officially the Army's Intelligence Support Activity, based at Fort Belvoir, in Virginia—which sent clandestine officers around the world with special equipment to intercept communications. With their arrival, the database of suspicious cell-phone numbers that the U.S.–Pakistani team used to track down al Qaeda around Peshawar and in the tribal areas expanded dramatically. Twelve numbers turned into one hundred, one hundred into twelve hundred. Names of Algerians, Libyans, Saudis, and others that neither the CIA nor the ISI had heard before were added to the roster, and the "list grew like crazy," Munir said. Most of the foreigners that Munir and the Americans were hunting had moved into Pakistan between December 2001 and April 2002, having escaped from the American bombing campaign at Tora Bora and the Shah-i-Kot Valley, in eastern Afghanistan. They were Arabs and Uzbeks and Chechens and natives of other Central Asian countries. Some were looking to make their way back to the Arab states of the Persian Gulf. Some were simply looking for a new home and began laying down roots by marrying local Pashtun women.

Each day the ISI and CIA operatives in Peshawar would pore over a thick stack of transcripts from intercepted conversations and then use the intelligence to plan raids to capture militants in and around Peshawar. The intelligence from the intercepts went only so far, and with a soda-straw view of the war, the spies in Peshawar sometimes made arrests they would never have made if they'd had access to more information. Once, in June 2003, they traced the cell phone of an Algerian operative, Adil Hadi al Jaza'iri, to a large public swimming pool near Peshawar. When they arrived there they found more than a

hundred men in the pool. Without a photograph of al Jaza'iri there was no way they could make the arrest. One of the ISI operatives called the phone number they suspected belonged to al Jaza'iri and watched as a bearded man swam to the side of the pool to pick up his ringing cell phone. A team of Peshawar policemen rushed to the man, dripping wet in his swimsuit.

But they had accidently arrested a double agent. Unbeknownst to them, al Jaza'iri had been informing on al Qaeda for Britain's MI6. The Algerian man was shipped to Guantánamo Bay, and British intelligence had one less informant.

Years later, Munir keeps many of the spy stories to himself, sticking to a code he also expects his American partners to honor. He thinks about the respect that the two spy services once had for each other, respect that might even have been something approaching trust. It was a "thoroughly enjoyable" time, he said, and a moment that he knows can never be re-created because of the years of suspicion that would follow.

The success of the operations led by Asad Munir and the CIA officers around Peshawar, together with the capture of senior bin Laden lieutenants like Khalid Sheikh Mohammed and Ramzi bin al-Shibh in other Pakistani cities, led many top Bush officials to believe that the partnership was working. The al Qaeda figures in Pakistan were being whisked out of the country to Afghanistan, to Thailand, to Romania and other countries that had allowed the CIA to construct secret prisons on their soil. The CIA was sending millions of dollars to the ISI when the bills for Islamabad's support came due. So lucrative had the arrangement become for the Pakistanis that a joke circulated in Islamabad that for each terrorist the ISI helped capture, two new ones needed to be created to keep the racket going.

As Asad Munir saw it, the vague ambitions the ISI had in 2001 to maintain its ties to the Afghan Taliban and the Haqqani Network

had, by 2003 and 2004, morphed into a carefully crafted strategy to use these groups to Islamabad's advantage for a postwar Afghanistan. The Pakistani analysis had been proven wrong: The war in Afghanistan had not turned out to be a short affair. Moreover, the decision by the Bush administration to invade Iraq in 2003 was proof to many in the Pakistani military and intelligence services that Washington had lost interest in Afghanistan and would once again make a chaotic exit from the country. Pakistan needed to protect itself.

"The Americans came to Afghanistan without having a plan in totality: 'How do we enter and how do we exit?'" said Munir. "They were not interested at that time in the Taliban. Their focus was on al Qaeda.

"Pakistan did have second thoughts that these people, the Americans, are not going to secure Afghanistan," he said. "We thought, 'They will leave, and we will have to live with the Afghans.'"

He paused, taking another drag from his cigarette.

"We have our own interests and our own security concerns."

3: CLOAK-AND-DAGGER MEN

"Certainly we don't need a regiment of cloak-and-dagger men, earning their campaign ribbons—and, indeed, their promotions—by planning new exploits throughout the world. Theirs is a self-generating enterprise."

—*Senator Frank Church, 1976*

There was a time, not very long ago, when the CIA was out of the killing business.

When Ross Newland joined the spy agency, in the late 1970s, the CIA wasn't looking to pick any fights abroad. Newland was fresh out of graduate school, and the CIA was reeling from the body blows it had absorbed from congressional committees that had investigated the agency's covert actions since its founding, in 1947. Congress was tightening its control over secret activities, and chastened CIA leaders began to refocus the agency's activities on stealing the secrets of foreign regimes—traditional espionage—rather than overthrowing them or trying to kill their leaders.

President Jimmy Carter, who had campaigned to put an end to the CIA's overseas adventures, had installed Admiral Stansfield Turner at Langley partly to rein in a spy agency he thought had run amok. New-

land and a generation of CIA case officers who joined the agency during this period were told that the CIA would only invite trouble if it got back into the work of killing. By the end of his career, Newland would see the agency come full circle on the matter of lethal action, and he would come to question the wisdom of the CIA's embrace of its role as the willing executioner of America's enemies.

The CIA had been established with a relatively simple mission: collect and analyze intelligence so that American presidents could know each day about the various threats facing the United States. President Truman had not wanted the agency to become America's secret army, but since a vague clause in the National Security Act of 1947 authorized the CIA to "perform such other functions and duties related to intelligence affecting the national security," American presidents have used this "covert action" authority to dispatch the CIA on sabotage operations, propaganda campaigns, election rigging, and assassination attempts.

From the start, critics questioned whether the United States needed a spy service separate from the Defense Department. In defending the agency's independence, CIA directors have pointed out what they have that the Pentagon does not. It has a cadre of undercover officers who can carry out covert missions overseas where the hand of the United States is hidden. The CIA answers directly to the president, the argument goes, and can carry out his orders more quickly, and more quietly, than the military. The residents of the Oval Office have turned to covert action hundreds of times, and often have come to regret it. But memories are short, new presidents arrive at the White House every four or eight years, and a familiar pattern played out over the second half of the twentieth century: presidential approval of aggressive CIA operations, messy congressional investigations when the details of those operations were exposed, retrenchment and soul-

searching at Langley, criticisms that the CIA had become risk-averse, then another period of aggressive covert action. Sometimes the cycle began at the very start of a presidency. During his first week in office, President John F. Kennedy told his advisers he didn't believe that the CIA was aggressive enough in Vietnam and set in motion a secret war against Hanoi that would eventually become the largest and most complex covert action of its time.

The CIA's ambivalence about carrying out assassinations went back to the spy agency's predecessor, the Office of Strategic Services. Created in 1942 under the leadership of its fierce commander, William J. Donovan, the OSS was a paramilitary organization first, espionage service second. Donovan's "glorious amateurs" spent much of World War II sabotaging railways, blowing up bridges, and arming Nazi resisters throughout the European theater. Still, even Donovan got cold feet at the end of the war about a program to train assassins to kill Nazi leaders. By 1945, the OSS had trained about one hundred Wehrmacht deserters to hunt down German leaders—from Adolf Hitler and Hermann Göring down to every SS officer above the rank of captain. For those organized killings, the agents working for the "Cross Project" would be paid two hundred dollars per month. But the teams were never sent into Germany; Donovan wrote to his staff that such a "wholesale assassination" program would "invite only trouble for the OSS." Instead of killing top Nazis, Donovan said that they ought to be kidnapped and interrogated for intelligence. The war ended before any kidnappings could take place.

Decades later, the Senate committee led by Frank Church, of Idaho, had originally intended to look only at domestic abuses by the agency, such as illegal wiretaps. But in early 1975, President Gerald Ford made an offhand comment to reporters, saying that if investigators dug deep enough, they might uncover a number of CIA attempts

to assassinate foreign leaders. When his remarks went public, the Church Committee made assassinations the principal focus of its hearings.

For six months, senators heard about plots to kill Patrice Lumumba, in the Congo, and to position an exploding seashell near where Fidel Castro snorkeled in Cuba. The iconic image of the hearings came when committee members passed around a pistol that the CIA had built to shoot poison darts and Senator Barry Goldwater pointed the gun into the air as he looked through its sights. CIA director William Colby tried to make clear that the weapon had never been used, but the image endured. Before the committee had even wrapped up its work, President Ford signed an executive order banning the government from carrying out assassinations of foreign heads of state or other foreign politicians.

If anything, President Ford's assassination ban was his attempt to put limits on his Oval Office successors, to prevent future presidents from being too easily drawn into black operations. The Church Committee pointed out that, for all the CIA's questionable activities during its early decades, it was always the White House encouraging reckless operations like coup attempts and killing foreign leaders. The CIA offered secrecy, and secrecy had always seduced American presidents.

As Senator Church wrote in his committee's final report, "once the capability for covert activity is established, the pressures brought to bear on the President to use it are immense." Church questioned whether America even needed the CIA at all. Instead of keeping a "regiment of cloak-and-dagger men" at the president's disposal, Church believed that the State Department would be more than capable of taking on covert operations if the need arose but should do so only in the case of dire emergency, perhaps to "avert a nuclear holocaust or save a civilization."

CHURCH DIDN'T GET his wish, but the CIA had been duly chastened by the time that Ross Newland graduated from Trinity College, in Connecticut, in the late 1970s. The son of an international businessman, he had spent most of his life in Latin America and Spain, and spoke fluent Spanish. Given his upbringing and interest in international affairs, Newland figured that he might be destined for a career as a diplomat, but he chose first to pursue a master's degree at the London School of Economics.

At an opulent holiday party in December 1978, at the residence of the American ambassador in Madrid, Newland was recruited to become a spy. He had flown from London to Madrid to see his parents, who were living in Spain, and during the party a man in his early fifties approached him and told him he worked at the embassy. After fifteen minutes of small talk, in both English and Spanish, the man asked Newland if he wanted to walk through the gardens of the residence and speak in private.

The man was Nestor Sanchez, the CIA's station chief in Madrid and a veteran clandestine officer whose storied career in the secret service was in its twilight. An ardent anticommunist, Sanchez had joined the CIA not long after its founding and had been at the center of many of the covert operations investigated by the Church Committee. He had helped engineer the successful 1954 coup against Jacobo Árbenz Guzmán, in Guatemala, and had given a poison-filled syringe disguised as a writing pen to a Cuban agent in an attempt to kill Castro.

Sanchez told Newland he might make a good CIA case officer and gave his name to the agency's station in London. Three months later, Newland was sitting in a bare room at CIA headquarters waiting for his psychological evaluation. A man walked in, sat down, and asked Newland only two questions.

"So, you grew up in Mexico?"

"Yes."

"What's the difference between an enchilada and a tostada?"

Though puzzled by the question, Newland nevertheless explained the difference between the two dishes. After a brief chat about Mexican food, Newland politely told his interviewer that they better start the psychological evaluation because he needed to get to his next interview.

"And he said, 'No, we're done,'" Newland remembers. Ross Newland was in the CIA.

He finished up at the London School of Economics and officially joined the spy agency on November 5, 1979. It was just a day after students in Iran stormed the American embassy and six weeks before Soviet paratroopers landed in Kabul as the vanguard of the hundreds of thousands of troops who would invade Afghanistan over the following months. The two events convulsed CIA headquarters, especially the fifty-three members of Ross Newland's class. Top agency officials ordered all trainees except those fluent in a language not spoken in the Muslim world to be funneled toward assignments in the Middle East or Central Asia.

Because he spoke Spanish, Newland was one of a dozen trainees excluded from the "draft." By the time Newland had completed his case-officer training, Ronald Reagan had become president and the CIA had a newfound interest in Latin America. Cocaine was flowing over the border into the United States, and the Reagan administration was deeply worried about the growing power of leftist guerrilla movements in Central America. Newland had a mentor in Nestor Sanchez, who by then had left Madrid and taken over the CIA's Latin America division. From his perch at headquarters Sanchez was able to guide Newland's early career, and he put him at the center of the action.

He was sent first to Bolivia, then the world's cocaine capital, where

he was directed to cultivate sources in the drug cartels. He spent much of his time in the Bolivian lowlands, posing as an American businessman and trying to make friends among the drug-runners in the city of Santa Cruz. He drank with them, bet on cockfights, met their wives and mistresses, and drove with them out of the city to eat duck with mango and pineapple in ramshackle bungalows along the road leading into the jungle.

When he wasn't in Santa Cruz, he was in the Bolivian capital of La Paz, awaiting the next coup attempt. The CIA station in Bolivia took pride in predicting each coup before it happened, and the agency officers there didn't want to blow their perfect track record. But Newland got a bracing dose of reality about his place in the world when the one successful military overthrow during his tour in Bolivia earned only a small mention on the inside pages of the *New York Times*. The previous four attempts hadn't even made it into the paper.

The Reagan administration had identified the Bolivian government as a partner in the war on drugs. But as he started to penetrate the Bolivian drug networks, Newland began to write intelligence reports about the rampant corruption among top officials in La Paz, many of whom were on the payroll of the cartels. The minister of the interior was protecting the drug kingpins from prosecution, and they were paying him off in ranches, jewels, and cash. The reports were hardly what the American ambassador in La Paz wanted to read.

For Newland, the experience in Bolivia was a first glimpse of how Washington's policy of propping up corrupt governments to serve a singular goal—in this case the war on drugs—could undermine long-term American interests. He also began to question whether the CIA should really be in charge of the drug war, or whether the Reagan administration had just leaned on the agency because messy wars are best fought in secret. Two decades later he would have similar questions about the CIA's role in the war against terrorists.

———

WHEN NEWLAND WAS DISPATCHED to Bolivia, the CIA's Latin America division was a relatively sleepy corner of the spy agency's Directorate of Operations. But it would soon become the center of the CIA's universe, largely because of dynamics many pay grades above Newland. In June 1981, Nestor Sanchez left the agency for the Pentagon. His replacement was Duane R. Clarridge, a gin-drinking and hard-charging spy of the old school who was exactly in the mold sought by William J. Casey, Ronald Reagan's newly installed CIA chief. Known to all as "Dewey," Clarridge grew up in a New Hampshire family of staunch Republicans (his nickname was a tribute to Governor Thomas E. Dewey, of New York) and earned degrees from Brown and Columbia before joining the CIA in 1955. He was eager to battle the Soviet Union on each shadowy front of the Cold War. By 1981, he had served undercover in Nepal, India, Turkey, and Italy, often posing as a businessman and using pseudonyms like Dewey Marone and Dax Preston LeBaron. With a high-octane personality and a preference for white suits and pocket squares, Clarridge attracted a following among younger undercover officers. He was fond of saying that the CIA's clandestine service "marches for the president," but his push for aggressive clandestine operations sometimes infuriated State Department diplomats. Clarridge's boss in Rome, Ambassador Richard Gardner, called him "shallow and devious."

When he returned to Washington, in 1981, Clarridge quickly developed a rapport with Casey. On Clarridge's first day back at CIA headquarters, Casey called him into his office and said that the Reagan administration was worried about Cuba and the Sandinista government in Nicaragua "exporting revolution" throughout Central America, particularly to El Salvador. Within a week, Clarridge came back with a plan:

Take the war to Nicaragua.

Start killing Cubans.

Casey, a former OSS man, embraced the plan immediately. He told Clarridge to draft a secret finding for the president to sign, authorizing a covert war in Central America. It was very early into his presidency, but Ronald Reagan was already accelerating covert activities both in Latin America and in Afghanistan, where he increased support to the mujahedeen fighting Soviet troops. Reagan was initiating a new turn of the cycle: The "risk-averse" CIA was once again running secret wars abroad.

Clarridge was just the man to be in charge of the Central American front, and he used a CIA slush fund to buy guns, ammunition, mules, and heavy weapons for the Nicaraguan Contras, the rebels resisting the government. He worked closely with the Pentagon's special-operations troops, and with an aide at the White House National Security Council, Lt. Colonel Oliver North, to build the Contras up into a guerrilla force he hoped would preoccupy the Sandinista government and prevent it from spreading its influence around America's backyard. The CIA's budget for Nicaragua was tiny; Clarridge and the agency's Latin America hands used to joke that the U.S. Navy pushed trash of greater value off its aircraft carriers in a single morning than the CIA had to spend in Nicaragua in an entire year.

ROSS NEWLAND AND MANY of his peers at the CIA saw the wars in Central America as exactly what the spy agency needed to avoid. But by 1985 Newland's work in the CIA's Latin America division brought him to the heart of the covert wars of the Reagan era. He arrived in Costa Rica just months after a secret CIA operation to mine Nicaragua's harbors had unleashed a fury in Congress and ultimately led

lawmakers to put new rules in place about when the intelligence committees were to be notified about CIA covert-action programs.

The mining operation, which Dewey Clarridge claims he dreamt
up over a glass of gin and a cigar, cost Clarridge his job as chief of the
Latin America division. He moved laterally inside the CIA's clandestine service, taking over CIA operations in Europe.

In Costa Rica, Newland saw firsthand the war that Dewey Clarridge had built. CIA officers in Costa Rica were managing the southern front of the Contra war; the northern operations were run out of
Honduras. Congress had, by then, banned the Reagan administration
from supporting the Nicaraguan rebels, but the CIA's station chief in
Costa Rica, Joe Fernandez, was working with Oliver North to deliver
supplies to the rebels.

Newland's job was to penetrate the government in the capital of
Managua in order to determine the plans and intentions of senior Nicaraguan political and military officials—traditional espionage work.
He met with agents, wrote intelligence reports about the strategy of
the Sandinista government, and put those reports into the stream of
classified cables going back to Langley.

What was bizarre, however, was that other CIA officers in charge
of running the Contras were doing the exact same thing. American
covert officers would make decisions about which Sandinista targets
the Contras should hit and then write up intelligence reports predicting which targets were about to be hit. The cables were sent back to
Washington, and, not surprisingly, the predictions were usually correct. The CIA was, in other words, generating its own intelligence.

"I thought this was so nuts," Newland recalled. "That's not the way
we were taught. But that's the way you do it in a paramilitary situation."

The American effort in Nicaragua steadily unraveled amid revelations that money had been diverted to the Contras from the sale of

HAWK missiles to Iran, a sale brokered by Oliver North in an attempt to secure the release of American hostages held in Beirut. Newland watched as the Iran–Contra investigation slowly ensnared his CIA bosses, past and present. His station chief in Bolivia, Jim Adkins, who had moved to Honduras to run Contra operations from the north, was fired from the agency when it emerged he had authorized helicopter flights to carry supplies into Nicaragua. Joe Fernandez was indicted on June 20, 1988, on counts of obstruction of justice and making false statements, although the charges were eventually dropped. Nestor Sanchez, Newland's first mentor at the CIA, was suspected of involvement in the illegal operations while working at the Pentagon but was never charged with a crime.

The Contra debacle was a searing experience for Newland. He disagreed with much of what he witnessed in Central America, but he was bitter that agency officers were being bled dry defending themselves while senior White House officials escaped punishment. But it taught him a lesson that he would apply years later, when President George W. Bush authorized the CIA to carry out the most extensive covert-operations campaign in its history, after the September 11 attacks. That lesson? Get everything in writing.

"When we got into things like lethal authorities, detention policies, all of these things, I made sure this was signed up and down Pennsylvania Avenue," he recalls. "Why? Because I had been there before."

IT WOULD BE ANOTHER five years before Iran–Contra investigators would catch up to Dewey Clarridge and indict him on perjury charges. But before that, he convinced Casey to upend the agency's bureaucracy to deal with a threat that neither the CIA nor the Pentagon had spent much time thinking about: Islamic terrorism.

In a two-year span beginning in 1983, terrorist groups with names

unfamiliar to most Americans went on a stunning international killing spree. The spate of attacks began when a bomb ripped through
the American embassy in Beirut and killed sixty-three employees,
including eight CIA officers. Later that year, a truck packed with explosives killed 241 Marines sleeping in their barracks in Beirut, an
attack that had been ordered by an underground terror cell called the
Islamic Jihad Organization (a cover name at the time for Hezbollah)
to protest the military's ill-advised deployment to Lebanon. In June
1985, Lebanese hijackers killed a U.S. Navy diver during the TWA
Flight 847 hostage standoff, and in October 1985 a Palestinian terrorist known as Abu Abbas hijacked the *Achille Lauro* cruise ship, ordering the killing of a sixty-nine-year-old American tourist named Leon
Klinghoffer. His body was thrown overboard.

Struggling for a response, Reagan officials considered giving the
CIA the authority to hunt and kill Lebanese terrorists using teams of
local hit men. Oliver North wrote a draft of a presidential finding that
included language giving the CIA authority to "neutralize" militants
with deadly force. Casey was intrigued by the idea of using Lebanese
hit men, but his deputy was appalled. John McMahon, who still bore
scars from the congressional investigations of the 1970s and had
grown weary of Casey's exploits, was enraged when he heard about
the plan. He was sure that creating hit squads violated President
Ford's assassination ban. "Do you know what intelligence means to
these people?" he asked Casey, referring to White House officials.
"It's tossing a bomb. It's blowing up people." And, he said, any blowback from a decision to start killing terrorists would be felt not at the
White House but at the CIA. "To the rest of the world," he warned
Casey, "it's not administration policy, it's not an NSC idea—it's those
crazy bastards at CIA."

But Casey was not convinced by McMahon's objections, and he
threw his support behind Oliver North's proposal. In November

1984, President Reagan signed a secret finding authorizing the CIA and the Pentagon's Joint Special Operations Command to go ahead with the training of Lebanese hit men. But the plan was never carried out, and the finding was ultimately rescinded by Reagan amid opposition from the State Department and the CIA's old guard. Former CIA director Richard Helms, weighing in from his retirement, told an aide to Vice President George H. W. Bush that the United States should not adopt the Israeli model of "fighting terrorism with terrorism."

Casey had hoped that the rash of terrorism would end as quickly as it began. But some CIA officers at the time thought that Casey simply didn't understand the new threat, and a bloody Christmastime attack at the El Al ticket counters inside the Vienna and Rome airports in 1985 destroyed any hope that terrorism would fade away. Palestinian gunmen doped up on amphetamines killed nineteen people during the airport spree. The grisliness of the attacks was driven home to Americans through the death of an eleven-year-old American named Natasha Simpson. A terrorist shot the girl at close range as she lay in her father's arms.

Shortly after the attacks in Vienna and Rome, Clarridge made his argument to Casey for a new CIA campaign against Islamic terrorism. Clarridge thought the agency was in a defensive crouch, and he won the director's blessing to begin an expansive new war.

Clarridge's proposal was to create a dedicated group inside the CIA devoted solely to international terrorism. It would be a "fusion center" where clandestine officers would work next to analysts, piecing together clues about possible threats and gathering intelligence in order to capture or kill terrorist leaders. What sounds like a standard bureaucratic reorganization was, at the time, quite controversial. The CIA is actually a fragmented, cliquish culture, more like a public high school than many inside the agency care to admit. Jockish paramilitary officers tend to shun the nerdy analysts, who regard the para-

military operatives as knuckle-draggers. At the top of the pyramid are the case officers—the spies who go out into the world—who believe they are doing the real work of the CIA and like to boast that they don't follow orders from desk jockeys at headquarters.

There was immediate resistance to Clarridge's idea from clandestine officers with Middle East experience. They believed that the center would be staffed by officers who didn't understand the nuances of the Islamic world and would create messes that the officers stationed overseas would have to clean up. Chasing terrorists, they sniffed, was police work, better suited to the FBI than the CIA. Finally, many officers simply didn't trust Clarridge and saw the center as empire building. The Counterterrorist Center was, therefore, born amid the similar tensions that the CIA would experience after the September 11 attacks—between case officers in Islamabad and CTC operatives at Langley, between those pushing for unilateral operations and those warning that such operations could shatter delicate relations with foreign intelligence services.

Casey ignored the internal objections and approved Clarridge's proposal, and the Counterterrorist Center began operations on February 1, 1986. The CTC's birth narrative was familiar: The White House was struggling with a problem it couldn't find an answer for, so it looked to the CIA for a solution. And the CIA was happy to oblige.

The creation of the CTC was also significant because, from the beginning, CTC officers worked closely with military special-operations troops and allowed the military to be a partner in clandestine missions. The Pentagon's Special Operations Command was founded one year after the CTC, and operatives from both organizations viewed each other as kindred souls, imbued with the spirit of Bill Donovan's OSS. Unlike other parts of the CIA, the Counterterrorist Center didn't turn up its nose at the military. The Pentagon's commandos were partners with the terrorist hunters at the CTC.

When the Counterterrorist Center began operations, there were no ongoing covert operations against international terrorist groups, and the CTC began working with Army paramilitary units like Delta Force to penetrate the Abu Nidal organization and Hezbollah. Lawyers working for President Reagan drew up secret legal memos concluding that hunting and killing terrorists did not violate the 1976 assassination ban, just as lawyers working for Presidents George W. Bush and Barack Obama would do decades later. These terrorist groups were plotting attacks against Americans, the lawyers argued, so killing them would be self-defense, not assassination.

But getting the legal authorities is only one step, and it doesn't guarantee that politicians will bless specific lethal operations. During the early years of the Counterterrorist Center, the White House had little political capital to spend convincing Congress of the need to kill terrorists in secret. The Iran–Contra investigations had sapped the energies from Reagan's national-security team and given more clout to advisers like National Security Advisor Colin Powell and Secretary of State George Shultz, who urged against any more overseas exploits. There was no longer the stomach for a fight, recalled Fred Turco, who was Dewey Clarridge's deputy at the CTC and later took over the center. "The wheels had fallen off for Reagan."

ROSS NEWLAND LEFT the jungles of Central America cynical about how the Iran–Contra scandal had shattered the agency's clandestine service. But unlike his CIA bosses, he had not become enmeshed in the unfolding scandal; in fact, he received a promotion. He and several of his contemporaries were elevated to become chiefs of overseas stations in Eastern Europe, jobs that put them in charge of agency operations in various Soviet satellite states. Still in his early thirties, Newland became the youngest station chief in the history of the CIA's

division handling Eastern Europe and the Soviet Union. In 1988, the CIA didn't see that as much of a risk.

"They put us there because they were pretty confident that nothing was going to happen," said Newland. "And, boy, did they fuck up."

Within a year, the Berlin Wall had crumbled and revolution had spread throughout Eastern Europe. As the CIA's top officer in Romania, Newland was in charge of keeping the Bush administration informed about the collapse of the regime of Nicolae Ceausescu, who fled Bucharest with his wife as crowds swelled in the streets during the week before Christmas 1989. On Christmas Day, with Romanian paratroopers holding Nicolae and Elena Ceausescu in custody, Newland found himself trying to convince the officers of the unit holding the couple not to execute them without at least conducting some kind of trial. At least, that's what Newland's bosses at Langley had told him to tell the Romanian troops. "And so we forced them to go through a trial, and it lasted, like, twenty minutes," he said. When that formality was dispensed with, the platoon commander asked for three volunteers to form a firing squad. But when the Romanian dictator and his wife were put up against the wall, their hands bound behind their backs, the entire platoon opened fire.

With the end of the Cold War came the end of the CIA's defining mission. Countering the advance of Communism had been the agency's lodestar, justifying decades of far-flung operations in Latin America, the Middle East, and Europe. The budget cuts to the Pentagon and CIA during the 1990s hit the agency's clandestine service particularly hard, with overseas stations shuttered and the total number of CIA case officers slashed. Overall spending on human-intelligence collection was cut by 22 percent over the decade. President Clinton, America's first baby-boomer president and a onetime Vietnam War protester, was a natural skeptic of the CIA and gave his spy chiefs little time during his first term. R. James Woolsey Jr., Clinton's first

CIA director, said that Clinton paid little attention to intelligence issues and had private meetings with his spy chief only once a year. "We
had very little access, frankly," Woolsey said. After he left the CIA he
joked that the man who crashed a stolen Cessna plane on the South
Lawn of the White House, in September 1994, was actually him trying to get a meeting with the president.

The agency was also still facing a reckoning for the aggressive operations in Latin America overseen by Dewey Clarridge in the 1980s. In
1996, an intelligence-oversight board issued a report detailing the
extensive human-rights abuses carried out for more than a decade by
CIA assets in Guatemala. It alleged that between 1984 and 1986
several CIA informants were alleged to have "ordered, planned, or participated in serious human-rights violations such as assassination, extrajudicial execution, torture, or kidnapping while they were assets—
and that the CIA was contemporaneously aware of many of the allegations." The Guatemala revelations had been trickling out for years,
leading CIA director John M. Deutch to impose new restrictions on
agency case officers consorting with unsavory characters. The drug
lords with whom Ross Newland had once bet on cockfights in Bolivia
would now be off-limits to CIA officers, as would terrorists who might
be attempting to kill Americans.

Deutch, a chemist with a Ph.D. from the Massachusetts Institute
of Technology, came to Langley from the Pentagon after President
Clinton removed James Woolsey from the CIA job in 1995. He
wanted to build spy satellites and overseas listening posts, not send
clandestine officers on swashbuckling secret missions. He didn't trust
the agency's clandestine service, and they treated him like a virus that
had invaded the host body.

One of his initiatives was to have the CIA work more closely with
the military on issues other than counterterrorism, which by the midnineties had returned to being an issue of little importance at the CIA.

Since the end of the Gulf War, in 1991, Pentagon generals had complained that the CIA had been useless in penetrating Saddam Hussein's regime before the war broke out and just as bad in helping the military hunt Iraqi forces in the desert. Deutch ordered CIA officers to serve in military command posts around the globe to make sure that the agency was giving its best intelligence on global threats.

Deutch believed that the CIA's role of supporting the military was so essential that in 1995 he also created a top-level job to serve as a liaison to the Pentagon, a post that would be held by a senior military officer. Some inside the agency joked that embedding CIA operatives inside military commands and flag officers inside the intelligence agency was the bureaucratic equivalent of a hostage swap.

The first military officer tapped for the CIA job was Vice Admiral Dennis C. Blair, a wiry Yankee from Kittery, Maine, who had graduated from the Naval Academy in 1968 and went on to Oxford University as a Rhodes scholar, where he became friends with a young Bill Clinton. Blair met resistance almost immediately from CIA officers who were skeptical about the three-star admiral with a dim view of the CIA's track record on covert action.

As Blair saw it, the agency should be focusing on collecting and analyzing intelligence, not on black operations that only served to get the United States in trouble. "Going back to the history of CIA covert operations, I think you can make the argument that if we had done none of them we would probably be better off, and certainly no worse off than we are today," Blair would say years later.

Some at Langley saw Blair as a Pentagon mole. But his presence also raised bigger fears that the Pentagon would consume the agency and that the CIA would lose its spot as the president's loyal intelligence service. The men, as Dewey Clarridge had said, marched for the president.

Blair soon found himself fighting battles with the CIA's Director-

ate of Operations on the biggest issue of the time, the war in the Balkans. One of the fights was over a new surveillance tool the CIA had borrowed from the Air Force to spy in Bosnia, a gangly, insect-like airplane called the RQ-1 Predator. The CIA had been flying the Predator to spy on Serbian troop positions, and senior agency officers proposed installing video screens inside the White House to allow President Clinton and his aides to watch the live drone feed. Blair admired the CIA's initiative in developing the Predator but thought it would be a waste of the president's precious time watching a drone feed. He suspected that the CIA's clandestine service was just trying to show off its new toy for President Clinton.

"What's the president going to do with it?" Blair remembers asking. "And they said, 'It needs to go into the White House in case the president wants to know what's going on in Bosnia.'

"And I said, 'That's ridiculous! The president is not going to look through this little soda straw!'"

Deutch ultimately sided with Blair, and the CIA never fed the Predator video into the White House. It was a silly fight, but for Blair, that episode and other battles he fought with the agency's clandestine service were telling reminders that the Directorate of Operations would try to bite any arm trying to block its direct path to the Oval Office.

More than a decade later, with another Democratic president in charge, Blair would try once again to get between the CIA and the White House. It would be fatal to his career.

4: RUMSFELD'S SPIES

"We seem to have created our own CIA, but like Topsy, uncoordinated and uncontrolled."

—*Deputy Secretary of Defense Frank Carlucci, 1982*

"Given the nature of our world, isn't it conceivable that the Department ought not to be in a position of near total dependence on CIA in situations such as this?"

—*Secretary of Defense Donald Rumsfeld, 2001*

In November 2001, as teams of American Green Berets, CIA operatives, and Afghan warlords were dislodging the Taliban forces from Kabul and Kandahar, Donald Rumsfeld flew to Fort Bragg, North Carolina, a sprawling base in Fayetteville that for years had been home to large numbers of the military's special-operations troops. It was primarily meant to be a day for glad-handing, with Rumsfeld meeting with the Special Forces commanders to thank them for what had been, thus far, a surprisingly easy invasion of Afghanistan.

After a morning of congratulations and PowerPoint presentations, Rumsfeld was driven to a walled-off compound straddling Fort Bragg and adjacent to Pope Air Force Base. It was the home of the Joint

Special Operations Command (JSOC), a highly classified organization comprised mostly of Army Delta Force operatives and members of the Naval Special Warfare Development Group, commonly called SEAL Team Six. JSOC was a small operational arm of the larger U.S. Special Operations Command, and at the time the Pentagon refused to acknowledge the group even existed.

JSOC put on a show for the visiting defense secretary. To demonstrate its ability to insert commandos into countries undetected, soldiers parachuted out of a plane and landed right in front of Rumsfeld. One of them, wearing a suit and carrying a briefcase, shed his parachute and walked away from the landing zone in his wingtip shoes. Rumsfeld was also taken to a "shoot house," where he watched a practice hostage-rescue operation—the JSOC operatives pretending to kill off all hostage-takers without harming the captives. Rumsfeld was immediately sold.

By that point, the special-operations group was well experienced in showing off for visiting officials. Years earlier, in 1986, Representative Dick Cheney went to Fort Bragg for a day of meetings with Delta Force commanders and heard about how Delta Force was using databases to mine information about possible terrorism threats. In the middle of a briefing about LexisNexis—the now-ubiquitous news-and-document database that was then a novelty—Cheney asked the military briefer to search the database for his name. The top story was a news article about a bill in the House of Representatives that Cheney had sponsored and how another congressman had said the day before that he would vote against it.

Cheney was livid. He ordered the watch officer to track down the congressman and then, from inside the operations center, he screamed at the man over the phone. "We had to clear the place out," remembered Thomas O'Connell, then a top JSOC intelligence officer, who said that Cheney seemed like "a changed man" when he saw the power

of using databases to gather information about specific individuals. From that point on, said O'Connell, "Cheney was in his comfort zone dealing with special operators."

Seventeen years later, on a similar pilgrimage to Fort Bragg, Cheney's old mentor Donald Rumsfeld also thought he was getting a glimpse of the future. Accompanying Rumsfeld on the trip was Robert Andrews, who had been at Rumsfeld's side almost constantly in the weeks since the September 11 attacks. Andrews was the Pentagon's top civilian official in charge of special operations, and, like Virgil in Dante's *Inferno*, he had been guiding Rumsfeld through a dark world, which had expanded dramatically since Rumsfeld's first tour as defense secretary, during the Ford administration.

Rumsfeld couldn't have found a more experienced guide. A folksy native of Spartanburg, South Carolina, Andrews graduated with a chemical-engineering degree from the University of Florida in 1960 and joined the Army as part of an ROTC commitment he thought would keep him in uniform for just two years. Instead, by 1963 he had joined the Green Berets and began what would turn into five decades immersed in the world of special operations and intelligence. The following year, he left for Vietnam as a young Special Forces captain, bound for the first of two tours as part of a covert paramilitary unit running a secret war against North Vietnam with sabotage, assassination, and black propaganda. The group, known officially by the bland bureaucratic name Military Assistance Command, Vietnam—Studies and Observation Group (MACV–SOG), conducted the largest and most intricate covert operations the United States had carried out since the days of the OSS.

Andrews returned from Vietnam and wrote a book, *The Village War*, about the extensive intelligence networks in South Vietnamese hamlets that the Communists had set up during the early 1960s and used to outmaneuver South Vietnamese and American forces during

the war. The book was based almost exclusively on interrogation reports of captured North Vietnamese Army and Viet Cong soldiers and the accounts of North Vietnamese defectors. Andrews's book was widely read inside the CIA, and in 1975, just after Saigon fell to troops from the North, he was asked to work at Langley as the head of a team scrubbing the agency's classified analysis of Vietnam.

"Essentially, it was looking at intelligence failures," recalled Andrews, who came to realize that America's problems in Vietnam had as much to do with a deep ignorance of the culture and psychology of the Vietnamese as any specific military blunders. He stayed at the CIA for five years before leaving to work in the defense industry and begin writing a string of spy thrillers and mysteries, including one called *The Towers*. The book was about a former CIA operative frantically trying to defuse a terrorist plot inside the United States. On the cover was a picture of the World Trade Center.

Andrews was sixty-four years old when he returned to the Pentagon in 2001, and he was sitting by Rumsfeld's side on September 25, when General Charles Holland, head of U.S. Special Operations Command (SOCOM), provided the first briefing about how the military would fight its war against al Qaeda. Rumsfeld had ordered Holland to come up with a plan for a worldwide campaign beyond the al Qaeda stronghold of Afghanistan, and when Rumsfeld gathered his aides around a conference table, he had expected to be told that might be possible.

The briefing got off to a promising start, when Holland showed a map and ticked off the list of countries—Afghanistan, Pakistan, Somalia, Yemen, Mauritania, even parts of Latin America—where the military believed Osama bin Laden's lieutenants were hiding. Rumsfeld became animated and interrupted the general.

"How soon can we begin operations in these countries?" he asked.

Holland considered the question. After a pause, he told Rumsfeld exactly what the irascible defense secretary didn't want to hear.

"Well, it would be difficult, because we don't have any actionable intelligence," Holland replied.

There was another problem: SOCOM wasn't even prepared to fight that kind of war—or any war, for that matter. The command's job was only to train special-operations troops, get them ready to fight, and send them off to the Pentagon's other regional military headquarters in the Middle East, the Pacific, and elsewhere. The regional commanders jealously guarded their own patches of the globe and looked dimly at the prospect of SOCOM running its own missions on their turf.

Things then went from bad to worse when Rumsfeld asked Holland another question, one he figured might get an acceptable response. When would special-operations troops get into Afghanistan and begin the war there?

"When we get clearance from the CIA," Holland replied.

Robert Andrews looked over at Rumsfeld, whom Andrews recalled was in the process of "screwing himself into the ceiling." In a matter of minutes, he had been told that not only did his expensive special-operations troops lack any intelligence about al Qaeda; they also couldn't even go to the battlefield without getting permission from George Tenet and the CIA.

This was something that frustrated Rumsfeld frequently during the months after the September 11 attacks, so often that he once complained to General Tommy Franks, commander of U.S. Central Command and the general in charge of the Afghan war, that even though the Defense Department was many times the size of the CIA, the military was like "little birds in a nest, waiting for someone to drop food in their mouths." Days after the war in Afghanistan began he

had dashed off an acerbic memo to Joint Chiefs chairman General Richard Myers. "Given the nature of our world," Rumsfeld wrote, "isn't it conceivable that the Department ought not to be in a position of near total dependence on CIA in situations such as this?"

Rumsfeld had long been critical of the intelligence agency. In 1998, when he was chairman of an independent commission to assess the ballistic-missile threat to the United States, he wrote a letter to Tenet that was a withering indictment of CIA judgments about the missile capabilities of Iran and North Korea. But now, in the midst of a new war, he realized he envied the spy agency's ability to send its operatives anywhere, at any time, without having to ask permission. "You can legitimately trace the change in warfare back to the realization that we didn't have the intelligence to fight the war we wanted to fight," said Andrews about his boss's decisions in the year after the September 11 attacks.

Rumsfeld concluded that the only answer was to make the Pentagon more like the CIA.

DONALD RUMSFELD'S CONCERNS weren't entirely new. In 1980, after a fiery debacle in the Dasht-e Kavir, Iran's Great Salt Desert, the Pentagon decided it needed more of its own spies.

The clandestine mission that April to rescue fifty-two hostages imprisoned in the American-embassy compound in Tehran was snake-bitten from the start: Three of the eight helicopters involved in the rescue operation developed mechanical problems on the way to the remote landing strip; another crash-landed at the rendezvous point; and, shortly after commanders gave the order to abort the mission, a helicopter caught in a sandstorm collided with a military cargo plane, killing eight soldiers in an explosion that lit up the desert sky.

And yet the botched mission in Iran was not, in the military's view, simply a tragic confluence of naive expectations, poor planning, and failed execution. In the minds of some of the commandos who watched their friends die in the explosions in the desert, Operation Eagle Claw had been partly undone by the failure of the Central Intelligence Agency to provide tactical information about what to expect during the mission.

Even before its disastrous conclusion, the operation had been beset by fights between the CIA and the military about how to gather intelligence for the mission. The spy agency had already shown it was unable to understand the dynamics of the Iranian Revolution, with CIA director Stansfield Turner lamenting during National Security Council meetings that the agency had few sources in the country and was largely relying on American newspaper reports and the BBC for information. The Delta Force commander for the mission didn't trust the CIA officers assigned to collect intelligence in Iran before the operation, so he sent former Green Beret Richard Meadows into the country to conduct surveillance of the embassy compound where the hostages were being held. Traveling on a fake Irish passport and masking his West Virginia accent with a brogue, Meadows had cleared customs posing as "Richard Keith," a European automobile executive.

Of course, the American troops never even made it into Tehran to carry out the rescue. But generals at the Pentagon complained that the Defense Department had no ability to send its own people on clandestine spying missions to help pave the way for commando operations. In a memorandum to the head of the Defense Intelligence Agency in December 1980, one general on the Pentagon's Joint Staff wrote about a "serious and persistent information deficiency" and the need for a group of "reliable human observers." With the Pentagon making plans for a second rescue attempt in Iran, the Joint Chiefs of

Staff hastily created a group of such observers. It became known as the Field Operations Group.

The group bore the unfortunate acronym FOG, and did very little. The hostages were released on the day of President Reagan's inauguration, in January 1981, making another rescue attempt in Iran unnecessary. But even after FOG was disbanded, Army chief of staff Edward Meyer saw the need for a permanent cadre of Pentagon spies and, at one Pentagon meeting, barked, "I'll be damned if we ever get caught in another Iranian hostage situation where we can't find out what's going on or where we can't get into the country." The military's Intelligence Support Activity (ISA) was born.

These programs during the early 1980s weren't the Pentagon's first foray into the human-intelligence game. But previous spying efforts had been halting, in part because of resistance from top generals and admirals, who thought that soldiers shouldn't also be spies. But the Operation Eagle Claw fiasco gave greater leverage to those who wanted to expand the Pentagon's ranks of human spies, most prominently the Army's General Meyer. The Intelligence Support Activity opened an office inside the Pentagon with approximately fifty people but with ambitions of growing to five times that size. The unit's official blazon featured various symbols to represent the failed Iranian rescue mission and carried the phrase SEND ME, drawn from a passage from the Book of Isaiah: "Also I heard the voice of the Lord, saying, 'Whom shall I send, and who will go for us?' Then I said, 'Here am I! Send me.'"

The ISA was set up in 1981 with a large black budget, a brash, hard-charging Army colonel as its commander, and permission to carry out secret spying operations without even having to notify the Joint Chiefs of Staff. They were the perfect ingredients for a toxic recipe. The world of secret operations is filled with Type-A person-

alities, and a clandestine unit with unlimited funds and a vague mission is bound to push legal boundaries. The ISA run by Colonel Jerry King was no exception.

Almost from the beginning, King launched a number of off-the-books operations around the globe. Undoubtedly the most colorful was an operation to funnel money and equipment to a retired Green Beret planning a private mission to rescue American POWs suspected of being held in Laos. For several years, James "Bo" Gritz had been traveling to Southeast Asia to gather information about possible POWs, trips that were bankrolled by Texas tycoon H. Ross Perot. By early 1981, shortly after the creation of the ISA, Gritz believed he had found hard evidence that dozens of POWs were being held at a camp in central Laos. The information had come from a satellite image of the camp taken years earlier, in which the figures B and 52 seemed to have been formed—a possible signal from POWs to whomever might be watching from the sky.

He began planning a rescue mission and even gave it a code name: Velvet Hammer. Gritz assembled a team of twenty-five retired Special Forces soldiers, trained them at a camp in Florida, and sent a separate group to Thailand to lay the groundwork for the mission into Laos. As Gritz prepared for the mission, many members of the ISA contacted him and offered their support: tens of thousands of dollars' worth of camera equipment, radios, plane tickets to Bangkok, and polygraph equipment to determine whether local sources providing information about the POW camp might be lying. The ISA also gave satellite photos and other intelligence information to Gritz's team.

Colonel King had begun supporting Gritz without notifying top Pentagon officials. That turned out to be a problem, as the Joint Chiefs of Staff all the while had secretly been drawing up their own plans for a rescue mission at the exact same camp in Laos. The Joint

Chiefs' plan called for sending a reconnaissance team of Laotian mercenaries across the border from Thailand into Laos to determine whether there were indeed any POWs being held there. If the mercenaries found proof that the POWs were at the camp, the Pentagon would launch a rescue operation modeled after the Iranian hostage rescue mission, sending a Delta Force team into the camp.

When top Pentagon and CIA officials learned about Gritz's parallel rescue mission, secretly supported by the ISA, they threatened to shut the group down. They thought that Gritz's freelancing had endangered the official rescue operation and that Colonel King had gone beyond his brief. As it turned out, no rescue missions were carried out on the camp in Laos, and no definitive proof was ever found that POWs were held there. Secretary of Defense Caspar Weinberger ordered the Pentagon inspector general to investigate all of the ISA's operations. Besides the Gritz episode, the ISA had also been secretly running undercover operations in Panama City to monitor General Manuel Noriega and was involved at the margins of an extensive network of front companies used for covert military activities around the world. The network of companies, part of a program called Yellow Fruit, helped enable some of the secret deals of the Iran–Contra scandal that came to light several years later.

The inspector general's report on the ISA was blistering. It portrayed the group as a rogue unit with little adult supervision and documented profligate spending by the intelligence unit, including a string of bizarre purchases: a Rolls-Royce, a hot-air balloon, and a dune buggy. The report stunned both Weinberger and Deputy Secretary of Defense Frank Carlucci. In May 1982, Carlucci wrote a memo calling the report "disturbing in the extreme." Carlucci had arrived at the Pentagon from the CIA, where he had been Admiral Stansfield Turner's deputy and had seen the toll that years of unsupervised black operations had taken on the CIA.

"We should have learned the lesson of the '70s," Carlucci wrote in his memo about the inspector general's report, but instead "we have created an organization that is unaccountable." He made a comparison to the character of Topsy, from Harriet Beecher Stowe's *Uncle Tom's Cabin*, a young slave girl whose origins and growth nobody in the book could explain: "We seem to have created our own CIA," he wrote, "but like Topsy, uncoordinated and uncontrolled."

The following year, when American troops were planning to invade Grenada to rescue a group of medical students taken as hostages, the mission commander refused to include the ISA in the operation because he didn't trust the outfit or its leader, Colonel King. As it turned out, American commandos fumbled around the Caribbean island in October 1983 with little idea of where the medical students were being held. "Our intelligence about Grenada was lousy," recalled Dewey Clarridge, who was chief of the CIA's Latin America division at the time. "We were operating virtually in the dark."

If things weren't bad enough for the ISA, the CIA was also trying to gut its operations. The spy agency was suspicious of the military building an intelligence empire and dismissive of the idea that military officers could be any good at espionage. This partly reflected a wider insecurity at Langley about the Pentagon. Since its founding, in 1947, the CIA had been the Pentagon's smaller sibling, dwarfed by the Defense Department's manpower and muscle in the Washington budget wars. The CIA director didn't even control most of America's big-ticket intelligence programs; the constellation of spy satellites and global listening posts that accounted for 80 percent of what the United States spent on spying was funded through the Pentagon's budget. During his first stint as defense secretary, under President Ford, Rumsfeld fought frequent turf battles with the CIA and White House, arguing that if he was paying for these programs, he was going to control them.

If there was one area where the CIA figured it had an advantage over the Pentagon, it was in the realm of human spying. So when the Pentagon created a program like the ISA, many at the CIA saw it as a direct threat to the agency's existence. CIA leaders whispered into the ears of members of the congressional intelligence committees that the Pentagon's spies were amateurs and were tripping over CIA case officers overseas. Covert operations could be blown, they said, and undercover officers might die.

Of course, the fact that the CIA was trying to undermine Pentagon spying efforts made military leaders trust the CIA even less and want to expand their own spying operations even more. During one meeting in 1983, when CIA director William Casey met with the Joint Chiefs inside the Pentagon's secure conference room, known as "The Tank," General Meyer was, as usual, complaining that the CIA never did anything to help the military. Casey tried to quiet the general by pointing out that his predecessor, Admiral Stansfield Turner, had been a military man. But General Meyer would have none of it. "Mr. Casey, what you say is true," he said. "But that son of a bitch didn't do a goddamned thing for the military during all his time at CIA."

EVEN AFTER THE INSPECTOR general's report, and even after Carlucci tried to get rid of Colonel King's group, it never went away. In fact, the unit would eventually become a cornerstone of Rumsfeld's efforts to dramatically expand the Pentagon's spying operations. By late 2001, the ISA had evolved into the secret spying unit, codenamed Gray Fox, that began working with Asad Munir and Pakistani spies in western Pakistan. Based just beyond the Washington beltway, at Fort Belvoir, Virginia, Gray Fox comprised several hundred operatives working undercover in overseas assignments. They specialized in

planting eavesdropping devices in hard-to-reach places—the devices could then link up to the large listening stations that the National Security Agency had set up around the globe.

But in 2001, the group was such a little-discussed, fringe organization that it had been nicknamed "The Secret Army of Northern Virginia." When Rumsfeld first met the commander of Gray Fox and learned details of the group's operations, he said, "If I had known you guys were doing all this before 9/11, I'd probably have thrown you all in jail." But with Rumsfeld now consumed with improving and better coordinating the Pentagon's somewhat meager human spying capabilities, he ordered an increase in Gray Fox's budget and closer coordination between the spying unit and Joint Special Operations Command, the secretive unit that had so impressed Rumsfeld during his trip to Fort Bragg in November 2001. Since that day, Rumsfeld increasingly had come to see JSOC as exactly the secret army he needed to fight a global war.

But JSOC in 2001 was in no position to be Rumsfeld's Praetorian Guard for a worldwide conflict. Delta Force and SEAL Team Six were niche forces, comprising no more than several hundred operatives and unable to sustain themselves for operations lasting more than two days. Delta Force trained almost exclusively for hostage-rescue missions, and SEAL Team Six had spent years training for the mission of securing America's nuclear arsenal inside the country if the need should ever arise. Neither had had the training or equipment for far-flung operations lasting weeks or months.

"Rumsfeld just got the notion that [JSOC] has this capability to get in anywhere, kill all the right people and save all the right people—why not use this thing?" said Robert Andrews. "What he didn't realize was that it wasn't set up for sustained combat operations."

But Rumsfeld saw the appeal in JSOC's independence. It could

be a strike force answering directly to the defense secretary and the president, not under the control of some four-star general worried about his turf. It could be like the CIA's Directorate of Operations— unburdened by the weight of a hidebound military bureaucracy. If Rumsfeld could throw money at the command, allowing Delta Force and SEAL Team Six to enlarge their ranks and buy enough equipment for lengthy overseas deployments, he figured he could send it virtually anywhere.

But was it even legal for him to do that? The Pentagon's activities are governed by Title 10 of the United States Code, and Congress historically has tried to limit how the military operates outside of declared war zones. This is partly born from concerns that American soldiers operating beyond battlefields could be caught and tried as spies rather than granted the usual Geneva Convention protections. By contrast, the president can order the CIA (which is governed by Title 50) to send its officers anywhere in the world. Under those rules, if a CIA officer is caught spying in a hostile country, the American government might deny any knowledge of his activities and let him rot in jail.

After the Iran–Contra scandal of the 1980s, Congress tried to place even more restrictions on secret operations. The Intelligence Authorization Act of 1991 mandated that all covert actions be authorized by a written presidential finding, explaining the need for the secret activity, and that the White House notify the House and Senate intelligence committees shortly after the finding is issued to the CIA. And yet the 1991 act contained a significant loophole: It exempted the Pentagon from these burdensome requirements if the military was conducting secret operations it considered to be "traditional military activities."

The law offered little guidance as to what constituted "traditional

military activities," partly because the George H. W. Bush White House and Pentagon had successfully lobbied Congress to keep the language vague. These activities were ultimately defined as any operations carried out by the military that were connected to "ongoing" or "anticipated" hostilities. In other words, the Pentagon could justify sending troops to any country in the world if it could make the case that the United States was at war inside that country—or might be at some point in the future.

These arcane provisions were little discussed for a decade, until the days after the September 11 attacks when Congress gave President Bush a sweeping mandate to wage war all over the globe. According to the provisions of the Authorization for Use of Military Force (AUMF), the United States was not at war *with* any one particular country but at war *in* any country where al Qaeda was operating. The measure, in effect, gave Rumsfeld the license he was looking for to carry out a global war.

Still, it took time for the defense secretary to exploit these new powers. Not long after the fall of Kabul, in late 2001, the energies of senior leaders at the Pentagon turned almost immediately to planning for an invasion of Iraq. And beyond the al Qaeda safe havens like Pakistan, the Pentagon had difficulty figuring out where else the United States could hunt al Qaeda. In the counterterrorism vernacular, the requirement was to "find, fix, and finish" terrorists. But as Rumsfeld would admit years later, "We had the ability to finish. We just couldn't find and fix things."

RUMSFELD AND HIS TEAM were feeling quite sure of themselves during the first half of 2003. The invasion of Iraq had seemed, at first, to confirm much of Rumsfeld's vision for a new way of war. The

march to Baghdad that had lasted barely a month was conducted with a relatively small invasion army—testing the defense secretary's philosophy that advances in technology, twinned with a war plan that emphasized speed over muscle, could win the wars of the twenty-first century. His skepticism about the CIA's intelligence had also led him, the year before the invasion, to set up a small shop at the Pentagon— overseen by Under Secretary of Defense for Policy Douglas J. Feith— to sift through raw intelligence to prove that Saddam Hussein was in league with Islamic terrorists. Once American troops had reached Baghdad, many of Rumsfeld's aides had convinced themselves, it was only a matter of time before they would find definite proof of a link between Hussein and Osama bin Laden and a post facto justification for the invasion. Ultimately, American troops found no such evidence, and the conclusions of Rumsfeld's intelligence shop were largely discredited.

But with Saddam Hussein gone and the administration divided about whether Syria ought to be the next target of the Bush administration's "regime change" strategy, Rumsfeld's planning for the global special-operations war intensified. Robert Andrews had left the Pentagon, and Rumsfeld replaced him with Thomas O'Connell, another veteran of the paramilitary wars of Vietnam and a former Gray Fox commander. O'Connell had deployed to Vietnam in 1970 as a military adviser to the Phoenix Program, the controversial CIA-led campaign to turn the tide of the war by capturing and assassinating Viet Cong leaders. He had spent most of his adult life in the special-operations-and-intelligence world, and he had been JSOC's top intelligence officer when Representative Dick Cheney visited the command in 1986.

His job interview with Rumsfeld had gone particularly well, mostly because O'Connell's views on the Pentagon's authorities and the role

of special-operations troops were exactly what Rumsfeld wanted to hear. "If we're at war, why do I have to put my people under CIA authority?" Rumsfeld asked O'Connell early on during the meeting.

"You don't," O'Connell replied quickly. "You have the power to send U.S. forces into any part of the world that you want."

In O'Connell's mind, Congress had given the Pentagon broad authorities to carry out a global war to gather intelligence or launch killing operations, and Rumsfeld ought to use them. He saw parallels to the Vietnam War, when President Nixon started a secret bombing campaign in Cambodia and Laos because he believed those countries had become safe havens for enemy fighters. But the difference, O'Connell thought, was that Rumsfeld had even more authority than Nixon had, because now Congress had essentially given the Pentagon its blessing to send troops wherever it believed al Qaeda fighters were hiding.

At the time, Rumsfeld was also looking for leverage in his fights with the CIA and he decided to consolidate all of the military's disparate and often haphazard intelligence-gathering operations into one office. He tapped his loyal aide Stephen Cambone as the first under secretary of defense for intelligence, giving the brainy and prickly Cambone extraordinary power to oversee all Pentagon spying efforts. Rumsfeld would even revamp the civilian line of succession in the Pentagon hierarchy in the event he and his deputy died or were incapacitated. Cambone, the intelligence chief, was put next in line and given an office right next to Rumsfeld's.

Rumsfeld appointed as Cambone's deputy Lt. General William "Jerry" Boykin, a Delta Force veteran who had been in the Iranian desert in 1980 during the botched operation to rescue the American hostages. Boykin was a born-again Christian who wore religion on his sleeve and occasionally spoke about the war against Muslim extrem-

ists in biblical terms. He often called it a war against "Satan" and once told a church congregation that in the early 1990s he knew that his hunt for a Somali warlord would be successful because he "knew that [his] God was a real God and [the Somali's] was an idol."

Boykin was also evangelical about pushing the military to the edge of its legal authorities. Since the Beirut hostage crises of the 1980s, he had been frustrated that Pentagon bureaucrats had been too timid about making use of groups like Delta Force. As he did with O'Connell, Rumsfeld peppered Boykin with questions during his job interview about the limits of the defense secretary's authorities to send troops outside of war zones. Boykin gave a similar response as O'Connell had: You have the authority, and you ought to use it. You don't need to put your troops under the control of the CIA.

Rumsfeld got a boost in his efforts to build an empire for unconventional warfare in the summer of 2004, when the 9/11 Commission recommended in its final report that the CIA be stripped of all of its paramilitary functions and that the Pentagon serve as the only agency carrying out clandestine warfare. The commission had excoriated the CIA for its inability to kill Osama bin Laden and thought that the agency's clandestine operations were in disarray. The panel recommended that the CIA improve intelligence collection with less reliance on foreign spy services, overhaul the way it conducted analysis, and perform "non-military" covert actions, like propaganda campaigns. Secret wars and drone strikes, the commission believed, were the job of the Pentagon.

"Whether the price is measured in either money or people, the United States cannot afford to build two separate capabilities for carrying out secret military operations, secretly operating standoff missiles, and secretly training foreign military or paramilitary forces," recommended the commission in its final report, published in July 2004.

That, of course, was exactly what Rumsfeld thought, and days after the report was released he asked Tom O'Connell to get more information about what led to the recommendation. After speaking with John Lehman, the former Navy secretary and a 9/11 commissioner, O'Connell reported back that the commission had found the CIA's approach to paramilitary operations "muddled." In a memo to Rumsfeld, O'Connell wrote that Lehman had told him the 9/11 Commission was struck by the CIA's "unwillingness to take risk" and the fact that the agency was "reluctant to pull the trigger when opportunities were presented." The biggest problem, Lehman had told O'Connell, was that the Pentagon had the capabilities for hunting-and-killing operations, but the CIA had the authorities.

Rumsfeld put Cambone in charge of investigating whether this recommendation could be enacted, and soon Cambone was asking deeper questions about whether CIA operations should be pared down even further. In late September 2004, Cambone wrote to Rumsfeld that he wasn't sure it made sense for the CIA to be carrying out *any* covert action—which he said could be viewed as an "operational activity not unlike that of a Combatant Commander." In other words, maybe the Pentagon should be taking over covert action as well. The problem, Cambone wrote, was that the CIA was in charge of *both* covert action and analysis, creating the potential for "bias" when assessing the efficacy of a specific covert action. Put differently, the CIA was set up to grade its own work.

The point might have been self-serving, but it got to the heart of a more profound question: Can an agency in charge of a targeted-killing campaign against al Qaeda provide dispassionate assessments about the impact that very campaign was having on the strength of al Qaeda? It was a question Obama officials would face years later after the spy agency escalated its drone war in Pakistan.

In the end, both Rumsfeld and CIA director Porter Goss advised

President Bush that the Pentagon didn't need to wrest secret military operations away from the CIA. Rumsfeld had become convinced that he could do what he wanted—even if the CIA was doing it in parallel—under the banner of "traditional military activities." Goss had also waged a quiet lobbying campaign to protect the CIA's turf, urging White House officials not to consider the 9/11 Commission's recommendation. It was a temporary moment of agreement for the Pentagon and CIA and hardly an end to the battles between the two agencies.

Already by 2004, small teams of JSOC operatives had begun fanning out on spying missions across the globe, to South America and Africa and Asia and the Middle East. They went to France to try to gather intelligence about Islamic militant groups there, and one team had to leave Paraguay in a hurry after one of Rumsfeld's spies pulled a gun in the middle of a bar fight. As one former Pentagon official who helped oversee the program put it, "We had all these guys running around trying to be James Bond, and it didn't work very well."

Some of the teams, given the innocuous-sounding name Military Liaison Elements, were stationed inside American embassies. Others stealthily entered foreign countries and began their spying missions without notifying the American ambassador or CIA station chief in the country. Because the whole world was now a war zone, Pentagon officials figured, the special-operations teams would answer to military commanders, not to the civilian ambassador.

One afternoon, the American ambassador to Jordan, Edward W. Gnehm, was sitting in his office when the embassy's defense attaché walked in and put a note on his desk. It was a message from the Pentagon, sent directly to the attaché and meant for only him to see. A military intelligence team would soon be arriving in Jordan, the note read, and the team would be gathering information about the stability

of the Jordanian regime. By no means, the message read, were the ambassador or the CIA station chief to be told about the Pentagon's activities in Jordan.

The defense attaché sitting in the ambassador's office had, of course, ignored this admonition. After the meeting, Gnehm promptly told the CIA station chief, who, as Gnehm remembered it, "hit the roof."

5: THE ANGRY BIRD

"This is a political war and it calls for discrimination in killing. The best weapon for killing would be a knife, but I'm afraid we can't do it that way. The worst is an airplane."

—*Lt. Colonel John Paul Vann,*
American officer in Vietnam

Officers inside the operations room at the CIA's Counterterrorist Center watched video of the Toyota Land Cruiser bumping over the desert road in Yemen's Ma'rib province, the legendary birthplace of the Queen of Sheba. It was an uncomfortable ride for the six men crammed into the dusty four-by-four, but nothing about the truck typically would have raised suspicions among Yemeni police or soldiers on that day in November 2002. But from the backseat of the truck, a cell phone belonging to Qaed Salim Sinan al-Harethi was betraying the location of the most wanted man in Yemen. An armed CIA Predator was flying overhead.

The United States had fingered al-Harethi as the mastermind of the 2000 bombing of the destroyer U.S.S. *Cole*, an attack that killed seventeen sailors as the ship was refueling in the Gulf of Aden. The attack had put al-Harethi near the top of the Bush administration's list of al Qaeda operatives marked for death, and when a team of American special-operations troops landed in Yemen in the spring of

2002, they made hunting al-Harethi a priority. But al-Harethi was a veteran of the mujahedeen war in Afghanistan during the 1980s, and whatever survival skills he hadn't learned while battling the Soviets he had honed during a decade of hiding from the secret police in the United Arab Emirates and from the shock troops loyal to Yemeni president Ali Abdullah Saleh. In 2000, Osama bin Laden had sent al-Harethi to Yemen to plan the *Cole* bombing and to set up al Qaeda training camps. More than once, al-Harethi had embarrassed President Saleh by escaping capture just as Yemeni troops were closing in.

The mercurial Saleh had immediately seen the financial benefits of siding with the United States in its new war but had insisted that the Bush administration do it on his terms. He had managed to stay in power in Yemen since the 1970s by navigating the shoals of tribal blood feuds and Shi'ite separatists, and he wasn't about to let America begin a stealth war in his country without getting something in return. On a trip to Washington two months after the September 11 attacks, he managed to wrangle $400 million in aid during meetings with President Bush, Rumsfeld, and CIA director George Tenet. He gave his blessing to a small group of American special-operations troops coming to Yemen but insisted that they fire weapons only in self-defense. Without telling Saleh, the Pentagon also sent operatives from Gray Fox, the Army spying unit that specialized in intercepting communications, along with the commandos.

And yet Saleh had been an easy sell when it came to the Predator.

In spring 2002, Ambassador Edmund Hull requested a meeting to get the Yemeni president to agree to drone flights in the country. By then, Hull knew Saleh well enough to know about his wild mood swings and what talking points might best advance the spy agency's case. A group of CIA officers, who had arrived from Langley days earlier, brought a laptop computer with an animated video demonstrating how the drones worked. The video included graphics of Hellfire mis-

siles hitting cars and mud compounds. Saleh broke into a smile as he watched, and he seemed proud that Yemen would be the first place outside of Afghanistan that the CIA was preparing to use the Predator.

But the Americans still had to find al-Harethi, who eluded surveillance by switching between five different cell-phone numbers. The Gray Fox team had identified several of them, but al-Harethi was always careful enough to use the phones sparingly. On November 4, however, the surveillance net got its first big catch.

The cell phone in the back of the Land Cruiser was beaming its signal into the skies, and Gray Fox operatives sent a flash message to analysts at the National Security Agency's sprawling headquarters, at Fort Meade, Maryland. Separately, the CIA had dispatched an armed Predator from its drone base in Djibouti, just across the Red Sea from Yemen. As the Predator moved into position above the Land Cruiser, an analyst at Fort Meade heard al-Harethi's voice over the cell phone, barking directions to the driver of the four-by-four. With confirmation that al-Harethi was in the truck, the CIA was now authorized to fire a missile at the vehicle. The missile came off the Predator drone and destroyed the truck, killing everyone inside. Qaed Salim Sinan al-Harethi was eventually identified in the rubble by a distinguishing mark on one of his legs, which was found at the scene, severed from his body.

President Saleh's government was quick to issue a cover story: The truck had been carrying a canister of gas that triggered an explosion. But inside the Counterterrorist Center, the importance of the moment was not lost. It was the first time since the September 11 attacks that the CIA had carried out a targeted killing outside a declared war zone. Using the sweeping authority President Bush had given to the CIA in September 2001, clandestine officers had methodically gathered information about al-Harethi's movements and then coolly incinerated his vehicle with an antitank missile.

BY THIS TIME, many inside the spy agency had forgotten that the CIA had never really wanted the armed drone. It had been considered a blunt and unsophisticated killing tool, and many at the CIA were glad that the agency had gotten out of the assassination business long ago. Little more than a year before the Yemen strike, a debate was still raging as spies fought with spies about the morality of using drones to kill terrorists. Charles E. Allen, a longtime CIA analyst and a fierce advocate for the Predator, would later describe the whole period as a "bloody struggle."

By the late 1990s, Ross Newland's generation of CIA officers, who had joined the agency after the revelations of the Church Committee and President Ford's ban on assassinations, had ascended to leadership positions at Langley. The rise to power of the post-Church generation had a direct impact on the type of clandestine operations the CIA chose to conduct around the world. The agency's paramilitary branch had been allowed to wither, a reflection of the CIA's antipathy toward returning to the wars of the past. The CIA was even divided about whether it could justifiably kill Osama bin Laden. One former head of the Counterterrorist Center would later tell the 9/11 Commission that he would have refused a direct order to kill bin Laden in the years before the September 11 attacks.

"The corporate view inside CIA was 'We don't want to do covert action. And if we do covert action, we want it to be neat and clean. We don't want to be involved in killing people. Because we're not like that. We're not Mossad,'" said Richard Clarke, who served in both the Clinton and Bush administrations as the top White House official responsible for counterterrorism.

By 2000, the year that Newland left undercover operations in the field for a senior management job at Langley as a CIA liaison to the

Pentagon, bin Laden had repeatedly shown he could strike at the time and place of his choosing, from the American-embassy bombings in Kenya and Tanzania in 1998, to the attack on the *Cole* in Yemen two years later. The Clinton administration had few good ideas when it came to figuring out where the al Qaeda leader was at any given time and then killing him before he went somewhere else.

Inside the White House Situation Room, discussions about bin Laden turned into abstract debates about whether the White House might be violating the 1976 ban on assassinations by choosing one killing method over another. Clarke remembered one meeting when National Security Advisor Sandy Berger became so enraged by the debates, he shouted at everyone in the room. "He said, 'So, you guys are perfectly OK if Bill Clinton kills bin Laden with a Tomahawk missile, but if Bill Clinton kills him with a 7.62-millimeter round in the middle of the eyes, that's bad? Could you tell me the difference between killing him with a Tomahawk and an M16?'

"Berger was about to have a heart attack," said Clarke. "He was all sweaty and red in the face and yelling at them."

President Clinton wasn't amused by the lack of options. "You know," Clinton told Joint Chiefs chairman General Hugh Shelton, "it would scare the shit out of al Qaeda if suddenly a bunch of black ninjas rappelled out of helicopters into the middle of their camp."

Not having ninjas at its disposal, the Pentagon had agreed to station two submarines in the Arabian Sea that could fire Tomahawk cruise missiles into Afghanistan on short notice. But without fresh intelligence about bin Laden's whereabouts, the submarines were of little use, and top admirals began agitating to move them elsewhere.

The CIA had one Taliban source feeding information to the Americans, but his tips were usually twenty-four hours old, insufficient for White House approval of missile strikes into Afghanistan. Flailing for ideas, clandestine officers met with American defense contractors about building blimps or hot-air balloons to take pictures of Afghanistan at thirty thousand feet but scrapped the idea when they considered the diplomatic calamity if wind gusts from the Hindu Kush mountains were to push a blimp hundreds of miles off course and into China—possibly over a nuclear reactor.

Clarke had a frosty relationship with George Tenet and James Pavitt, the head of the CIA's Directorate of Operations, and decided to go around them for new ideas. He called senior CIA analyst Charles E. Allen, who had been at the agency for four decades and by then was in his midsixties. Bright, iconoclastic, and ornery, Allen bore scars from the agency's past battles; the Iran–Contra scandal had dealt his career a glancing blow. But he had also emerged as something of a legend among CIA analysts for being a lonely voice in 1990, predicting that Saddam Hussein would invade Kuwait. Clarke asked Allen to conduct an independent review of various options for spying in Afghanistan.

Allen went to the Defense Department for ideas and met with officers working for the Pentagon's Joint Staff. They discussed far-fetched ideas, such as putting a giant telescope on a mountaintop and training it on bin Laden's Derunta training camp, near Jalalabad, where al Qaeda had experimented with chemical weapons. But there was another, more realistic option. Allen was told about a series of secret tests the Air Force had been conducting in the desert. There was a chance, Pentagon officials said, that the CIA could find bin Laden using a drone.

By 2000, the MQ-1 Predator was well known inside the small, geeky fraternity of military engineers and intelligence analysts working at the experimental fringes of electronic spying. The Predator had already had some success as a spying tool in the Balkan wars, spotting Serbian troop concentrations and hunting Bosnian Serb leaders. Drone pilots operated the planes out of a hangar in Albania that the CIA had rented in exchange for two truckloads of wool blankets. The drone video was beamed into the office of CIA director R. James Woolsey Jr., who communicated with the pilots through a crude e-mail link. Woolsey had managed to get a small stash of money to fund the project from Representative Charlie Wilson, the hard-drinking Texas congressman who had used similar budget trickery to fund the CIA's war in Afghanistan during the 1980s.

The mountainous terrain in the Balkans had made it impossible to fly the drones using "line of sight" technology—with the pilot operating the drone through a direct signal to the airplane—so during the 1990s the military had made strides flying the Predators by bouncing a signal off a satellite hurtling through space. But the Predator couldn't carry a weapon. It also looked like a gangly insect and had a loud engine that made it sound like a flying lawnmower. Unlike most planes, its stabilizers pointed down rather than thrusting up into the sky, and when one major trade magazine published its first story about the Predator, the photo was upside down. But a handful of Air Force officers inside the service's flyboy culture saw the potential in unmanned systems and began advocating for the Predator.

Allen brought the Predator idea back to Richard Clarke at the White House. They figured that both Tenet and Pavitt would be against the idea, so they waited to tell them about the Predator option until a plan had been cobbled together to send the Predator into Afghanistan. Without telling Tenet, Clarke called a White House meeting and invited the Predator's biggest advocates: Charlie Allen, CTC chief Cofer Black, and Richard Blee, the head of the CTC's bin Laden hunting unit, which had been given the code name Alec Station.

Blee was a career case officer who had served in several CIA stations in Africa, and shortly after he took over Alec Station, in 1999, he led a team into Afghanistan's Panjshir Valley to reestablish CIA contact with Ahmad Shah Massoud, the leader of the Northern Alliance, whom al Qaeda would end up killing just two days before the September 11 attacks. Blee was smart and intense but occasionally sullen, leading some of his colleagues to think of him as aloof. He had grown up a CIA brat, the son of a head of the CIA's Soviet division who had battled with the agency's legendary head of counterintelligence, James Angleton, over the direction of clandestine operations against the Soviet Union. David Blee won the fight and successfully penetrated the KGB with dozens of highly placed moles during the 1970s. Now his son was at the front of a very different CIA war.

By Memorial Day weekend 2000, Clinton's national security adviser, Sandy Berger, thought that the CIA had dickered around too long about the Predator and demanded a decision on the drone flights. General John Gordon, the CIA's deputy director, arranged a hasty meeting at Langley that quickly degenerated into a shouting match. Pavitt, who by then had been told about the Predator option, made it clear he opposed having CIA spy flights over Afghanistan. "Where would the drones be based?" he asked, and "what if they were shot down?" The CIA shouldn't be operating its own air force, Pavitt said. The meeting, one participant said, became "a really ugly scene."

After the session, Allen called Clarke to tell him about Pavitt's opposition. Clarke thought Pavitt's worries were ludicrous and that the plan presented almost zero risk. "You know," he told Allen, "if the Predator gets shot down, the pilot goes home and fucks his wife. It's OK. There's no POW issue here."

Tenet was also skeptical when he heard about the Predator days later, and he didn't relish the prospect of asking Uzbekistani strongman Islam Karimov to allow the CIA to base Predators at an old Soviet air base near the Afghan border. At the time, the idea of the CIA establishing military-style bases anywhere in the world seemed crazy—and a drain on the agency's limited budget for covert action.

By June, however, Clarke had won the argument, and the White

House had approved moving Predators to the Karshi-Khanabad Air Base, in Uzbekistan. But CIA officers had another problem: how to get enough satellite bandwidth for the drone flights. Air Force engineers by that point had devised a way to fly the Predator from thousands of miles away by bouncing the signal off a satellite and relaying the feed through a ground station in Germany. This allowed the CIA to station Predator pilots very close to home, in a converted race-car trailer set up in a parking lot at Langley. But the agency still had to rent bandwidth from commercial satellite companies, which proved harder than expected. With news organizations sucking up all of the satellite bandwidth in their preparations to cover the Olympic Games in Sydney, the Predators were almost grounded as the CIA frantically searched for a satellite company with transponder space to rent.

The spying flights began in September 2000, and the CIA flew more than a dozen drone missions over Afghanistan in the fall before the winter winds in the mountains began buffeting the Predator's fragile airframe, making the flights too risky. Several times, Clarke drove out to Langley to watch the video beamed into the trailer in the parking lot. "It was just science fiction; it was unbelievable," he said. During one flight over bin Laden's Tarnak Farms training camp, near Kandahar, the Predator spotted a truck convoy driving into the camp. Out walked a tall man in long white robes. The video was grainy, but every person standing around the video monitor at the CIA was convinced that the camera was trained on bin Laden.

CIA analysts scrambled to alert the Pentagon and the White House to get approval to launch missiles from the submarines. But officials at the National Security Council demanded to know whether bin Laden was going to be at Tarnak Farms for at least six hours—the time it would take to go through the launch protocols and for the Tomahawk missiles to fly from a submarine in the Arabian Sea to southern Afghanistan. The CIA had no clue, and so Sandy Berger and his staff declined to approve the strike. The CIA had only two options: predict bin Laden's whereabouts six hours in advance or find a weapon that could hunt the al Qaeda leader and kill him immediately.

INDIAN SPRINGS AIR FORCE AUXILIARY FIELD was at the time a small, decaying base in the Nevada desert, some thirty-five miles northwest of Las Vegas. It was one of a myriad of benighted military outposts built during World War II and then forgotten by the Pentagon. In the 1950s and '60s the base had been a supply hub for the underground nuclear tests nearby, and helicopters stationed at Indian Springs were occasionally flown over the test sites at Mercury and Yucca Flats to monitor for radiation leaks. Save for the occasional training by the Thunderbirds, the Air Force's demonstration squadron, Indian Springs was a desolate backwater.

The base also had a bird problem. The skies above Indian Springs were filled with birds, and the Air Force had restricted how often fighter jets could take off from the base due to concerns that the birds could get sucked into jet engines and cause deadly crashes. But as a drone proving ground, Indian Springs was ideal: The aircraft didn't fly much faster than the birds. At Indian Springs, a small group of test pilots was trying to turn the Predator from a hunter into a killer.

The housing at the base was scheduled for demolition because the walls of the bungalows were filled with asbestos, so the Predator team traveled each morning from their rented houses in the Las Vegas suburbs to a command post set up at Indian Springs inside an abandoned church building. Curt Hawes, one of the Predator pilots at the base in 2000 and 2001, recalls that his group had a vague idea that the drone testing had been accelerated because the CIA urgently wanted to use the Predator to kill bin Laden, but most of the details about the debate back in Washington were kept from the group at the base.

Funding for the program had been channeled through the Air Force's "Big Safari" office, a classified division based at Wright-Patterson Air Force Base, in Dayton, Ohio, in charge of developing secret intelligence programs for the military. Big Safari's mandate was to cut through Pentagon bureaucracy to get certain weapons from the drawing board to the field more quickly than usual, which sometimes meant that they went into combat before they were entirely ready. Such was the case in 2000 with the early model Predators, aircraft with a haphazard control panel that some pilots likened to the scattered features of a Mr. Potato Head doll. Just one of the significant design flaws was that the button that killed the engine on the drone was only a quarter inch from the button that launched the Hellfire missile—creating the possibility for human error with deadly consequences.

The bigger problem, however, was that nobody was quite sure what launching the missile might do to the drone itself. Would the force of the missile rupture the airframe or rip the Predator's wings in midflight? In January 2001, a test was conducted in the high desert of China Lake, California, to find out. Three days after President Bush was sworn into office, Air Force engineers chained a Predator to a concrete pad on top of a small mountain and fired a Hellfire missile from the drone. The missile hit a target tank in its path, and the Predator was undamaged. Live flight tests could proceed.

Hours before dawn on February 16, 2001, Curt Hawes left the command post in the abandoned church at Indian Springs and drove twenty miles into the desert. He had gone over the preflight checklist in his mind the night before, sitting in his bedroom in Las Vegas. His eyes closed, he practiced the moves his hands would make as he controlled the Predator joystick and fired a missile.

Maybe for the first time in the history of American flight, the drama surrounding a landmark test had nothing to do with concerns about whether the pilot would survive. Curt Hawes didn't wake up on the morning of February 16 as Chuck Yeager had before he squeezed into the cockpit of the Bell X-1, hoping he wouldn't be the latest test pilot to die trying to break the sound barrier. Hawes faced no risk whatsoever, which is exactly why it was a watershed moment: The United States was developing a new weapon for war that required no one actually going to war.

The test was planned for early morning, when the desert winds would be calmest. Shortly after sunrise, Hawes took control of the Predator from the team that had launched the drone off the runway at Indian Springs. He slowly made it descend to two thousand feet, the highest altitude from which a Hellfire missile had ever been fired. He lined up the shot with the help of a laser beam pointed at a target tank in the desert, the laser directed by an Army contractor on the ground. Pressing the button, he launched the Hellfire missile.

What Hawes remembers was the silence. He was a pilot, but he was miles away from his plane. He couldn't hear the sound of the Hellfire's rocket engine firing or feel the plane buffet when he launched the missile. His video screen flickered from the missile's heat trail, and he watched the missile propel toward the target tank for a direct hit.

The engineers had decided not to use a live warhead for the test, so there was no explosion. The dummy missile struck the tank's turret six inches to the right of dead center, denting the armor and spinning the turret thirty degrees. The test was declared an unqualified success. By 7 A.M., it was done, and the Predator team met at the little casino adjacent to the Indian Springs base for a celebratory breakfast.

Air Force leaders were giddy, and by the second test, five days later, they had arranged for a group of generals to gather at the Pentagon to watch the Hellfire shot through a video feed sent from Nevada. This time, Curt Hawes flew the Predator using a satellite, creating a two-second lag between his joystick movements and the actual movements of the plane. This made the Predator more difficult to control, but once again the Hellfire scored a direct hit. This time, the missile carried a live warhead, and when it found its target a small ball of fire rose into the morning sky.

The age of armed, remote-controlled conflict had begun with little fanfare. The Air Force issued a short press release, which led to a small story in a local Las Vegas newspaper. A congressman from Nevada called to congratulate the Predator team, but the engineers and pilots were disappointed when a CNN crew that was rumored to be coming to film the test didn't show up. CIA officials had been trying to keep the entire operation a secret and were angry that the Air Force even put out a press release. CNN was never allowed on base.

Curt Hawes didn't know any of these details. All he heard was that "other parties" had intervened to keep his work a secret.

BUT THOSE "OTHER PARTIES" couldn't decide what to do with the armed drone. Even after the successful missile tests, the CIA remained divided at the top about whether to send armed Predators to Afghanistan to hunt for Osama bin Laden. Pavitt, head of the CIA's clandestine service, was a one-man Greek chorus arguing forcefully against the CIA running the Predator program. He wanted to spend his black budget on hiring more case officers, not buying drones. He would repeatedly ask a question during meetings that now seems quaint after the billions of dollars that have poured into counterterrorism programs since the September 11 attacks: Was the $2 million for each Predator going to come out of the CIA or the Pentagon budget?

But he also voiced a much deeper concern, one shared by other members of Tenet's staff. What exactly were the repercussions of the

CIA getting back into assassinations? "You can't underestimate the cultural change that comes with gaining lethal authority," said John McLaughlin, then the CIA's deputy director. "When people say to me, 'It's not a big deal,' I say to them, 'Have you ever killed anyone?'" he said. "It is a big deal. You start thinking about things differently."

Moreover, the United States was scolding other countries for the exact same thing it was debating whether to undertake. When Israel's government was killing off Hamas leaders in 2000 and 2001 during the second Palestinian intifada, American ambassador to Israel Martin Indyk said that "the United States is very clearly on the record as being against targeted assassinations. . . . They are extrajudicial killings and we do not support that."

George Tenet was ambivalent and repeatedly said he thought it should be the military, not the CIA, that pulled the trigger on a weapon of war. During one discussion about whether a CIA officer should be allowed to authorize Predator strikes, both Charles Allen and Alvin "Buzzy" Krongard, the agency's third-ranking official, volunteered to pull the trigger themselves. This infuriated Tenet. He later told the 9/11 Commission he scolded Allen and Krongard, telling them they had no authority to fire a Hellfire missile, and neither did he.

Sitting near Tenet's side during all the debates about the Predator, Lt. General John Campbell was a bit like an anthropologist watching the fighting rituals of a strange species. He had spent his career in the Air Force and had moved to Langley the previous summer to take over as the agency's director of military support. Campbell believed strongly that the CIA should embrace the Predator, but now, when he thinks back to the internal fights over armed drones in the summer of 2001, he understands that the agency was wrestling with the most basic questions about what it wanted to be.

"In the military culture, if you're following a legal order—and as an officer you're expected to follow a legal order—then you're pretty much protected in the long term for any personal liability for the things you do," he said. "The CIA is different. They have much less protection. They can be operating under the provisions of a presidential finding where you get a piece of paper with the president's signature that says, 'I authorize you to do these things.' Then, the next administration can come in and Justice decides that the finding was questionable and maybe even illegal—and guess what?—those guys are personally liable for the things they did.

"Something like the Predator, where you're specifically targeting individuals, dredges up a whole list of concerns about the future ramifications," said Campbell.

Campbell's deputy at the time was Ross Newland, who had a front-row seat for the Predator fights. As he sat in the meetings, Newland knew he was watching another turn of the familiar cycle: A "risk-averse" CIA was once again about to wade back into secret war. He supported the Predator program and thought that the Bush administration should use it to kill bin Laden as soon as possible, but he also couldn't help but think back to his days as a counternarcotics officer in Bolivia. An unprepared CIA had been assigned the mission of chasing drug-runners because nobody else wanted to do it. Two decades later, Newland could see the same thing happening with terrorism.

Weeks later, when the September 11 attacks killed nearly three thousand Americans, thorny questions about assassination, covert action, and the proper use of the CIA in hunting America's enemies were quickly swept aside. Within weeks, the CIA began conducting dozens of drone strikes in Afghanistan.

America had found, in the armed Predator, the ultimate weapon for a secret war. It was a tool that killed quietly, a weapon unbound by the normal rules of accountability in combat. Armed drones would allow American presidents to order strikes on remote villages and desert camps where journalists and independent monitoring groups could not go. The strikes were rarely discussed publicly by a spokesman standing at a podium, but they were cheered in private by politicians from both parties hoping to flex American muscle without putting American lives at risk.

Rare is the technology that can change the face of warfare. In the first half of the past century, tanks and planes transformed how the world fought its battles. The fifty years that followed were dominated by nuclear warheads and ICBMs, weapons of such horrible power that they gave birth to new doctrines to keep countries from ever using them. The advent of the armed drone upended this calculus: War was possible exactly because it seemed so free of risk. The bar for war had been lowered, the remote-controlled age had begun, and the killer drones became an object of fascination inside the CIA.

During the summer of 2002, Ross Newland visited the small gift shop at the CIA's headquarters. Looking to buy some presents for friends, he walked amid the rows of shelves filled with mugs, fleece jackets, and T-shirts emblazoned with the CIA logo. Then he made an unexpected find: a golf shirt with a small drone embroidered on the left side. The Predator still was one of the CIA's most classified programs, but the spy agency was now hawking images of the drones on souvenirs.

THE KILLING OF AL-HARETHI in Yemen later that year showed that the CIA, with a pliable foreign ally, could wage war far beyond war zones. Bush officials were so pleased about the strike in Yemen that news of the attack quickly leaked out, puncturing the thin cover story put out by Yemeni officials about the exploding gas can. Paul Wolfowitz, deputy defense secretary, even praised the strike on CNN.

President Saleh was furious when he heard about Wolfowitz's comments. His government had been made to look like fools and liars, and he demanded that American spies and diplomats in Yemen appear in his office immediately. Since Washington couldn't keep a secret, he told them, America's hidden war in Yemen would be scaled back. He ordered the Predator flights to stop immediately.

And they did, for nearly eight years. It wouldn't be until 2010, with Yemen in turmoil and Saleh losing his grip on power one finger at a time, that another American president would order drones back over the skies of Yemen. By then, Saleh was hardly in any position to object.

6: A TRUE PASHTUN

"Things fall out of the sky all the time."

—*Pervez Musharraf*

Why is this bird following me?"

Nek Muhammad Wazir sat inside a mud building in South Waziristan, surrounded by his followers and talking on his satellite phone to a BBC reporter. Looking out the window, the young commander with long, jet-black hair noticed something hovering above, glinting in the sun. He asked one of his lieutenants about the coruscating metal object in the sky.

Nek Muhammad had just humbled Pakistani troops, and the CIA was following him. He had emerged as the undisputed rock star of Pakistan's tribal areas, a brash member of the Wazir tribe who had raised an army to fight government forces in the spring of 2004 and brought Islamabad to the negotiating table. His rise had taken Pakistan's leaders by surprise, and now they wanted him dead.

Nek Muhammad, age twenty-nine, was part of a second generation of Pakistani mujahedeen who saw no cause for loyalty to the ISI that had given succor to their fathers during the war against the Soviets. Many Pakistanis in the tribal areas viewed President Musharraf's alliance with Washington after the September 11 attacks with disdain, and saw the Pakistani military as no different from the Americans—whom they believed had launched a war of aggression in

Afghanistan just like the Soviets had years earlier. Nek Muhammad gave Pakistan's government its first taste of what would be a growing problem in the coming years: a militancy that extended its reach beyond the western mountains and into the settled areas of the country, near Pakistan's biggest and most important cities. It was militancy that Islamabad eventually would be unable to control.

Born near Wana, the bustling market hub of South Waziristan, Nek Muhammad was sent at an early age to one of the religious seminaries that had sprung up in the area during the 1980s to educate the illiterate youth of the Federally Administered Tribal Areas. He dropped out after five years and spent the early 1990s surviving as a petty car thief and a shopkeeper in the Wana bazaar. He found his calling in 1993, when he was recruited to fight alongside the Afghan Taliban and against Ahmad Shah Massoud's Northern Alliance in the civil war then raging in Afghanistan.

He rose quickly through the Taliban's military hierarchy, winning a reputation for never conceding in battle, even when his commanders ordered him to pull back. He cut a striking figure on the battlefield, with his long, thin face and unkempt beard brushing the top of his collarbones and his black hair flowing from his white turban. He looked less like a typically scruffy tribal militant and more like a Pashtun version of Che Guevara.

Nek Muhammad seized an opportunity to become a host for the Arab and Chechen al Qaeda fighters who moved into Pakistan to escape the barrage of American bombs in Afghanistan in 2001 and 2002. Local tribesmen considered it their religious duty to shelter the fighters, but some also saw the potential for profit, charging the foreigners inflated rents to stay in the protected dwellings of Wana and Shakai, a farming region of large shade trees and steep river valleys. For Nek Muhammad, it was partly a get-rich scheme, but he also saw another use for the arriving fighters. With their help, over the next two years he launched a string of attacks on Pakistani Frontier Corps installations and American firebases across the border in Afghanistan.

CIA officers in Islamabad urged Pakistani spies to lean on the Waziri tribesmen to hand over the Arab and Chechen fighters, but Pashtun tribal custom prohibited such treachery. Reluctantly, Musharraf ordered his troops into the forbidding mountains to hunt down the foreigners and deliver rough justice to Nek Muhammad's men. It wasn't the military's first foray into Waziristan, but for Musharraf there was a new urgency: In late 2003, al Qaeda's second-in-command, Ayman al-Zawahiri, issued a fatwa ordering the Pakistani president's killing for helping the Americans. On two occasions in December 2003, assassins came close to fulfilling the order, and Musharraf thought that a quick, punishing military campaign in the mountains might put a stop to the attacks on Pakistani soil.

But it was only the beginning. In March 2004, Pakistani helicopter gunships and artillery bludgeoned Wana and the surrounding villages. Government troops shelled pickup trucks that were carrying civilians away from the fighting and destroyed the compounds of tribesmen suspected of harboring foreigners. One tribesman told a reporter that when Pakistani troops looted his house, they took not only his clothes but his pillow covers and his shoe polish. Lt. General Safdar Hussain, the commander who led the battle, declared the operation an unqualified success. It had destroyed a militant base, he said, and a network of tunnels containing sophisticated communications equipment.

But for Pakistan's government, the game hadn't been worth the candle. Military casualties were higher than anticipated. During one battle, on March 16, when troops laid siege to a fortress belonging to Nek Muhammad and two other senior militants, fifteen Frontier Corps troops and one Pakistani regular-army soldier were killed. Fourteen other soldiers were taken hostage, and dozens of army trucks, artillery pieces, and armored personnel carriers were destroyed. In

Islamabad, clerics of the influential mosque Lal Masjid issued a message calling for the people of South Waziristan to resist the army's offensive and for Pakistani troops to be denied Islamic burials. Obeying the order, some parents refused to accept the bodies of their slain sons. In Waziristan, tribesmen who already opposed the military's deployment into the mountains were furious about the indiscriminate assault on Wana. Attacks against Frontier Corps posts increased, and Islamabad began looking for a way out.

On April 24, 2004, Pashtun tribesmen danced in a circle and banged drums as President Musharraf's military envoys arrived at the madrassa school in Shakai, near Wana, where Nek Muhammad's men were waiting for them. General Hussain came in person, a sign of just how desperate Musharraf was to sue for peace. Tribesmen presented AK-47s to the military men, a traditional gesture of peace, and General Hussain hugged Nek Muhammad and hung a garland of bright flowers around his neck. The two men sat next to each other and sipped tea as photographers and television cameramen recorded the event.

When the formalities were finished, the general addressed the hundreds of men sitting cross-legged in the dirt, dressed in flowing shalwar kameez and wearing flat woolen pakul hats. The general told the crowd that the United States had been foolish to make war in Afghanistan. "When America's World Trade Center was hit by a plane, how many Afghan pilots were involved?" the general asked. "Since there were no Afghan pilots, why is there this situation in Afghanistan?"

He suggested that the government of Pakistan, by brokering the peace deal, was protecting the people of South Waziristan from the American bombs.

"If the Pakistan government had not made such a wise choice, then just like America invaded Iraq and invaded Afghanistan, they also would have invaded the tribal areas," he said. The crowd cheered wildly.

Nek Muhammad also spoke of peace. "Whatever happened, happened," he said before a bank of microphones. "Be it our fault or the army's, we will not fight each other again."

There was little doubt which side was negotiating from strength. Nek Muhammad would later brag that the government had agreed to meet inside a religious madrassa rather than in a public location, where tribal meetings were traditionally held. "I did not go to them; they came to my place," he said. "That should make it clear who surrendered to whom."

Judging by the terms of the truce, he was right. The government agreed to pay reparations for the carnage in South Waziristan and to free all the prisoners who had been captured during the offensive. The foreign fighters in the mountains were granted amnesty as long as they pledged to give up attacks on Pakistani troops and raids into Afghanistan—a provision that was essentially unenforceable. Nek Muhammad and his followers also promised not to attack Pakistani troops but did not renounce attacks into Afghanistan. Later, Nek Muhammad said that he would not give up jihad in Afghanistan until the country was free from foreign occupation.

Not everyone in Pakistan's government thought that the peace deal was a wise move. By 2004, Asad Munir had retired from the ISI and taken a job as a civilian administrator in Peshawar, overseeing security and development in the tribal areas. The former station chief who had worked closely with the CIA in 2002 and 2003 watched as Pakistani generals debated whether to negotiate with Nek Muhammad. He warned that appeasing the tribal militants would only expand their reach into the settled parts of Pakistan. The peace deals that were brokered in the tribal areas beginning in 2004, Munir now believes, led to the rise of a powerful, deadly group in the country, a group that came to be known as the Pakistani Taliban.

"If [Pakistani troops] had just carried through with the operation in 2004, both in South and North Waziristan, the Taliban would not have spread" to areas much closer to Islamabad, he said. "With every peace deal, they gained strength and controlled more areas, and people started to take them as the rulers because the state was not interfering."

Nevertheless, government officials in Islamabad boasted that the peace deal had driven a wedge between Pakistani militants and al Qaeda fighters. Nek Muhammad continued to deny publicly that there were any al Qaeda operatives in the tribal areas. "There is no al Qaeda here," he said. "Had there been a single al Qaeda fighter here, the government would have caught one by now."

The Shakai peace arrangement propelled Nek Muhammad to new fame. He was the man who had brought the government to its knees, and he began comparing himself to famous Wazir tribesmen who had repelled British forces from the mountains. Within weeks, the truce was exposed as a sham and Nek Muhammad resumed attacks against Pakistani troops. Musharraf once again ordered his army back on the offensive in South Waziristan.

CIA officials in Islamabad had been lobbying the Pakistanis for months to allow Predator flights in the tribal areas, and Nek Muhammad's repeated humiliation of Pakistani troops presented an opportunity. The CIA's station chief in Islamabad paid a visit to General Ehsan ul Haq, the ISI chief, and made an offer: If the CIA killed Nek Muhammad, would the ISI allow regular drone flights over the tribal areas? "Nek Muhammad really pissed off the Pakistanis," recalled the former station chief. "They said, 'If you guys can find him, go get him.'"

But the access came with limits. Pakistani intelligence officials insisted that they approve each drone strike before it happened, giving them tight control over the killing list. After tense discussions about where exactly the drones could fly, Pakistani spies insisted that the drones be restricted to narrow "flight boxes" in the tribal areas, knowing that more extensive access would allow the CIA to spy in places where Islamabad didn't want the Americans to go: Pakistan's nuclear facilities, and mountain camps where Kashmiri militant groups were trained for attacks against India.

The ISI also insisted that all drone flights in Pakistan operate under the CIA's covert-action authority—meaning that the United States would never acknowledge the missile strikes and Pakistan would either take credit for individual kills or remain silent. President Musharraf didn't think it would be difficult to keep up the ruse. During the negotiations he told one CIA operative, "In Pakistan, things fall out of the sky all the time."

Even if the CIA had not been constrained, the agency at that time would not have been able to carry out a more extensive killing campaign in the tribal areas. The Americans had hardly any intelligence sources in the area and precious little information about where bin Laden and other al Qaeda leaders might be hiding. CIA analysts suspected that bin Laden and Ayman al-Zawahiri were somewhere in the tribal areas, but vague suspicions and sketchy third-hand reports were hardly enough to make effective use of the Predator. The ISI wasn't much better connected. The Pakistani spy service had extensive source networks in the cities to help track down al Qaeda leaders like Khalid Sheikh Mohammed, but in South Waziristan and the other tribal agencies the ISI did not have reliable contacts.

Lucky for both the American and Pakistani spies, Nek Muhammad wasn't exactly in deep hiding. He gave regular interviews to the Pashto channels of Western news outlets, bragging about humbling the mighty Pakistani military. These interviews, by satellite phone, made him an easy mark for American eavesdroppers, and by mid-June 2004 the Americans were regularly tracking his movements. On June 18, one day after Nek Muhammad spoke to the BBC and wondered aloud about the strange bird that was following him, a Predator fixed on his position and fired a Hellfire missile at the compound where he had been resting. The blast severed Nek Muhammad's left leg and left hand, and he died almost instantly. Pakistani journalist Zahid Hussain visited the village days later and saw the mud grave at Shakai that was already becoming a pilgrimage site. A sign on the grave read, HE LIVED AND DIED LIKE A TRUE PASHTUN.

After a discussion between CIA and ISI officials about how to handle news of the strike, they decided that Pakistan would take credit for killing the man who had humiliated its military. One day after Nek Muhammad was killed, a charade began that would go on for years. Major General Shaukat Sultan, Pakistan's top military spokesman, told Voice of America that "al Qaeda facilitator" Nek Muhammad and four other militants had been killed during a rocket attack by Pakistani troops.

FOUR MONTHS after the drone strike, a general with sad, hollow eyes and stooped shoulders took control of Pakistan's ISI. Beyond the basics of his biography, American spies knew little about the phlegmatic, chain-smoking Ashfaq Parvez Kayani. He was born into a military family and raised in Jhelum, an arid region of Punjab. He received his army commission in 1971, the year Pakistani forces were defeated during a thirteen-day war with India that led to Pakistan losing the territory that would eventually become Bangladesh. Like most Pakistani officers, Kayani believed that Pakistan fought a daily struggle for its own survival and that the country could make no military decisions without determining first how those decisions would affect its ability to defend itself against India.

And yet Kayani was controlled where others were hotheaded. After militants based in Pakistan launched a deadly attack on India's parliament in New Delhi in late 2001 and it looked as if the two nuclear rivals might go to war, Kayani was the army commander in charge of marshaling Pakistani forces along the border with India. He won praise inside Pakistan for quietly managing the tense situation, staying in contact with his Indian counterparts, and preventing the simmering dispute from escalating into nuclear war. He won General Musharraf's loyalty two years later, when he was in charge of the investigations into the December 2003 assassination attempts on the president.

It wasn't long after Kayani took over the ISI that he had earned a grudging respect at CIA headquarters for being something of a master manipulator—this was a compliment—and a man who always kept his most important agendas a secret. During meetings, he could go long stretches without speaking a word, appearing to be asleep. Then, when a subject came up that agitated him, he would speak passionately for several minutes and then return to his somnolent state. He golfed obsessively and went everywhere trailing a cloud of cigarette smoke.

He rarely spoke about himself, and when he did it was difficult to understand what he was saying, because of his tendency to mumble. Where his ISI predecessor, General ul Haq, was dapper and suave, General Kayani was rumpled and unpretentious. During trips to Washington, D.C., he insisted that his limousine driver take him to Marshalls, the discount-clothing chain, where he would shop for suits and ties. Above all, he could wait patiently for what he wanted. One top American spy recalled a lengthy meeting with Kayani during which the Pakistani general spent half an hour meticulously rolling a cigarette between his fingers. Then, after taking one puff, he gently stubbed it out.

General Kayani took over the ISI at a time when Pakistani leaders were becoming increasingly convinced that the Americans had lost their stomach for the fight in Afghanistan. The Iraq war had diverted

Washington's attention away from Afghanistan, and soldiers, spies, and politicians in Islamabad believed it was only a matter of time before the rising violence in Pakistan's western neighbor would threaten the government in Islamabad. According to several Pakistani officials in positions of authority at that time, it was during this period when the ISI decided to take a more active role with the Afghan Taliban, hoping to steer Afghanistan toward a political future that was acceptable to Islamabad.

General Kayani was consumed with the past, and he understood that Afghanistan's bloody history was prologue to America's war in that country. He had been studying Afghanistan for decades and was an expert in the dynamics that helped Afghan insurgents vanquish a superpower in the 1980s. In 1988, as a young Pakistani army major studying at Fort Leavenworth, in Kansas, Kayani wrote a master's thesis about the Soviet war in Afghanistan titled "Strengths and Weaknesses of the Afghan Resistance Movement." By then, the Soviet Union had endured nearly a decade of war in Afghanistan, and Soviet premier Mikhail Gorbachev had already begun to pull out his troops. Over ninety-eight pages of clear, straightforward prose, Kayani examined how the Afghan Resistance Movement (ARM) had bled the vaunted Soviet army and increased "the price of Soviet presence in Afghanistan."

Kayani was, in essence, writing the playbook for how Pakistan could hold the strings in Afghanistan during the occupation of a foreign army. Pakistan, he wrote, could use proxy militias to wreak havoc in the country but also to control the groups effectively so that Islamabad could avoid a direct confrontation with the occupying force.

In a country without national identity, Kayani argued, it was necessary for the Afghan resistance to build support in the tribal system and to gradually weaken Afghanistan's central government. As for Pakistan, Kayani believed that Islamabad likely didn't want to be on a "collision course" with the Soviet Union, or at least didn't want the Afghan resistance to set them on that path. Therefore, it was essential for Pakistan's security to keep the strength of the Afghan resistance "managed."

By the time he took over the ISI in 2004, Kayani knew that the Afghan war would be decided not by soldiers in mountain redoubts but by politicians in Washington who had an acute sensitivity to America's limited tolerance for years more of bloody conflict. He knew because he had studied what had happened to the Soviets. In his thesis, he wrote that "the most striking feature of the Soviet military effort at present is the increasing evidence that it may not be designed to secure a purely military solution through a decisive defeat of the ARM.

"This is likely due to the realization that such a military solution is not obtainable short of entailing massive, and perhaps intolerable, personnel losses and economic and political cost."

In 2004, Kayani's thesis sat in the library at Fort Leavenworth, amid stacks of other largely ignored research papers written by foreign officers who went to Kansas to study how the United States Army fights its battles. This was a manual for a different kind of battle, a secret guerrilla campaign. Two decades after the young Pakistani military officer wrote it, he was the country's spymaster, in the perfect position to put it to use.

7: CONVERGENCE

"Deniability is built in and should be a big plus."

—*Enrique Prado*

On a cold afternoon in early 2005, CIA director Porter Goss was attending a ceremony for a class of agency case officers graduating from "The Farm," the CIA's training base at Camp Peary, in southern Virginia. It was a standard ritual for CIA directors to make the trip down to the base for the graduations, and the ceremonies were a brief moment of normalcy for the graduates before they began their lives of cover identities, deceit, and, occasionally, extreme danger. But the ceremony was cut short after one of Goss's aides came to him with an urgent message. Within minutes, the CIA director and his bodyguards had loaded back into a Blackhawk helicopter and were flying north. But instead of returning to Langley, Goss flew directly to the Pentagon to meet with Donald Rumsfeld. There was about to be a military assault into Pakistan.

A Pakistani agent working for the CIA had delivered the American spies a rare tip: There was to be a high-level meeting of al Qaeda officials in Bajaur, one of the desolate tribal areas of northwestern Pakistan. The agent had been tracking Abu Faraj al-Libi, the third-ranking official in al Qaeda, who had occasionally been spotted riding around the mountain villages of Pakistan on a red motorcycle. The agent told his CIA handlers not only that al-Libi would be at the gathering but also that Osama bin Laden's deputy, Ayman al-Zawahiri, might attend.

A plan of attack was hastily put together, and Goss and Rumsfeld considered the risks. Three dozen Navy SEALs would jump out of a C-130 cargo plane and parachute into a drop zone not far from where the meeting was supposed to take place. The SEALs would attack the compound, grab as many people as possible, and take them to a staging area where everyone would be spirited back over the Afghanistan border in helicopters. Goss urged that the military carry out the mission, and he had the backing of Lt. General Stanley McChrystal, a rail-thin and intense ascetic who had taken over Joint Special Operations Command in 2003.

But Rumsfeld and his top intelligence aide, Stephen Cambone, resisted the plan. It was too risky, they said, and Rumsfeld demanded that dozens more Army Rangers be added to the mission so they could bail out the SEALs in case something went wrong. The invasion force swelled to more than 150 troops, and Rumsfeld decided there was no way an operation that size could be kept from President Pervez Musharraf. Another objection came from the CIA's station chief in Islamabad, who had been awakened in the middle of the night and told that a large group of well-armed Americans were about to enter the country. "This is a really bad idea, Stan," the station chief told McChrystal, who had been the one to call him. "You might kill a couple of al Qaeda guys, but it won't be worth it.

"You're invading Pakistan," he said.

All the while, the SEALs were sitting inside the C-130 at Bagram Air Base, waiting for the final orders to launch the mission. They waited for hours before the mission was finally scrubbed.

Rumsfeld's concerns about the assault were largely about intelligence. The information came from one CIA source, and the defense secretary thought that a single strand of information was a shaky basis for a high-risk mission into the snowy mountains of western Pakistan. He also didn't trust the CIA's track record, and in early 2005 the spy agency was having difficulty convincing anyone—especially Rumsfeld—about the credibility of its intelligence analysis. American spy agencies were still reeling from the Iraq war debacle, when they had judged that Saddam Hussein was keeping stockpiles of chemical and biological weapons, and a cloud of suspicion hung over all of the CIA's assessments for several years afterward. As much as Goss was frustrated by how the discussions about the Bajaur operation ended, there was nothing he could do. Rumsfeld didn't trust even a CIA judgment that there was an 80 percent chance that al-Zawahiri was at the meeting, and Rumsfeld was the one in charge of the troops. As one aide to Goss described it, "It was like your dad telling you that you can't have the car for the weekend."

But beyond the questions about the reliability of the intelligence, the episode was also a bleak reminder that, several years after the September 11 attacks, the war against international terror groups remained haphazard and chaotic. Neither the CIA nor the Pentagon had a coherent plan for the secret wars outside of Iraq and Afghanistan. Both agencies were still locked in turf battles, set to prove to the White House that they ought to be in charge of the global manhunt. And, increasingly, they were mimicking each other: the CIA, after Nek Muhammad's killing in Pakistan, becoming ever more a lethal, paramilitary organization, and the Pentagon ramping up its spying operations to support a special-operations war. There were no clear ground rules. When an emergency came up, like the intelligence about the al Qaeda meeting in Bajaur, there was no plan in place to act on it.

IF THERE WAS ONE EVENT that had catalyzed the CIA's escalation of lethal operations, it was the completion of a devastating internal report in May 2004 by the spy agency's inspector general. The 106-page report by John Helgerson kicked out the foundation upon which the CIA detention-and-interrogation program had rested, and it raised questions about whether CIA officers might face criminal prosecution for the brutal interrogations carried out inside the agency's network of secret prisons. It suggested that interrogation methods like waterboarding, sleep deprivation, and exploiting the phobias of prisoners—such as confining them in a small box with live bugs—violated the United Nations Convention Against Torture, which prohibits "cruel, inhuman, or degrading treatment or punishment." The CIA had subjected several detainees to waterboarding—wherein the prisoner was hooded and immobilized on a wooden plank while water was poured over his face, creating the sensation of drowning—and in one month alone had used the technique on Khalid Sheikh Mohammed, the chief planner of the September 11 attacks, 183 times.

Waterboarding was one of a number of interrogation techniques that had been authorized by the Justice Department, but Helgerson's report also detailed a pattern of freelancing in the black sites, what the inspector general called "unauthorized, improvised, inhumane, and undocumented" detention-and-interrogation techniques. There were instances of interrogators conducting mock executions to scare the detainees into talking; one CIA interrogator pointed a spinning drill at a prisoner's head.

The CIA's secret prison program had grown from a single, spartan facility in Bangkok, Thailand, to an archipelago of jails throughout the world. Jose Rodriguez, the head of the Counterterrorist Center, had intended the prisons to be a more permanent alternative to the Thailand site, which had originally been code-named "Cat's Eye" but later renamed when CIA officers thought the designation seemed racially insensitive. Thailand was where the CIA had held its first two prisoners, Abu Zubaydah and Abd al-Rahim al-Nashiri, but as the

CIA and its partner spy services began rounding up dozens of prisoners in Afghanistan, Pakistan, and other countries, Rodgriguez and CTC officers decided the spy agency needed far more prison space.

The CIA's detention-and-interrogation program would become the most infamous and divisive aspect of the Bush administration's strategy against al Qaeda, but the way the CIA set up the black prisons was somewhat prosaic. Rodriguez ordered a team at the Counterterrorist Center to work with engineers and outside contractors, and when the prisons were near completion the CIA hired a small supply company to provide toilets, plumbing equipment, earplugs, bedding, and other prison supplies. The contractors bought some of the equipment at Target and Walmart and flew it to the jails: one of them in a nondescript building on a busy street in Bucharest, Romania, and another in Lithuania. The waterboards were bought locally, constructed from lumber purchased near some of the secret sites.

The jails were small—intended to house about half a dozen detainees—and the cells had some special features designed specially to accommodate the brutal methods used by CIA interrogators, such as flexible, plywood-covered walls that might soften the impact of someone being slammed into a wall. The detainees were prevented from communicating with one another and were kept in solitary confinement for twenty-three hours a day. The remaining hour was for exercise, when CIA security officers wearing black ski masks removed the prisoners from their cells. By 2004, CIA prison wardens had imposed a system of reward and punishment. Detainees who were considered well behaved received books and DVDs. The entertainment was taken away if the prisoner misbehaved. The CIA, an espionage service created after World War II to inform American presidents about the world around them, had become the Department of Secret Corrections.

Concerns about the CIA's interrogation program had been percolating in parts of the Bush administration even before Helgerson's report, but still only a small circle of officials were aware of the secret prisons. This had sometimes led to bizarre discussions between the White House and the CIA. In June 2003, for instance, the White House was set to commemorate a day set aside by the United Nations to support torture victims. The White House press office had prepared a bland statement about how the United States is "committed to the world-wide elimination of torture" and was "leading the fight by example."

But the United States wasn't, in fact, leading by example, and the draft statement unnerved some senior officers at the CIA. Scott Muller, the agency's top lawyer, told the White House he was concerned about the press release, given that the kinds of interrogation methods that President Bush had authorized for the CIA were widely considered torture. The concern at Langley, Muller said, was that the CIA could be turned into a scapegoat were the political winds to shift. The press release never went out.

The report by Helgerson hinted at some of the angst inside the CIA. Several officers involved in the detention program, it stated, worried they might "be vulnerable to legal action in the United States or abroad and that the U.S. government will not stand behind them." The White House and Justice Department had blessed the program, and George Tenet had lobbied for the CIA to take charge of the prisoners, but some of the older hands at Langley felt sure they had seen the movie before: during the Church Committee investigations and the Iran–Contra scandal. A day of reckoning would come, they believed, when the Bush White House would use the inspector general's report as a noose to hang the CIA.

The report was the beginning of the end for the detention-and-interrogation program. The prisons would stay open for several more years, and new detainees were occasionally picked up and taken to the secret sites, but the agency would eventually stop using waterboarding and some of the other roughest interrogation techniques. Senior officials at Langley began looking for ways to offload the prisoners to the Pentagon, but those who couldn't be transferred languished in the secret jails as the Bush administration frantically searched for an endgame for the prison program.

The greatest impact of Helgerson's report was felt inside the CIA's Counterterrorist Center, which was at the vanguard of the spy agency's global terror hunt. The CTC had focused on capturing al Qaeda operatives, interrogating them either in CIA jails or outsourcing interrogations to the spy services of Pakistan, Egypt, Jordan, and elsewhere, and then using the fruits of the interrogations to hunt down more terror suspects. This strategy, the thinking went, would one day lead the CIA to Osama bin Laden.

But now the ground had shifted, and counterterrorism officials were forced to rethink the strategy for the secret war. Armed drones, and targeted killing in general, offered a new direction for a spy agency that had begun to feel burned by its years in the detention-and-interrogation business. Killing by remote control was the antithesis of the dirty, intimate work of interrogation. It somehow seemed cleaner, less personal. Targeted killings were cheered by Republicans and Democrats alike, and using drones flown by pilots who were stationed thousands of miles away from the war made the whole strategy seem risk-free. After the killing of Nek Muhammad in Pakistan—carried out just a month after John Helgerson's report was completed—the CIA began to see its future: not as the long-term jailers of America's enemies but as a military organization that could erase them.

IN 2004, Jose Rodriguez even tried to resurrect a killing program that had been proposed, and then abandoned, during the first year after the September 11 attacks. It was the plan to cobble together paramilitary hit squads to kill terror suspects across the globe, from Europe to the Middle East to South Asia. Vice President Dick Cheney had given his approval for the program when Rodriguez and fellow CTC officer Enrique Prado presented the plan to the White House in December 2001. Unlike what people saw in movies, the CIA had no in-house cadre of assassins, and the program would have brought the spy agency more in line with its glamorized Hollywood version. But George Tenet had never authorized any missions, and the plans had been temporarily shelved.

Like Rodriguez, Prado was a veteran of the CIA's Latin America division, and he had played a leading role in Nicaragua's Contra war during the 1980s. He transferred to the Counterterrorist Center in 1996, and during the months after the September 11 attacks Prado had been a tutor of sorts for Rodriguez about the workings of al Qaeda. After the meeting with Cheney in December 2001, Prado had been put in charge of recruiting CIA officers to train for the killing missions.

When Rodriguez decided to reopen the program in 2004, his close friend Prado had left the CIA for Blackwater USA, the private military company that was in the midst of a dramatic expansion with the help of millions of dollars in contracts from the State Department, the Pentagon, and the CIA. So Rodriguez arrived at an astonishing solution: He decided to outsource the killing program to Blackwater employees.

The company's founder, Erik Prince, was already a favorite son in the Bush administration and was looking to burrow deeper into America's clandestine establishment. Prince had arrived on the scene with impeccable timing. The CIA couldn't find enough of its own personnel to meet the demands of its large covert stations in Kabul and Baghdad, and the spy agency turned to Blackwater's private guards for secret missions—from protection of CIA officers to intelligence gathering to snatch-and-grab operations—that once had been reserved only for fully trained CIA employees. Eventually, the CIA even hired Blackwater to load bombs and missiles on Predator and Reaper drones in Pakistan.

Prince regularly invited top CIA officers to the Kentucky Derby, or down to Blackwater's headquarters, in eastern North Carolina's Great Dismal Swamp, for a day of shooting at the company's expansive training grounds. And he successfully poached top CIA officials, including Prado and Cofer Black, the former head of the Counterterrorist Center, with big salary offers. Prado, now working for Blackwater, had the opportunity to sell programs back to the government that he had originally developed while at the CIA.

Prince did not see the outsourcing of war as anything novel, merely an evolution of a centuries-old phenomenon. During one visit to Langley, he pitched senior CIA officers on a Blackwater "quick-reaction force," a cadre of operatives the CIA could use to carry out paramilitary assignments in the far reaches of the world. He began his presentation with a sweeping statement. "From the earliest days of the American republic," he said, "the nation has relied on mercenaries for its defense." CIA officials ultimately rejected the plan.

Blackwater's reputation for reckless behavior, cemented during a September 2007 incident during which Blackwater operatives killed seventeen Iraqis at a traffic stop in Baghdad, would eventually turn Prince and his company into symbols of America's misadventures in Iraq. He would lament that Democrats in Congress painted him as a war profiteer even as he was "paying for all sorts of intelligence activities to support American national security out of my own pocket." This was true, but often the money that Blackwater spent on secret projects was like an R&D fund, used to develop products and services that could be sold to the government for millions of dollars. He pitched CIA case officers in Pakistan on ideas for stealth aircrafts, and Asia operatives on a plan to smuggle CIA informants out of China by having them swim underwater using a Navy SEAL–style rebreather all the way to the submersed vessel. There was a problem with this plan: Most of the CIA's informants in China were eighty-year-old generals who would never have survived an underwater swim with a rebreather.

Former CIA officers who joined Blackwater were aggressive in their attempts to expand the company's business with the spy agency. On at least one occasion, a top CIA lawyer had to call the company to warn that ex-spies were on the edge of breaking "revolving door" laws that restrict retired government employees from lobbying their former agencies. Beyond Blackwater's work for the CIA, Prado considered selling the Drug Enforcement Administration on a plan to use a network of foreign spies Blackwater had cultivated that could "do everything from surveillance to ground truth to disruption operations," according to an internal Blackwater e-mail. "Deniability is built in and should be a big plus," he wrote.

It was a desire for "deniability" that led Jose Rodriguez to take the extraordinary step of outsourcing a lethal CIA program to an American company. The CIA signed Prince and Prado to a personal services contract, and the two men began devising plans to carry out surveillance of potential targets, including some of the same men—like Pakistani nuclear scientist A. Q. Khan—whom the CIA had first proposed killing in 2001 during the meeting with Cheney. Prince and Prado would oversee the program, and the hand of the United States would, in theory, be hidden. Prince and Prado envisioned that the Blackwater hit teams would ultimately be under CIA control, but once they were given missions they would have a large degree of autonomy. "We were building a unilateral, unattributable capability," Prince later said during an interview with *Vanity Fair.* "If it went bad, we weren't expecting the chief of station, the ambassador, or anyone to bail us out."

As it happened, they never needed to be bailed out. Like the first iteration of the assassination program, no killing operations were carried out during this phase of the hit-team program. Prince and Prado had overseen the training of the Blackwater teams, but Prince blames "institutional osteoporosis" for why the Blackwater assassins were never dispatched to kill terrorists.

Given the support the program had from senior managers like Rodriguez, why not? Amazingly, it wasn't because of legal concerns either at the CIA or the White House. Lawyers at the CIA had given their approval to involve Prince and Prado in the killing operation, but senior CIA officials were ultimately unconvinced that the agency would be able to keep its role in the program hidden. Blackwater had developed a web of subsidiary companies to hide its CIA work, but it likely would not have been difficult for foreign governments to untangle the web and trace operations back to Prince and, ultimately, the CIA.

"The more you outsource an operation, the more deniable it becomes," explained one senior CIA officer involved in the decision to terminate Blackwater's role in the assassination program. "But you're also giving up control of the operation. And if that guy screws up, it's still your fault."

The ill-conceived Blackwater phase of the killing program remains—like the earlier iteration of the program—a closely guarded government secret. Even in retirement, former Counterterrorist Center officer Hank Crumpton is prohibited by the CIA from giving details about the time that he worked on the first phase of the program. But in an interview, he said he found it puzzling that the United States still seemed to make a distinction between killing people from a distance using an armed drone and training humans to do the killing themselves.

If the country is going to allow the CIA to do one, he said, should it really be queasy about allowing the other? "How we apply lethal force, and where we apply lethal force—that's a huge debate that we really haven't had," he said. "There seems to be no problem with a Hellfire shot against a designated enemy in a place like Afghanistan, the tribal areas of Pakistan, Somalia, or Yemen." In those places, he said, it seems like just another part of war.

But, he asked, what if a suspected terrorist is in a place like Paris, or Hamburg, or somewhere else where drones can't fly, "and you use a CIA or [military] operative on the ground to shoot him in the back of the head?

"Then," he said, "it's viewed as an assassination."

STILL, each hit the CIA took for its detention-and-interrogation program pushed CIA leaders further to one side of a morbid calculation: that the agency would be far better off killing, rather than jailing, terror suspects. In late 2005 Congress passed the Detainee Treatment Act, which included a provision banning "cruel, inhuman, and degrading" treatment of any prisoner in American custody, including CIA black sites. There was now the potential that covert officers working at the CIA prisons could be prosecuted for their work, and the specter of criminal investigations and congressional hearings hung over Langley.

These fears already had led Jose Rodriguez to order the destruction of dozens of videotapes that gave a minute-by-minute chronicle of the ordeals of al Qaeda operatives Abu Zubaydah and Abd al-Rahim al-Nashiri during CIA interrogations. Rodriguez, who had been promoted yet again and now had the powerful job of head of the Directorate of Operations—running all CIA covert-action and espionage operations across the globe—worried that the faces of the undercover officers were clearly visible on the tapes. With the toxic details of the prison program leaking out, he thought the officers might face both legal and physical jeopardy. In early November 2005, he sent a secret cable to the CIA's Bangkok Station, where the tapes were being kept in a safe, and ordered that they be fed into an industrial-strength shredder. Seven steel blades went to work on the tapes, pulverizing them into tiny shards that were vacuumed out of the shredder and dumped into plastic trash bags.

But even after destroying vestiges of the early days of the prison program, the CIA faced more uncertainty with the passage of the new law by Congress. Days after the Detainee Treatment Act was passed, CIA director Porter Goss wrote a letter to the White House. The CIA would shut down all interrogations, he wrote, until the Justice Department could render a judgment about whether the CIA techniques violated the new law.

White House officials were incensed when they received the letter. National Security Advisor Stephen Hadley thought Goss's memo was pure posturing—the CIA trying to cover its back in the event of future investigations. Hadley called the CIA director at home on Christmas Day and accused him of not being a "team player." But Goss wouldn't budge, and it became clear to officials in the White House that all of the hyperventilating at the CIA, Washington's most paranoid institution, wasn't going to subside unless something was done to calm the spies down.

The job fell to Andrew Card, President Bush's chief of staff. Card drove out to Langley intending to soothe the fears at CIA headquarters, but his visit was a disaster. Inside a packed conference room, Card thanked the assembled CIA officers for their service and their hard work but refused to make any firm declarations that agency officers wouldn't be criminally liable for participating in the detention-and-interrogation program.

The room became restless. Prodded by his chief of staff, Patrick Murray, Porter Goss interrupted Card.

"Can you assure these people that the politicians will not walk away from the people who carried out this program?" Goss asked. Card didn't answer the question directly. Instead, he tried to crack a joke.

"Let me put it this way," he said. "Every morning I knock on the door of the Oval Office, walk in, and say, 'Pardon me, Mr. President.' And, of course, the only person the president can't pardon is himself."

Card giggled after he said this, but his joke landed with a thud. The White House chief of staff, when asked whether President Bush would protect CIA officers from legal scrutiny, had suggested that the most they might be able to rely on is a presidential pardon after the indictments and the convictions were handed down.

At the CIA, pardon jokes don't go down well.

SOME OF PRESIDENT BUSH'S AIDES began to see the CIA as a problem. The agency's director was doing battle with the White House over the detention program, and Vice President Cheney had become convinced that CIA analysts secretly opposed the war in Iraq and were leaking negative assessments about the war to members of Congress and the press. As much as Bush and Cheney had originally tried to resist pressure by the 9/11 Commission to create a director of national intelligence to take control over all sixteen American spy agencies, some at the White House saw an ancillary benefit of the new position: It put the CIA in its place.

A weakened CIA presented an opportunity for Donald Rumsfeld. The worsening situation in Iraq had dampened some of the triumphalism among Rumsfeld and his staff, but the defense secretary continued with his efforts to wage war far from declared war zones—in countries that historically had been the CIA's turf. In 2004 Rumsfeld issued a secret directive—known internally at the Pentagon as the "Al Qaeda Network Execute Order"—that expanded the powers of special-operations troops to kill, capture, and spy in more than a dozen countries. The order gave Joint Special Operations Command, the unit based at Fort Bragg that Rumsfeld had come to identify as a new model army for the post–September 11 era, broad authority to launch operations across an arc of territory from North Africa all the way to the Philippines. It allowed them to go into Syria, Somalia, and Pakistan. Under the new authorities, the missions were highly classified, seldom publicly acknowledged, and irregularly briefed to members of Congress.

Joint Special Operations Command was now one of the brightest stars in the Defense Department firmament, and the budget for special operations more than doubled over six years, reaching nearly $8 billion in 2007. This was still just a sliver of the Pentagon's budgets for buying ships and jets, but the infusion of money allowed JSOC not only to build more platoons of secret troops but also to spend money on supplies and logistics that would allow Navy SEALs and Delta Force operatives to sustain clandestine operations for days or weeks on end. No longer was JSOC capable merely of twenty-four-hour hostage-rescue missions. It could run wars of its own.

JSOC was proving as much in Iraq. There, Lt. General Stanley McChrystal's task force had been handed the mission of attacking the al Qaeda franchise in the country led by Jordanian terrorist Abu Musab al-Zarqawi. Wave upon wave of deadly violence was washing over the country, and al-Zarqawi's al Qaeda in Mesopotamia had claimed responsibility for devastating attacks on American troop convoys and Shi'ite holy sites. Within months of the beginning of the insurgency, it became clear to commanders on the ground that the war would be sucking American troops into the country for years, and Rumsfeld and his senior intelligence adviser, Stephen Cambone, gave JSOC a long leash to try to neutralize what had become the Iraqi insurgency's most lethal arm.

The mantra of the task force, based inside an old Iraqi air-force hangar at Balad Air Base, north of Baghdad, was "fight for intelligence." In the beginning, the white dry-erase boards that McChrystal and his team had set up to diagram the terror group were blank. McChrystal realized that much of the problem came from the poor communication between the various American military commands in Iraq, with few procedures in place to share intelligence with one another. "We began a review of the enemy, and of ourselves," he would later write. "Neither was easy to understand." Just how little everyone knew was apparent in 2004, amid reports that Iraqi troops had captured al-Zarqawi near Fallujah. Since nobody knew exactly what the Jordanian terrorist looked like, he was released by accident.

But a campaign plan eventually developed. Night raids against al-Zarqawi's network were designed not just to kick down a door and spray gunfire in all directions. McChrystal believed that what was important was not body count but the intelligence that could be gathered through interrogations and computer forensics at the spot of the raid. The intelligence trail could then be followed to the next suspected safe house, where more senior al Qaeda operatives were hiding. Put a needle into one vein, the theory went, and you can learn about the entire system.

McChrystal tried to ensure that his task force wasn't crippled by the same rivalries that had hurt special-operations missions in Afghanistan. He courted CIA officers in Iraq and convinced a senior CIA officer to sit beside him each morning for the task force's daily battlefield update. Thousands of miles away, analysts working in a nondescript government building in Fairfax, Virginia, each day sifted through the intelligence from the previous night's raids in Iraq that had been extracted from thumb drives, cell phones, and computer hard drives. Over time, the dry-erase boards filled up with the names and aliases of al-Zarqawi's operatives. The various names were connected by lines drawn with black marker—everyone's best guess about how an amorphous terror network carried out its business.

JSOC's rapid growth was aided by an internal Pentagon study commissioned by Rumsfeld and completed in 2005. The report recommended that the military "must increase capabilities and capacities to conduct sustained operations in multiple, sensitive, non-permissive, and denied areas." Translated from militaryspeak: Wage simultaneous secret wars in as many places as possible. Written by former JSOC commander General Wayne Downing and Michael G. Vickers—a former CIA clandestine officer who had gained a degree of fame when his role in running guns to Afghanistan during the Soviet war was detailed in the book *Charlie Wilson's War*—the report had instant currency with Rumsfeld. Its primary conclusion was that special-operations troops should take a greater role in the Bush administration's war against al Qaeda and other terror groups. Special-operations troops were well positioned in Iraq and Afghanistan, it concluded, but not the wars of the future. "The future fight," it read, "will take place in countries with which we are not at war."

The Pentagon had even begun carrying out risky spying missions inside Iran. Taking advantage of the commercial traffic crossing Iraq's eastern border into Iran, special-operations troops were paying agents to cross the border using phony cover stories to collect intelligence about military installations inside western Iran. The foreign agents were both Iranian Muslims and Coptic Christians who could easily get past Iranian border security, telling stories about their plan to buy truckloads full of fruit or other merchandise inside Iran. With such limited cross-border forays, it was difficult for the Pentagon to get truly valuable intelligence from these missions, and the Pentagon wasn't authorized to conduct any sabotage operations or to kill Iranian Revolutionary Guard troops.

The real goal, said a senior Pentagon intelligence official during that period, was to build up as much of an intelligence network as possible inside Iran—a network that could be tapped if President Bush or one of his successors decided to invade the country. Like so many other military missions in undeclared war zones, the operations in Iran were justified as "preparation of the battlefield."

The work of soldiers and spies was becoming increasingly blurred. The CIA still had more expansive authorities than the Pentagon to carry out missions anywhere in the world, but after Rumsfeld's 2004 order it became harder to see real differences between the mission of the military and the mission of the CIA. McChrystal had developed a good rapport with American spies inside of Iraq, but the military's missions into Iran had not been coordinated with the CIA, and with so many secret operatives crawling around the world's darkest corners, the lack of coordination created the potential for a major catastrophe.

OR A MISSED OPPORTUNITY. After Donald Rumsfeld called off the 2005 Bajaur mission in Pakistan because he thought that the hastily planned operation was freighted with too much risk, both the Pentagon and CIA conducted an inquest to figure out what had gone wrong and to make sure the debacle wouldn't be repeated. The review determined that there were no established procedures in place for authorizing an emergency mission into a country beyond Iraq and Afghanistan. The Pentagon and CIA were carrying out parallel secret operations across the globe, but neither the defense secretary nor the CIA director had the authority to take charge when an opportunity arose to launch a secret mission into a country such as Pakistan. Over the next year, the Pentagon and CIA tried to work out a division of labor, carving up the world and determining who was in charge of each front of the secret war.

Stephen Cambone led negotiations for the Pentagon, and deputy CIA director Vice Admiral Albert Calland was in charge of the CIA team. Whether the CIA or JSOC would be in charge of secret operations in a particular country depended on a variety of factors: How willing was that country to allow special-operations troops on its soil? What was the strength of the relationship between the CIA and a country's spy service? Just how prickly might a specific CIA station chief be about ceding control in his country to JSOC?

Because of the Bajaur episode, Pakistan was at the top of the list for the negotiators. President Musharraf had given his blessing to drone strikes, but he still vehemently opposed American combat operations in the tribal areas. It was fine for things to "fall out of the sky," but not for them to come marching over the border from Afghanistan. Trying to sell Musharraf on special-operations ground campaigns in places like North Waziristan and Bajaur was, most people in Washington agreed, a hopeless endeavor.

The CIA proposed a solution. In order to get special-operations troops inside Pakistan, they would simply be turned over to the CIA and operate under Title 50 covert-action authority. Special-operations troops would be "sheep-dipped"—the SEALs would become spies. Special-operations troops would be able to launch operations into Pakistan, and Musharraf would never be told. As one former CIA officer described the arrangement, the special-operations troops "basically became the CIA director's armed platoon." The exact same trick would be used six years later, when helicopters carrying teams of Navy SEALs took off from Jalalabad, Afghanistan, and crossed the border into Pakistan for the raid that would kill Osama bin Laden. That night, the SEALs were under CIA authority, and CIA director Leon E. Panetta was technically in charge of the mission.

In other countries, it was JSOC that was in control, and commando missions escalated in countries like the Philippines, where special-operations troops were already posted. In 2006, an American military drone fired missiles at a suspected terror camp in the jungles of the southern Philippines, based on intelligence that Umar Patek, one of the ringleaders of a 2002 terrorist attack in Bali, was hiding at the camp. The missile strike, which the government of Manila announced publicly as a "Philippine military operation," missed Patek but killed several others. The military was never able to determine how many of them were followers of Umar Patek and how many were women and children.

The ballooning budgets for special operations also allowed JSOC to buy new eavesdropping equipment that gave commandos the ability to collect intelligence inside Pakistan from the sky. Beechcraft airplanes would regularly take off from airstrips in Afghanistan, fly over the spine of mountains separating Afghanistan and Pakistan, and turn into flying cell-phone towers. Inside the Beechcraft planes, a device called a "Typhoon Box" housed dozens of phone numbers that military spies suspected were used by Pakistani militants. The device could identify when one of the numbers was being used and pinpoint its location. Even if a phone was switched off, JSOC had the ability to turn the phone on; it would then give away the precise coordinates of whoever was carrying it.

AFTER THE NEW DEALS were struck with the CIA, JSOC operatives that had been "sheep-dipped" and turned into CIA officers could act on the intelligence with ground operations in Pakistan. One year after the mission into Bajaur was scotched, the CIA once again picked up information about a gathering of military leaders, once again in the Bajaur Agency, in the tribal areas.

The tiny village of Damadola had been under surveillance for some time, since al Qaeda captive Abu Faraj al-Libi told Pakistani intelligence officers he had once met Ayman al-Zawahiri at the house of Bakhptur Khan, a Damadola villager. The CIA had carried out a drone strike in Damadola in January 2006, narrowly missing al-Zawahiri. And, months later, when the intelligence tip came in about another meeting in Damadola, a team of Navy SEALs was sent into the village.

With the new procedures in place, CIA and military officials took only hours to analyze the intelligence and approve the operation. General John Abizaid, commander of United States Central Command, was in Washington when the CIA received the intelligence tip, and Abizaid jumped into a black SUV and raced to Langley in a motorcade. Shortly after Abizaid and Porter Goss had agreed on the final details of the raid, helicopters took off from Afghanistan and delivered the SEALs over the border into Bajaur.

The troops stormed the compound, wrestled several people to the floor, and bound them with plastic handcuffs. The prisoners were loaded into the helicopters and brought back into Afghanistan.

Inside the Counterterrorism Center at Langley, CIA officers gathered around a television screen to watch a video feed from a Predator, which was circling above the compound in Damadola—a staring, unblinking eye allowing spies thousands of miles away to watch the operation unfold. The SEALs captured no senior al Qaeda leaders on the operation. But the Damadola mission proved they could get into Pakistan undetected, conduct a snatch operation, and return to the other side of the border without Pakistan's government ever being wise to the mission.

8: A WAR BY PROXY

"Me and my nation against the world. Me and my clan against my nation. Me and my family against the clan. Me and my brother against the family. Me against my brother."

—*Somali proverb*

B y spring 2006, the CIA operatives in Nairobi, Kenya, were loading unmarked cargo planes with rocket-propelled grenades, mortars, and AK-47s and flying the shipments to airstrips controlled by Somali warlords. Along with the weapons, they sent suitcases full of cash, about two hundred thousand dollars for each warlord as payment for their services in the fight against terrorism. For a group of men who had been trying to kill one another at various times over the years, the warlords had no qualms about working together once the CIA opened up its coffers. They even managed to come up with a Washington–friendly name for their partnership: the Alliance for the Restoration of Peace and Counter-Terrorism (ARPCT). The name was unintentionally ironic, given the brutal history of some of the warlords, like Abdi Hasan Awale Qeybdii and Mohamed Qanyare Afrah. Even in parts of the CIA, the group became the butt of jokes. Some American spies compared the acronym ARPCT with SPECTRE, the global terrorist organization from the James Bond films.

Jose Rodriguez had signed off on a plan developed by spies in

Nairobi to escalate a program of running guns and money to the war-lords, who had convinced the Americans they would help battle a burgeoning radical threat in the chaotic, impoverished nation.*** The collection of warlords, some of the same men who had dispatched gunmen to kill Army Rangers and Delta Force commandos in 1993, had been on the CIA's payroll in 2002. They had helped the CIA hunt down members of al Qaeda's East Africa cell, some of whom had been smuggled out of Somalia to CIA black sites. But the covert operation in 2006 was a more formal arrangement, and it turned into a Washington-sanctioned boondoggle for the warlords.

The spiraling chaos in Iraq had not only drawn soldiers and spies away from the war in Afghanistan; it had also inspired a new generation of young Muslims to take up arms against the United States. At that time, drafts of a classified intelligence report circulating through American spy agencies laid bare the metastasizing problem of radicalization in the Muslim world. The final report concluded that Iraq had become a "'cause célèbre' for jihadists, breeding a deep resentment of U.S. involvement in the Muslim world and cultivating supporters for the global jihadist movement."

The report, a National Intelligence Estimate, predicted that an increasingly decentralized global jihad movement would splinter even further, with regional militant groups proliferating. The landscape was changing dramatically, and countries in North Africa, East Africa, and impoverished parts of the Arabian Peninsula were becoming increasingly unstable.

In Yemen, twenty-three militants linked to al Qaeda escaped from a local jail using spoons and broken table legs to dig a tunnel. They likely had help from members of Yemen's security services who were

---

*** In 2005, the CIA changed the name of the Directorate of Operations to the National Clandestine Service. Rodriguez was the head of the NCS.

sympathetic to the prisoners' cause from the days of the Soviet war in Afghanistan. As one Yemeni official explained the inside job to the *New York Times*, "You have to remember, these officers used to escort people from Sana'a to Pakistan during the Afghan jihad. People made relationships, and that doesn't change so easily." Interpol issued an urgent global alert seeking the arrests of the twenty-three men, but most did not go far. They stayed in Yemen, forming the core of a group that would eventually name itself al Qaeda in the Arabian Peninsula.

Then there was Somalia, and the rise to prominence of a small, stubby man with almond-shaped eyeglasses and, protruding from his chin, a tuft of hair that he dyed with red henna. Hassan Dahir Aweys led the shura council of Somalia's Islamic Courts Union, a loose federation of clan elders, businessmen, and magnates who had joined together to bring order to Somalia's chaos by imposing Islamic sharia law. The courts, which for years had been dominated by moderates, were widely popular in Somalia because they offered a reprieve from decades of warlordism. But by late 2005, Aweys's influence over the ICU had turned the organization into a larger version of his sharia court in the port city of Merca: a platform for preaching an uncompromising brand of Islam that regularly meted out punishments like stoning adulterers and severing the hands of thieves.

Aweys had been on an American list of top terror suspects for years, and the CIA had linked him to the al Qaeda cell in East Africa that had carried out the 1998 embassy bombings in Kenya and Tanzania. And yet he operated in plain sight, making high-profile trips to Dubai and moving openly among cities in Somalia. Under his command were a band of young, committed gunmen who had taken to calling themselves "al Shabaab"—Arabic for "The Youth." The group would roam the streets of Mogadishu, hunting and killing anyone believed to have pledged allegiance to Somalia's Transitional Federal

Government, a weak and corrupt organization created by the United Nations that had little control inside the country. Locals suspected of spying for the Americans were shot on sight.

The CIA had not kept a permanent station inside Somalia for years, so the job of monitoring events inside the country fell to the clandestine officers in neighboring Kenya. The CIA station in Nairobi had grown significantly since the September 11 attacks, getting more money and personnel after CIA director Porter Goss decided that the agency needed to beef up its presence in Africa and reopen some of its previously shuttered stations on the continent. During the final months of 2005 and into 2006, alarming cables from spies in Nairobi arrived in Langley warning about the growing influence of the red-bearded Hassan Dahir Aweys and the al Shabaab gunmen. Some of the reports concluded that the young radicals inside the Islamic Courts Union, including a gangly veteran of the Afghanistan war named Aden Hashi Farah Ayro, could feather the nest for al Qaeda operatives to set up a new base in Somalia.

But as much as Osama bin Laden and his followers might have wanted to establish a home in Somalia, the group over the years had confronted some of the same problems in the war-ravaged country that the Americans had. Put simply, al Qaeda didn't understand Somalia, and a plan by the group to flee to Somalia once the war in Afghanistan had begun had failed miserably. Arab militants who arrived in the country had trouble navigating the dizzying array of clans and subclans knit into the fabric of Somali culture, and found themselves being extorted by clan elders at every turn. Rather than unite under a single banner to expel Westerners from the country, Somalis decided they would rather fight one another. Al Qaeda militants, adherents to the radical Wahhabi strain of Islam, could not relate to the more moderate Sufism that the vast majority of Somalis practice. Somalis had a reputation for being tremendous gossips, and the foreign visitors grew angry that they couldn't keep secrets. All told, the chaotic African country by the sea seemed very different from the mountains of Pakistan and Afghanistan.

This was hardly clear at the time to anyone in military or intelligence circles in Washington, and the alarming CIA reports out of Nairobi started getting attention at the White House. But what exactly was to be done if Somalia was going the way of Afghanistan? With the ghosts of the Black Hawk Down episode—the 1993 Battle of Mogadishu—still haunting the halls of the Pentagon, Army generals already had made it clear they might resign before the United States attempted another significant military intervention in Somalia. Besides, the wars elsewhere were sapping the ranks of soldiers and Marines, and the Pentagon could hardly spare troops for the Horn of Africa beyond what it had committed to the bare-bones task force in Djibouti, operating out of a former French Foreign Legion camp there. With the Bush administration convinced that Somalia was a problem that needed to be solved, the White House turned to the CIA to find a proxy army to fight a new war for Mogadishu. So was born the Alliance for the Restoration of Peace and Counter-Terrorism.

The warlords of the ARPCT were hardly discreet about their ties to Washington and bragged openly about how much the CIA was paying them. But the tradecraft used by the Americans was also shoddy, making it readily apparent that the alliance was a CIA front. The gun shipments and money drops were broadcast in the local press. Agency officers supplied the warlords with contact information to use when they needed more supplies, and rumors spread through the capital that the CIA men had even given out an e-mail address to use when the warlords needed more guns and money.

The clumsiness of the CIA had divided officials inside the American embassy in Nairobi, a fortress built after the 1998 bombing had destroyed the previous building. The entire operation was being run by the CIA's station chief in Kenya, but diplomats at the compound began writing cables back to State Department headquarters warning about blowback from the covert support to the warlords. In one of the cables, Leslie Rowe, the embassy's second-ranking officer, described the anger among African officials about the CIA effort. Michael Zorick, the State Department's political officer for Somalia, sent a scathing cable to Washington criticizing the warlord policy and complaining that the CIA was running guns to some of the biggest thugs in Somalia. Soon afterward, Zorick was reassigned to Chad.

Just as some of these officers had warned, the covert operation blew up in the CIA's face. Instead of weakening the Islamists, it tipped the balance in Somalia in the other direction. Somalis began to embrace the Islamic Courts Union as the way to rid the country of foreign influence and finally bring an end to the warlord rule that had Balkanized the country. During a meeting of American ambassadors from East Africa and Yemen in May 2006, the American officials could already see things unraveling inside Mogadishu. With nobody able to agree about what the next steps should be, the ambassadors agreed on the importance of "changing the conversation" from the fighting in the Somali capital toward "positive U.S. steps" to help restore Somali institutions.

What had once been a standoff turned into a rout, as the Islamists drove the CIA-backed warlords out of Mogadishu. The ICU consolidated its power in the capital. Even more disastrous for Washington, the Battle of Mogadishu gave even greater influence inside the ICU to Hassan Dahir Aweys and the radical band of al Shabaab gunmen.

Hank Crumpton, the former spy at the CIA's Counterterrorist Center, watched the disaster unfold from his desk at the State Department, where he had taken a job as the coordinator for counterterrorism. The job carried the lofty title of ambassador-at-large but was hobbled by its location inside an underfunded and occasionally dysfunctional diplomatic machinery. For Crumpton, the CIA's warlord adventure in Somalia was a classic example of Washington turning to covert action when a problem seemed too difficult to solve in a different way. What do you do when you can't figure out what to do in Somalia? "Here's some money. Here's some weapons. Now go," he said.

"Absent a foreign policy, covert action isn't going to work," he said. "And if you can describe to me the U.S. government's foreign policy in Somalia in 2006, or even now, I will give you a ten-dollar bill."

The CIA's station chief in Nairobi took the brunt of the withering internal criticism. Jose Rodriguez pulled the officer from Kenya, and the CIA decided it had had enough with Somalia for the time being. With the Islamic courts now in power in Mogadishu, Bush officials began speaking about Somalia as a new terror state. Jendayi Frazer, the State Department's senior official for Africa policy, made public speeches during the last half of 2006 about direct connections between the ICU and al Qaeda and bluntly labeled the ICU "terrorists."

THE COLLAPSE of the CIA effort in Somalia had, for the moment, exhausted the Bush administration's options for dealing with the rise of the Islamists there. But where governments feared to tread, new opportunities were emerging for private military companies and would-be contractors eager to wade into the anarchy in East Africa.

The conditions were perfect: The United States government was unwilling to send many of its own into Somalia, but it was eager to spend money so others could. By the middle of 2006, Somalia was turning into the outsourced war.

Just a week after the CIA-backed warlords fled Mogadishu, a commercial jet carrying a middle-aged woman from the horse country of Northern Virginia landed in Nairobi. Michele Ballarin was the president of Select Armor, a small company with a contract to sell body armor to the Los Angeles Country Fire Department but one that had found no success winning any big Pentagon deals. But her ambitions were far grander than being a fourth-tier defense contractor. When she landed in Kenya in June 2006, she was scheduled to have a private meeting with Abdullahi Yusuf Ahmed, the man leading Somalia's UN-backed government-in-exile from his luxurious hotel suite in Nairobi.

It seemed a strange thing that a woman who had the appearance of a wealthy heiress would have an audience with the leader of Somalia's feckless Transitional Federal Government. But Ballarin had traveled to the Horn of Africa several times before and had developed something of a cult following in some sectors of the Somali political class. She claimed to train and breed Lipizzaner stallions—the famous white horses that performed dressage—and wore her wealth wherever she went. She traveled with Louis Vuitton bags, expensive jewelry, and Gucci clothing. If the idea was to dazzle the residents of one of the world's poorest countries, it had the intended effect. Somalis began referring to her by a one-word moniker, the Arabic word for "princess." They called her "Amira."

It was a long way from West Virginia, where she had first made a name for herself during the 1980s as a Republican candidate in a staunchly Democratic state. She had tried to piggyback on Ronald Reagan's popularity in the hopes of winning a congressional seat representing Morgantown, the location of West Virginia University. Just thirty-one at the time, she had funded much of her 1986 campaign with money from her first husband, a man several decades older than her who had landed on the Normandy beaches on D-Day and amassed a small fortune as a real-estate developer. But she also hustled to raise money on the campaign trail by showing off her skills as a concert pianist during political fund-raisers. Trying to paint the Democratic incumbent as out of step with the values of West Virginian families, she criticized her opponent during the final weeks of the campaign for his vote to spend taxpayer money to print *Playboy* in Braille. She even made hay of his refusal to show up to one debate by cutting up a piece of cardboard, pasting his face on it, and debating him anyway. She was roundly defeated in the election.

After the death of her first husband, she married Gino Ballarin, a former bartender at Manhattan's 21 Club who went on to own and manage the private Georgetown Club, in Washington. The couple threw parties at their home in Virginia, eventually earning themselves a listing in *The Green Book*, a directory of "socially prominent Washingtonians" that was a bible for the city's old-money elite. In 1997, she spoke to a reporter about how pleased she was to get into *The Green Book* with all her friends, neighbors, and other "supporters of equine sports."

"The book symbolizes old ways of doing things which have really rattled against change," she said. "It symbolizes a gentler way of going about living."

The Ballarins by then were living on an estate in Markham, Virginia, with the grand name Wolf's Crag. It was once the home of Turner Ashby, a Confederate cavalry commander who gained fame during Stonewall Jackson's Shenandoah Valley campaign and earned the nickname "The Black Knight of the Confederacy." But Michele Ballarin seemed to have bigger plans than living a genteel life of polo matches and lawn parties. During the 1990s and early 2000s she began a number of business ventures, from real-estate development to international finance to selling body armor.

As she describes it, it was a casual meeting with a group of Somali Americans set up by a friend of hers from the Freemason lodge in

Washington that sparked her interest in the war-racked country, and the transformation of Michele into Amira began. She started traveling to Africa, and soon the devoutly Christian woman who played the organ at her church each Sunday became entranced by the teachings of Sufism, a mystical branch of Islam once dominant on the Indian subcontinent and North Africa. Sufism had lost ground after the breakup of the Ottoman Empire had spawned more muscular forms of Islam, but it is still practiced widely in Somalia. Ballarin became convinced that promoting Sufi groups inside the country was the best way to diminish what she saw as a toxic influence of strict Wahhabism that had gained a foothold in the Horn of Africa with the help of rich Saudi donors, who sent money there to build radical schools and mosques.

Her public work in Somalia made her appear like just another rich do-gooder pushing airy-fairy development projects, but there was a darker, edgier side to her projects. When the Islamic Courts Union took control in Mogadishu, she saw an opportunity to take advantage of the vast ungoverned areas in Somalia to set up bases for a resistance movement to drive the Islamists out of power, as well as to nurture business ventures in the country. The horsewoman of Virginia would insert herself into the chaos.

At the meeting with President Abdullahi Yusuf Ahmed, Ballarin discussed her plan to set up a base in Somalia's northern port city of Berbera. The city was home to an abandoned airstrip that NASA had once designated as an emergency landing strip for the space shuttle, and Ballarin figured that the site could be turned into a hub for commercial traffic and a location to train anti–al Shabaab forces. President Ahmed, a political figurehead seeking refuge inside a plush hotel in Nairobi, was hardly in a position to sign off on Ballarin's plan. But when she emerged from the meeting, Ballarin was elated. Days later, she dashed off an e-mail to several of her business partners in the

United States, including Chris Farina, the head of a Florida-based private security firm called ATS Worldwide.

"Boys, successful meeting with President Abdullay Yussef [sic] and his chief of staff personnel," Ballarin wrote. "He has appointed his chief of presidential protocol as our go to during this phase." Later in the e-mail, Ballarin implied that the CIA was aware of her plans, and that she was planning to meet a CIA contact of hers in New York.

But Farina urged caution, writing back to warn that the plan shouldn't go off half-cocked. "A forced entry operation [into Mogadishu] at this point without the addition of follow-on forces who can capitalize on the momentum/initiative of the initial op will result in a replay of Dien Bien Phu," he wrote, referring to the French debacle in Indochina in 1954.

Farina also told Ballarin that perhaps the CIA wasn't the best partner for their efforts—perhaps wise advice, given what had just happened in the country. A better bet, he said, was the Pentagon.

She eventually took his advice, but it would be another two years before she managed to convince the Pentagon to fund her adventures inside Somalia.

THE ISLAMIC COURTS UNION'S takeover in Mogadishu at first brought a calm to the capital that it had not known for years. A city that warlords had divided up was now open. Children who had grown up within a mile of the sea but who had never actually seen the water, because it meant crossing into the zone of a rival warlord, were free to spend the day at the beach.

But a series of pronouncements that summer by the al Shabaab wing of the Islamic Courts Union, which had in effect seized control of the ICU movement, turned many Somalis against the new leaders. Foreign films were banned, as were soccer games. Women were forced

to veil their faces. Most unpopular of all was a ban on khat, the nar-
cotic green leaf that almost all Somali men chewed daily to bring on
a mild, pleasant haze.

The concerns in Washington about the imposition of sharia law in
Mogadishu were stoked by a stream of intelligence fed to the Bush
administration by Ethiopian officials, who feared that a new al Qaeda
safe haven might be emerging on their eastern border. Animosities
between Ethiopians and Somalis ran deep. During the 1970s the two
countries fought a territorial battle over the Ogaden region of Ethiopia that became a proxy conflict of the Cold War—with the United
States supporting Somalia and the Soviet Union giving military supplies to the Ethiopians. But the fall of the Soviet Union reshuffled the
alliances in Africa, as it did in so many other parts of the world. During the 1990s, with Washington worrying about the spread of Islamic
fundamentalism, Ethiopia and its Christian majority came to be seen
as natural allies for the United States.

So, during the summer of 2006, when Ethiopian officials began to
talk openly about the possibility of invading Somalia to dismantle the
Islamic Courts Union and al Shabaab, some in Washington saw an
opportunity. The strategy to arm a ragtag collection of warlords had
failed, but maybe the Ethiopian army could become America's new
proxy force in Somalia. Within weeks of the Islamist takeover in
Mogadishu, General John Abizaid, of U.S. Central Command, visited
Addis Ababa, Ethiopia's capital, during a tour of East Africa. During
meetings with military, CIA, and State Department officials at the
American embassy, he asked about what Ethiopia's military might
need if they were going to drive their tanks toward Mogadishu.

Abizaid made it clear that, while the United States would not push
Ethiopia to invade, it would try to ensure that an invasion was a success. He also met with Ethiopian officials and offered to share American intelligence about ICU military positions inside Somalia. Back in

Washington, Director of National Intelligence John D. Negroponte authorized spy satellites to be trained on Somalia to provide detailed pictures for the Ethiopian troops. "The idea," as one American official stationed in Addis Ababa, Ethiopia, in 2006 described it, "was to get the Ethiopians to fight our war."

The Ethiopian invasion would also provide cover for American commando missions into Somalia, launched from a base in the coffee-growing region of eastern Ethiopia. During the summer and fall of 2006, when it increasingly looked like Ethiopian troops might invade Somalia, Navy Seabees arrived at the base in Dire Dawa, three hundred miles east of Addis Ababa. Officially, the Seabees were there on a humanitarian mission: Treacherous rains had flooded the plains around Dire Dawa and sent a ten-foot wall of water crashing through the town, and the Seabees helped set up tents and give emergency medical care for the ten thousand people displaced by the floods.

But besides the humanitarian supplies, the C-130 transport planes arriving in Dire Dawa also began ferrying in war materiel for a group of Navy SEALs and Delta Force commandos who were trickling into Ethiopia as part of a secret JSOC unit called Task Force 88. Their plan was to use Ethiopia's invasion of Somalia as a cover to get into the country and hunt down senior ICU operatives.

The mission to Somalia had been authorized under Donald Rumsfeld's 2004 order permitting military commandos to infiltrate countries that had traditionally been off-limits to American soldiers. In early January 2007, just days after the first Ethiopian tank columns rumbled over the border and artillery batteries started pounding Islamic Courts Union military installations in southwest Somalia, Task Force 88 began its missions inside the country. Attached to the group were surveillance experts from Gray Fox, the Pentagon's clandestine spying unit that would eventually change its code name to Task Force Orange. The group carried specialized equipment allowing it to pinpoint the locations of ICU commanders by intercepting their telephone communications.

In addition to the special-operations troops, two AC-130 gunships armed with 105-millimeter cannons and Gatling guns arrived at the airstrip in eastern Ethiopia, and in early January the gunships launched an attack on a small fishing village in the swamplands of southern Somalia. They were acting on intelligence that Aden Hashi Farah Ayro, the young al Shabaab leader, was hiding in the village of Ras Kamboni. Hours after a barrage of missiles, American and Ethiopian troops sifted through the wreckage and found a passport of Ayro's stained with blood. The Americans assumed that Ayro would not have lasted long if he had been wounded in the strike, but nobody was sure where he had gone. The AC-130 gunships carried out a second strike two weeks later against a different Islamist commander, but the attack killed civilians instead of its intended target.

The clandestine missions in Somalia in early 2007 had mixed results. American troops and intelligence aided the Ethiopian offensive through southern Somalia and led to a swift retreat by Islamic Courts Union troops. But the JSOC missions had failed to capture or kill any of the most senior Islamist commanders or members of the al Qaeda cell responsible for the 1998 embassy bombings. And, beyond the narrow manhunt, the larger Ethiopian occupation of Somalia could fairly be called a disaster.

The Bush administration had secretly backed the operation, believing that Ethiopian troops could drive the Islamist Courts Union out of Mogadishu and provide military protection for the UN-backed transitional government. The invasion had achieved that first objective, but the impoverished Ethiopian government had little interest in spending money to keep its troops in Somalia to protect the corrupt transitional government. Within weeks of the end of fighting, senior

Ethiopian officials declared that they had met their military objectives and began talking publicly about a withdrawal.

The Ethiopian army had waged a bloody and indiscriminate campaign against its most hated enemy. Using lead-footed urban tactics, Ethiopian troops lobbed artillery shells into crowded marketplaces and dense neighborhoods, killing thousands of civilians. Discipline in the Ethiopian ranks broke down, and soldiers went on rampages of looting and gang rape. One young man interviewed by the nonprofit group Human Rights Watch spoke of witnessing Ethiopians kill his father and then rape his mother and sisters.

The occupation by the hated Ethiopian troops turned into a recruiting bonanza for al Shabaab, and the group grew in strength. Insurgents planted roadside bombs and used other guerrilla tactics that militants in Iraq and Afghanistan had used with great success. Foreign fighters flooded into Somalia. Jihadi internet sites invoked the name Abu-Raghal, an infamous traitor in the Muslim faith who had helped the Ethiopian army march on Mecca. The fighters came from Morocco and from Algeria.

And they came from Minnesota. Not long after the Ethiopian invasion, twenty American students from the Little Mogadishu neighborhood of Minneapolis boarded planes and went to Somalia to wage jihad against the Christian invaders. Among them was Shirwa Ahmed, a community-college dropout who loved basketball and spent most of his days doing odd jobs and memorizing the lyrics to rap songs. He had become so enraged by the arrival of the Ethiopians in Somalia that he made his way to the Horn of Africa, where he joined al Shabaab.

In October of the following year, he drove a car packed with explosives into a government building in Puntland, a region of northern Somalia.

He was the first-ever American suicide bomber.

9: THE BASE

"In a wilderness of mirrors. What will the spider do,
Suspend its operations, will the weevil
Delay?"

—*T. S. Eliot, "Gerontion"*

It didn't take long for Art Keller to learn what had become the first
rule for CIA officers serving in Pakistan: Each day you spend in the
country, you know less than you did the day before. By the time your
tour of duty is up, you know nothing.

By the middle of 2006, when Keller's helicopter touched down at
the CIA base near Wana, in the tribal agency of South Waziristan,
intelligence operations in Pakistan had become the twenty-first-
century version of James Jesus Angleton's "wilderness of mirrors."
Angleton, the legendary and ruthless former chief of counterintelligence at the CIA, had paraphrased his beloved T. S. Eliot to describe
the deceptions, double crosses, and divided loyalties of Cold War espionage. Decades later, the spy games in Pakistan were no less mad-
dening to play.

The boyish-looking Keller was an unlikely candidate to be dropped
into the middle of the Pakistani mountains at a time when al Qaeda
was turning the area into its new base of operations. He had never
stepped foot in Pakistan before, spoke none of the local languages,

and his expertise—in Iran's missile program—wasn't about to do him much good in Wana. But with the Iraq war taking CIA case officers with any Middle Eastern experience away from Afghanistan and Pakistan, the clandestine service was desperate for bodies. So Art Keller volunteered for Afghanistan. He was assigned to Pakistan.

"The ideal person you want sitting in the base there was someone who could speak Dari or Urdu or Pashto, with years of experience, and knows the target," he said.

"Instead, you get me."

Keller had joined the CIA in 1999 after a decade of meanderings through the military, college, and journalism. He had graduated high school with an interest in international affairs but without a clear idea about what he wanted to do in life, and joined the Army in the early 1990s because he was fairly certain it would be a risk-free way to earn money for college. "Eighteen months later," he said, "I'm sitting in the middle of the desert wondering, 'How did I end up here?'"

He played only a bit part in Operation Desert Storm, which swiftly expelled Iraqi troops from Kuwait. He had been assigned to a parachute-rigging company, but with no airborne operations during the war there was no need for the group's work. On the eve of the fighting, his unit was driven into the middle of the Saudi desert and told to guard a logistics base used to supply the American tank invasion into Iraq.

After leaving the Army, he attended the University of Northern Arizona and decided he should either become a reporter or join the CIA. He took a job in the sports department of *The Arizona Republic*, and just as he was about to be transferred to the political desk, the CIA contacted him and told him that his application had been accepted.

He drew an assignment in the agency's Counterproliferation division, working to halt the spread of mass casualty weapons, and his first overseas posting was to Vienna, where the headquarters of the International Atomic Energy Agency was located. Officers at the CIA's Vienna Station were expected to develop sources inside the IAEA to learn about its secret deliberations. But after the September 11 attacks, the CIA was also feeding the IAEA some of its most sensitive intelligence in order to get the international body to sanction regimes like those of Iran, Iraq, and North Korea.

Keller had developed an intimate understanding of Tehran's efforts to develop ballistic missiles, but at that time Iran was not at the top of the CIA's list of worries. In late summer 2002, Keller's boss in Vienna returned from a trip to Langley and approached a group of officers inside the agency's station.

"You know how there's been rumors about maybe there being an invasion and a war with Iraq?" Keller remembered him asking. "You're gonna hear some funny things coming out of headquarters because they're under incredible pressure to find evidence to justify this," he said.

"You know that scene in *Das Boot* when they're at the bottom of the ocean and the rivets are popping out of the submarine and shooting around inside?" Keller's boss asked. "That's what's going on at headquarters right now."

Keller would do two brief stints in Iraq after the ill-fated invasion, one of them as part of the Iraq Survey Group, the CIA-led team of weapons-hunters who spent 2003 and 2004 patrolling desert sites for Saddam Hussein's phantom chemical- and biological-weapons programs. Early on, Keller could tell that the effort was pointless: Iraqi scientists who had every reason to show the Americans the weapons stockpiles—and be rewarded by the CIA with cash and possibly resettlement—insisted to the survey group that the weapons didn't exist. But Keller and other officers would interview the same scientists two or three times, allowing Langley to pad the numbers about how many interviews the survey conducted. This also allowed President Bush and Vice President Cheney to say publicly that the weapons hunt in Iraq was still going on.

The dusty CIA base in South Waziristan where Keller arrived in 2006 was in the same town that Pakistani troops had hit with artillery and gunships during their battle with Nek Muhammad's fighters in 2004, and near the madrassa in Shakai where government troops had agreed to a cease-fire with the Waziri tribesmen. When Keller got there, another fragile peace deal was in place. This one had been negotiated by Pakistani troops and Baitullah Mehsud, another young guerrilla leader who had picked up the bloody banner when Nek Muhammad was killed in the 2004 CIA drone strike. Mehsud had never honored the terms of the agreement and had merely used the cease-fire to consolidate power in South Waziristan and plan hit-and-run attacks on Pakistani troops. But Pakistan's military leadership in 2006 did not want another battle in the tribal areas, so when Art Keller arrived in Wana there was little appetite among Pakistani soldiers and spies to kick a hornet's nest.

As a result, relations between CIA officers and the local ISI operatives in South Waziristan were dismal. When he landed at Wana, Keller learned just how bad they were when he was briefed by the man he would be replacing, a salty older officer named Gene. Gene told Keller that Pakistani troops were doing few patrols and spending nearly all of their days inside protected barracks. No matter how hard he pushed, Gene said, the Pakistani military and spies did not want to challenge the power of the ministate that Baitullah Mehsud was building in South Waziristan.

Mehsud, unlike Nek Muhammad, was no media hound. He gave few interviews and, following traditions of strict Islam, refused to be photographed. He had barely any education, not even significant time at a madrassa, but in 2006 he commanded a fiercely loyal band of some five thousand tribal gunmen. He brooked no dissent and had deserters hunted down and killed. There were even suspicions he had arranged for Pakistani troops to help capture his former mentor, Abdullah Mehsud, a one-legged fighter whom the United States had released from Guantánamo Bay in 2004, so Baitullah could take power in South Waziristan. When Pakistani troops surrounded Abdullah's home in Balochistan, he held a grenade up to his chest and pulled the pin.

Baitullah Mehsud's power and influence would expand dramatically when a collection of smaller military groups joined together under the name of Tehrik-i-Taliban Pakistan (TTP), known commonly as the Pakistani Taliban, with Mehsud as the group's leader. Unlike the Afghan Taliban, under the control of Mullah Omar and enjoying the quiet patronage of the ISI, the new group intended to drive the Pakistani soldiers and spies out of the tribal areas using suicide bombings in Islamabad, Karachi, and other cities as bloody calling cards. They called it "defensive jihad," a struggle to protect the tribal way of life from Pakistani military forces, whom they viewed as foreigners in their lands.

The group had few contacts or supporters beyond the tribal regions, but in Wana in 2006 it was clear who was in charge. Baitullah Mehsud's followers had been administering rough justice throughout South Waziristan, roaming around assassinating any tribal chiefs suspected of working with the Americans or the Pakistani government. Thieves were hanged in the village streets, adulterers were stoned, and vendors in the Wana bazaar openly sold gruesome DVDs in Urdu depicting the beheading of Pakistani army scouts. The snuff films were part propaganda and part intimidation, a blunt message that the military should stay in their barracks and cede control to the tribes. Baitullah Mehsud forced barbers in Wana to post signs in their shops saying that since facial grooming is forbidden under sharia law, beard trimming services were not available. Barbers who refused watched their shops burn down. Other evidence of militant control was more prosaic: Keller's base received supplies of fuel just once every two weeks, on the specific days the militants allowed the Pakistani army trucks to use the roads.

The CIA outpost was a brick compound inside a larger Pakistani military base near Wana. A small detachment of Pakistani special-operations troops guarded the American buildings, but Keller soon figured out that the troops were more jailers than protectors, because the CIA officers were never allowed off base. Inside the compound was a small cluster of rooms where the Americans ate, slept, and communicated with their bosses using secure radios and computers to keep the ISI from intercepting their transmissions. The small base reeked of raw sewage from plumbing leaks, and a barrage of plaster chips from the ceiling would often cover the beds, dishes, and communications equipment. Gene had once tried to persuade the CIA station in Islamabad to put up money for a squash court at the base. Given the popularity of squash within the ranks of Pakistan's military, he argued, the court might help the CIA officers built a rapport with their counterparts. The request was denied.

Keller's own relations with his main ISI counterpart were sour from the beginning, in no small part because of a prank that Gene played before he left South Waziristan. On the day of his helicopter flight out of Wana, Gene handed Keller a note scribbled in Urdu and told him to give it to the ISI officer during their first meeting. Keller had no idea what the message said, but he dutifully passed it along during the meeting. The ISI man, a member of the Khattak tribe, was not particularly amused. He translated the note for Keller.

"You can never trust a fucking Khattak," the note read.

"Gene thought that was hilarious," said Keller. "Thanks a lot, Gene."

GIVEN THE ACCUMULATING MISTRUST between the Americans and Pakistanis in Wana, most of the intelligence gathering that Keller oversaw during his time in South Waziristan occurred without the ISI's approval. Gene had passed along the names and contact information of the Pakistani agents that the CIA had cultivated in the region—a network that was now in Keller's hands to run. But for a white American spy in Wana, running a network of Pakistani agents without tipping off the ISI was not easy. The agents couldn't come on the CIA base or they would be spotted and arrested by the ISI, and any attempt by Keller to meet them off the base would also put them at risk.

By contrast, CIA officers working from the other side of the border in Afghanistan had a much easier time. By 2006, the agency had set up a string of small bases in eastern Afghanistan, in towns like Khost and Asadabad, from which agents were sent over the border into Pakistan to collect information in the tribal areas. The Americans could meet the agents at the base or in neighboring towns. The CIA started sending "targeting analysts" from Langley to the firebases in Afghanistan, charged with sifting through human source information gathered in the hinterlands and fusing it with intelligence gleaned from satellites or listening posts to try to pin down the locations of militants in Bajaur and Waziristan. Three years later, a meeting with a man the CIA believed was a high-level agent but in fact was working for the militants went horribly wrong at one of the bases, Camp Chapman, in Khost. Seven CIA employees were killed when the agent, a Jordanian doctor, detonated a suicide vest. It was the agency's deadliest day since the attack on the United States embassy in Beirut in 1983.

Without the option of meetings, Keller kept in touch with his primary agent entirely through computer communications, and he maintained an elaborate network of go-betweens, without any face-to-face contact with his sources during his months in South Waziristan. He compared the experience to that of Western reporters in Baghdad during the darkest days of the Iraq war: Unable to move freely through the streets, they relied on Iraqi stringers to gather information and quotes.

In his case, Keller would send off a message to CIA computer engineers, who would encrypt it and then send it to a Pakistani agent working for the CIA who had been given specialized communication equipment to receive his transmissions. The Pakistani man was paid several hundred dollars per month, but some of that money went to hiring other agents (or "subagents") to collect information about the movements of al Qaeda operatives in South Waziristan. The subagents knew nothing about whom they were working for, and possibly thought that their money came from the ISI. Sometimes Keller would be three or four layers removed from a subagent closest to the target of surveillance.

During Keller's time in South Waziristan, the CIA's primary target was an Egyptian chemist with the nom de guerre Abu Khabab al-Masri. A member of bin Laden's inner circle, al-Masri once ran al Qaeda's Derunta training camp, in Afghanistan, where the group had experimented with chemical weapons and other poisons. He was thought to be hiding in South Waziristan, and the United States had put a $5 million bounty on his head. But the CIA knew almost nothing about what he looked like; in early 2006 American officials admitted they had mistakenly been using the wrong photograph on a wanted poster for al-Masri. The picture on the poster was replaced with a black silhouette.

With so little to go on, the CIA officers in South Waziristan often had to lean heavily on unsubstantiated information from sources that had not been vetted. One of the tips Keller received was that al-Masri would occasionally visit a particular shop in the Wana bazaar. Keller asked his Pakistani agent to hire a subagent who lived in the vicinity and would have reason to visit the shop. An operation was set up to stake out the shop, determine if al-Masri was indeed a regular, and to take a picture of him. Then the plan was to install surveillance equipment to determine whom al-Masri might be trying to contact.

Keller never learned if the operation ultimately bore fruit, or if it was just one part of a wider operation to net al-Masri. Officers at individual bases were usually kept in the dark about operations in towns even as close as a dozen miles away, where there were other CIA bases, and he didn't have access to classified cable traffic in the rest of the country. Keller's was a worm's-eye view, and he dutifully sent his intelligence reports forward for the analysts at Islamabad to use as one piece of a mosaic.

It was a setup ripe for circular reporting. Once, a sub-source of Keller's passed along a tip that Osama bin Laden had been spotted in the Dir Valley, in the North-West Frontier Province. Keller tapped out a cable to Islamabad, suggesting that the CIA send an agent to Dir to investigate the tip.

When he received the cable, the Islamabad station chief was irate; bin Laden tips were like Elvis sightings, igniting interest all the way back to Langley. CIA officers in Pakistan were pushed to investigate even the murkiest rumor about bin Laden, and the Dir Valley tip had been checked out—and debunked—months earlier. Islamabad Station was now required to explain to excited CIA leaders why Keller's cable should be ignored. The CIA station chief flew out to Wana personally to chew Keller out, figuring it was worth the bumpy helicopter ride.

"This was a rumor that they had worked long and hard to drive a stake through," Keller recalled. "And, like a vampire, I had resurrected it."

UNBEKNOWNST TO KELLER, he was just one part of a large campaign by the CIA in 2006 to refocus the hunt for Osama bin Laden by dramatically expanding the number of case officers in Pakistan and Afghanistan. It was painfully evident to senior officers at Langley that the Iraq war had taken attention away from the al Qaeda manhunt, but the bin Laden hunt had also been beset by problems within the CIA. Clandestine officers posted in Islamabad had been clashing with officers from the Counterterrorism Center at Langley, whose preference for Predator strikes was derided by officers at Islamabad Station as the work of "boys with toys."**** The CIA station chief in Islamabad thought the drone strikes in 2005 and 2006—which, while infrequent at that time, were often based on bad intelligence and had resulted in many civilian casualties—had done little except fuel hatred for the United States inside Pakistan and put Pakistani officials in the uncomfortable position of having to lie about the strikes.

There had also been dysfunction back at headquarters. The battles between members of the Directorate of Operations—which oversaw the spies in the field—and Porter Goss's aides spilled into the public through media leaks, and the Directorate of Operations was also in turf fights with other branches of the agency. In late 2005, Porter Goss called a management retreat for all the agency's senior leaders, a move designed to soothe tensions among his leadership team. During the meeting, the CIA's deputy director for intelligence—the head of the analysts in charge of piecing together reports from the field—

**** The CIA's Counterterrorist Center was renamed the Counterterrorism Center in 2005.

complained openly about the arrogance of the clandestine officers, who he said could get away with whatever they wanted. Jose Rodriguez, the head of operations, exploded. "Wake up and smell the fucking coffee!" Rodriguez shouted, reminding everyone in the room that unlike the analysts, who saw the world from their desks, his undercover officers worked at "the pointy end of the spear."

Rodriguez's volatility occasionally created problems within the clandestine branch itself, and by early 2006 he was barely speaking with the man he had installed as chief of the Counterterrorism Center, Robert Grenier. Grenier, a former station chief in Islamabad, was polished and cerebral—in many ways the antithesis of Rodriguez. He had pushed to expand the CIA's counterterrorism aperture beyond Afghanistan and Pakistan, ordering more officers to focus on emerging threats in places like Southeast Asia and North Africa. Given the Counterterrorism Center's expansion since 2001, Grenier thought it needed to be restructured to eliminate redundancies. The CIA's bin Laden–hunting unit, formed in the 1990s and code-named Alec Station, was reorganized and renamed.

Rodriguez thought all of this was a distraction from the bin Laden hunt. He replaced Grenier with another officer from inside the CTC, a gaunt, chain-smoking workaholic named Mike.***** Mike had spent his early career as an undercover officer in Africa and had converted to Islam. His wardrobe tended toward shades of black and gray, as did his general demeanor. Some called him the "Prince of Darkness," and he would eventually preside over the CIA's most expansive killing operation since the Vietnam War.

When Mike took over the job, in 2006, his immediate mission was to carry out a plan to bolster the CIA's ranks in Afghanistan and Pakistan, eliminate the squabbling between the stations in Kabul and

---

***** Because Mike remains an undercover officer, only his first name is used here.

Islamabad, and reorganize the staff at CIA headquarters. Outside the main cafeteria at Langley, just past the Starbucks, giant structures resembling Quonset huts were built to house the growing staff devoted to the bin Laden hunt. As part of this new plan, dubbed Operation Cannonball, dozens of intelligence analysts were sent to Kabul and Islamabad to work in tandem with the case officers chasing slivers of leads on the whereabouts of al Qaeda leaders.

Most important, however, the CIA sent more undercover officers into the field—one of them Art Keller—to try to develop sources independent of the Pakistanis. With the United States fighting a public war in Afghanistan, it was easy enough to get more CIA officers into Kabul. The bigger problem was Pakistan, where the ISI closely monitored the number of visa applications for American officials hoping to enter the country and kept a close watch on the CIA officers sent to man the Islamabad station. Langley needed to come up with more exotic ways to mask the identities of the spies it wanted to get into Pakistan.

One opportunity came on the morning of October 8, 2005, when a massive earthquake in the mountains of Kashmir leveled the city of Muzaffarabad and caused landslides throughout northern Pakistan. Initial Pakistani government estimates put the death toll at nearly ninety thousand people, nineteen thousand of them children who died when schoolhouses collapsed on top of them. Billions of dollars of international aid poured into Pakistani Kashmir, and almost immediately a stream of American military helicopters crossed the border from Afghanistan to deliver humanitarian aid. The Chinook helicopters became a regular sight in Kashmir, and Pakistanis began referring to them in the local dialect as "angels of mercy."

But the Americans were not just on a mercy mission. In the months after the earthquake, the CIA used the relief effort in Kashmir to slip covert officers into the country without the ISI's knowledge. The American spies adopted covers of various civilian professions. ISI officials suspected that the aid mission might be a Trojan horse to get more CIA officers into Pakistan, but amid the devastation in Kashmir and the urgent need to maintain the stream of humanitarian relief, Pakistani military and intelligence officers were not in a position to challenge the credentials of all the Americans arriving in Pakistan.

It would be several years before the CIA would begin to reap the benefits of its enlarged presence inside Pakistan, which in any event was still relatively modest. One former top official at Langley estimates that the total number of undercover officers inside Pakistan grew by only about 10 to 20 percent during Operation Cannonball. CIA officials at that time worried that flooding the country with too many spies would encourage more surveillance by the ISI.

But the CIA had trouble masking a weakness. There were a finite number of seasoned officers to send to Afghanistan and Pakistan, and managers at Langley became so desperate for bodies that they took some newly minted case officers—recent graduates from "The Farm" at Camp Peary—and sent them to the field. "We had to put people out in the field who had less-than-ideal levels of experience," recalled one of those in charge of the operation, "but there wasn't much to choose from."

One aspect of the retooled hunt for Osama bin Laden was to try to penetrate the network of couriers that bin Laden used to transmit messages to his followers. The CIA had been gathering snippets of information about bin Laden's favored couriers, which had enabled the CIA to begin tracking al Qaeda operatives in Pakistan to develop a richer picture about the internal workings of the terror group's second and third tiers. When General Michael Hayden took over the CIA from Porter Goss, in the spring of 2006, the agency "had developed far more penetrations, far more knowledge of al Qaeda in 2006 than we ever had in 2001 or 2002," Hayden said. "We actually began to develop good sources of information."

It was shortly after a visit by Hayden to Pakistan in August 2006 that the CIA and ISI set up a joint operation to arrest Rashid Rauf, the kingpin of a terror plot to blow up a handful of jets crossing the Atlantic from London, using a lethal mixture of powdered chemicals and the breakfast drink Tang. Rauf had orchestrated the plot from the tribal regions, communicating with teams inside the United Kingdom who would carry out the mission. The plot had been in the works for years, and the plotters had become sloppy. Britain's MI5 had managed to set up surveillance nets to monitor the groups, and British spies used wiretaps to listen patiently as the plot unfolded.

When the ISI picked up information that the planners were about to carry out the attack, Pakistan's spymaster, General Ashfaq Parvez Kayani, told Jose Rodriguez that they were prepared to pick up Rauf as he rode in a bus from the tribal areas to the city of Bahawalpur, in Punjab. Rodriguez, who was visiting Islamabad at the time, ordered CIA officers to set up a surveillance post near Bahawalpur, where they could listen to Rauf's cell-phone communications and feed information to Pakistani troops, who made an uneventful arrest.

MI5 was furious, knowing that Rauf's arrest would alarm the plotters in Britain. British spies neither trusted nor relied on the ISI, an animosity that had seeds in the days of British rule in India before the partition with Pakistan, and the British suspected there was some ulterior motive in General Kayani's move to arrest Rauf. British police scrambled to roll up the twenty-five plotters before they scattered and wondered about the costs of having to make the arrests before they could gather more evidence to indict the suspects.

Still, foiling the August 2006 plot was a significant success, even though it got the CIA no closer to finding bin Laden. Going after the courier network was what Hayden described as a "bank shot" for finding bin Laden and often felt like chasing shadows—a mission bedeviled by misinformation and insufficient manpower.

For instance, in the years before Pakistani agents for the CIA tracked Abu Ahmed al-Kuwaiti to a sprawling compound in the leafy town of Abbottabad, where bin Laden turned out to be hiding, CIA interrogators had been led to believe that al-Kuwaiti was of marginal value. Khalid Sheikh Mohammed, the chief planner of the September 11 attacks, had told his interrogators that al-Kuwaiti had retired. But there was also a good deal of suspicion about what Khalid Sheikh Mohammed said, because he was one of the CIA detainees who had been subjected to the most extreme interrogation techniques, including waterboarding. When he was telling the truth and when he was merely telling interrogators what they wanted to hear was a matter of fierce debate inside the American government. One year later, a different detainee assured his interrogators that al-Kuwaiti was indeed bin Laden's main courier, information that the CIA was eventually able to corroborate elsewhere.

EVEN WITH THE INCREASE in the CIA's ranks in Pakistan, the agency hardly had the resources in the country to chase every lead, and ISI restrictions on surveillance used by the Americans made things even more difficult. During his time in South Waziristan, Art Keller began building a dossier on a suspected al Qaeda facilitator, nicknamed Haji Omar, who owned four compounds in the area that al Qaeda militants were said to frequent. Keller sent a cable to his bosses in Islamabad requesting aerial surveillance to monitor the comings and goings at Haji Omar's compounds. He didn't have nearly enough human sources to keep close watch on the compound, and human surveillance was always riskier.

The gist of the cable was, according to Keller, "This guy is involved in al Qaeda logistics, is definitely a courier, and maybe this is our guy. How else are we going to find out until we start watching him?" But with the South Waziristan peace deal in place, the ISI refused to allow Predator flights.

The dynamics in South Waziristan were giving Keller a glimpse of the byzantine apparatus of the ISI, where wheels turning clockwise have no contact with wheels going in the other direction. Operatives inside the ISI's Directorate C, the division of the spy agency responsible for counterterrorism operations, often helped CIA officers hunt al Qaeda operatives. Asad Munir, the ISI's former station chief in Peshawar, had been an officer from Directorate C. But these officers were sometimes at odds with the Pakistani spies of Directorate S, which had long been responsible for nurturing groups like the Taliban, the Haqqani Network, and Lashkar-e-Taiba, which Pakistan has seen as critical proxies for its defense against India. It was Directorate S that helped arm the mujahedeen during the Soviet war in Afghanistan, helped navigate the Taliban's rise to power during the 1990s, and in the years since 2001 has worked to see that various militant groups keep the focus of their violence inside Afghanistan, rather than turning their fury against Pakistan.

Almost nothing is written publicly about Directorate S, and even though the CIA worked with Directorate S operatives during the Soviet war, American spies have only an impressionistic portrait of its operations. Some inside the CIA have spent years obsessively gathering nuggets of information about Directorate S, and what American analysts generally agree on is that, since 2001, Directorate S has been at the vanguard of the ISI's quiet strategy to maintain ties with militant groups that could serve Pakistan's interests in the future.

Whether Directorate S routinely ordered lethal attacks against

American and NATO troops in Afghanistan is still a matter of some debate, but the American electronic-surveillance net over Pakistan—and, more specifically, ISI headquarters—frequently intercepted phone calls between Pakistani spies and Haqqani Network operatives. Pakistani officials usually either deny the evidence or say it is the work of rogue elements in the spy service, but in private have made a case that the spy agency needed to work with groups like the Haqqani Network to protect Pakistan's western flank. American spy agencies even intercepted one telephone call in 2008 during which General Kayani referred to the Haqqani Network as a "strategic asset." While "so many people inside the CIA say, 'The ISI is dirty,' and others say, 'The ISI can help us,'" said Keller. "It's actually both at the same time, and that's the problem."

Compared with South Waziristan, the dynamic between American and Pakistani spies during the summer of 2006 was only marginally different in North Waziristan, where the government had not yet signed a peace deal with militants. The CIA and ISI worked more closely together, and shared a base in an abandoned schoolhouse in Miranshah, less than a mile from the Haqqani Network's primary madrassa in the town. From there, American and Pakistani spies gathered intelligence to find another senior al Qaeda figure, Khalid Habib.

As the hunt for Habib gained momentum, the CIA reassigned Keller to North Waziristan. Even with the move, he remained in charge of the operations in South Waziristan and continued to run his sources via computer messages. He had been doing the same thing while stuck inside the base at Wana, so it mattered little if he was, in effect, telecommuting. Keller and other CIA officers directed Predators to monitor truck convoys and mud compounds outside of Miranshah in the hope of getting enough information to call in a strike on

Khalid Habib. The ISI collected its own intelligence from human sources, which was combined with the information from the Predators and electronic eavesdropping.

But the cooperation had its limits. When Keller arrived at Miranshah, he was given a piece of advice from the base chief.

"Don't tell anything to Pakistani army intelligence you don't want to get back to the Taliban," he said.

Pakistani army intelligence, a unit distinct from the ISI, was thought to have even deeper ties to the Taliban and the Haqqani Network than the ISI's Directorate S. Weeks before Keller had arrived in Miranshah, the ISI and CIA had raided the Haqqani madrassa but had come up with nothing. CIA officers later learned from sources that Pakistani spies had warned Haqqani militants that the raid was about to take place.

Though frustrated, Keller understood perfectly why Pakistan was so wary of dismantling the Haqqani Network. The United States was not going to be in Afghanistan forever, and turning the Haqqanis into enemies might lead to two possible outcomes for Islamabad, both horrible. The best case would be that Pakistani troops would find themselves bogged down in an endless war in the mountains against a group that could be a far more useful ally in the effort to blunt Indian influence in Afghanistan. The worst case was that the war could spread east, with the Haqqanis carrying out violence in Pakistan's settled territories.

Scared of either prospect, Pakistani military officers in mid-2006 quietly began discussing a peace deal in North Waziristan, similar to the one already in place in South Waziristan. Keller and his CIA colleagues warned their ISI counterparts that the deal could have disastrous consequences. Their views, though, had little impact. Pakistan's government brokered a cease-fire agreement in North Waziristan in September 2006. And it came about because of the secret negotiations of a familiar figure to many in Washington, Lt. General Ali Jan Aurakzai, the man President Musharraf had appointed as military commander in the tribal areas after the September 11 attacks and who had long believed that the hunt for al Qaeda in Pakistan and Afghanistan was a fool's errand.

Aurakzai had since retired from the military, and Musharraf had appointed him as the governor of the North-West Frontier Province, which gave him oversight over the tribal areas. Aurakzai believed that appeasing militant groups in the tribal areas was the only way to halt the spread of militancy into the settled areas of Pakistan. And he used his influence with Musharraf to convince the president on the merits of a peace deal in North Waziristan.

But Washington still needed to be convinced. President Musharraf decided to bring Aurakzai on a trip to sell the Bush White House on the cease-fire. Both men sat in the Oval Office and made a case to President Bush about the benefits of a peace deal, and Aurakzai told Bush that the North Waziristan peace agreement should even be replicated in parts of Afghanistan and would allow American troops to withdraw from the country sooner than expected.

Bush administration officials were divided. Some considered Aurakzai a spineless appeaser—the Neville Chamberlain of the tribal areas. But few saw any hope of trying to stop the North Waziristan peace deal. And Bush, whose style of diplomacy was intensely personal, worried even in 2006 about putting too many demands on President Musharraf. Bush still admired Musharraf for his decision in the early days after the September 11 attacks to assist the United States in the hunt for al Qaeda. Even after White House officials set up regular phone calls between Bush and Musharraf designed to apply pressure on the Pakistani leader to keep up military operations in the tribal areas, they usually were disappointed by the outcome: Bush rarely made specific demands on Musharraf during the calls. He would thank Musharraf for his contributions to the war on terrorism and pledge that American financial support to Pakistan would continue.

The prevailing view among the president's top advisers in late 2006 was that too much American pressure on Musharraf could bring about a nightmarish scenario: a popular uprising against the Pakistan government that could usher in a radical Islamist government. The frustration of doing business with Musharraf was matched only by the fear of life without him. It was a fear that Musharraf himself stoked, warning American officials frequently about his tenuous grip on power and citing his narrow escape from several assassination attempts. The assassination attempts were quite real, but Musharraf's strategy was also quite effective in maintaining a steady flow of American aid and keeping at bay demands from Washington for democratic reforms.

The North Waziristan peace deal turned out to be a disaster both for Bush and Musharraf. Miranshah was, in effect, taken over by the Haqqani Network as the group consolidated its criminal empire along the eastern edge of the Afghanistan border. As part of the agreement, the Haqqanis and other militant groups pledged to cease attacks in Afghanistan, but in the months after the deal was signed cross-border incursions from the tribal areas into Afghanistan aimed at Western troops rose by 300 percent. During a press conference in the fall of 2006, President Bush declared that al Qaeda was "on the run." In fact, the opposite was the case. The group had a safe home, and there was no reason to run anywhere.

ART KELLER LEFT PAKISTAN just before the North Waziristan deal took effect, his five-month tour of duty having ended. Before he left, he took care of one last piece of unfinished business: buying a gift for his best Pakistani agent in South Waziristan, a man he had never met. The man was an avid sportsman, and he wrote to Keller that surely the CIA could find a way to buy some American sports equipment for one of its few human sources in the tribal areas. After a flurry of cables between Wana, Islamabad, and Langley about the propriety of the request, the CIA finally relented and put the sports equipment on a flight to Pakistan, stored in the cargo hull with other sensitive material bound for the American embassy in Islamabad.

Two years later, after President Bush signed a secret order to escalate the CIA's covert war in Pakistan, Abu Khabab al-Masri was killed in a CIA drone strike, just twelve miles from the CIA base in Wana. Three months later, a missile fired from a CIA drone killed Khalid Habib as he sat in a parked Toyota station wagon in the village of Taparghai in South Waziristan. When the strikes occurred, Art Keller was back in the United States, retired from the CIA and living in Albuquerque. When he heard the news he had no idea whether any of the work he did in Pakistan in 2006—from spying at the Wana bazaar to sifting through bits of information at a schoolhouse in Miranshah—was at all helpful in bringing about the deaths of the two men.

Likely, he would never know.

10: GAMES WITHOUT FRONTIERS

"A Mighty Wurlitzer"

—*Frank Wisner*

For all the public's fascination with the coups, assassination attempts, and gunrunning that the CIA carried out during the first four decades of its existence, a far larger fraction of the spy agency's budget for covert-action programs during the Cold War was devoted to subtler tools of warfare. Black propaganda and psychological operations had once been a cornerstone of CIA covert action: from spreading money around Europe after World War II to sway elections to setting up CIA-funded radio stations in the Eastern Bloc and Southeast Asia. Frank Wisner, an OSS veteran who rose to become head of CIA clandestine operations, said that propaganda missions needed to be run by a deft, mature organization that could conduct several different influence campaigns at once—what he called a "mighty Wurlitzer" playing the martial music in a war of ideas. When the Cold War ended, the CIA no longer saw a need to invest heavily in black propaganda, or to train its officers in psychological warfare, and the programs became victims of the drastic budget cuts of the 1990s.

But it wasn't just about money. The advent of the Internet and the globalization of information had made all propaganda campaigns legally dicey for the CIA. United States law prohibits the spy agency from carrying out propaganda operations against American media outlets and from running influence campaigns against American citizens. Before the Internet the CIA could put foreign journalists on its payroll and plant phony stories in newspapers without worrying about the potential for these operations infiltrating the American media. But by the midnineties, Web surfers in New York and Atlanta could read news Web sites from Pakistan and Dubai. American news outlets began paying greater attention to foreign news, and citing the foreign press in their reports. As a result, it became harder for the CIA to convince congressional overseers, who have final approval for all covert actions by the agency, that a planned propaganda campaign wouldn't "blow back" to the United States.

But when the CIA let its propaganda efforts atrophy, the Pentagon sought to fill the void. The military faces similar restrictions against conducting propaganda operations on American citizens, but Congress has generally given the Defense Department wide latitude to carry out psychological-operations missions as long as they can be shown—however tangentially—to be supporting American troops in combat. The Pentagon's leash grew even longer after the September 11 attacks, when Congress in effect defined the world as a battlefield, and military leaders were confronted with the disorienting reality that America's enemies mostly lived in countries where the Army and Marine Corps couldn't go. The Defense Department assumed control of the "mighty Wurlitzer," spending hundreds of millions of dollars to influence opinion in the Muslim world, far from the shooting wars in Iraq and Afghanistan.

Which is how, in the spring of 2005, a beefy man with a box of Marlboros tucked into his breast pocket came to be walking among the booths set up by technology vendors at the National Association of Broadcasters convention in Las Vegas. He was posing as an office-supplies salesman, but it was a thin cover for a onetime Army psychological-operations officer who had spent a decade thinking of ways to wage warfare inside other people's heads.

It was good that Michael Furlong thrived on mental combat, because he was no longer cut out for the physical kind. He was built like a Russian matryoshka doll, with a wide frame that narrowed only slightly into his neck and head. He was diabetic and moved slowly, and yet he was a mound of nervous energy and tended to sweat profusely. He spoke in rapid bursts, fusing strings of sentences together while barely taking a breath. During meetings, he often buried his audience beneath a blizzard of military jargon, which often worked to his advantage. "Mike is supersmart," said one military officer who worked closely with Furlong. "But he speaks in such gibberish, and nobody would ask any questions because they didn't want to appear dumb and admit that they didn't know what he was talking about." At meeting's end, Furlong often left the room unchallenged, convinced he had just received approval for whatever exotic scheme he had just presented.

A Miami native, Furlong was drafted into the Army in 1972, just months before President Richard Nixon abolished the draft, but he deferred his service to earn a journalism and business degree from Loyola University, in New Orleans. After college, he spent his first four years of military service learning the basics of infantry combat at Fort Bragg, North Carolina, and then rose to command a mechanized infantry unit based in the California desert at Fort Irwin, where he excelled. One escarpment there still bears the name Furlong Ridge for his success in the desert war games. He became a military instructor during the mideighties, first at West Point and later at the Royal Military Academy in Sandhurst, England. After the Gulf War of 1991, Furlong returned to Fort Bragg as an Army major in the 4th Psychological Operations Group.

Like many officers, Furlong was paranoid about being left out of any overseas adventure in which the U.S. military was engaged and would sometimes joke to colleagues that his greatest fear was that the Pentagon would sideline him by assigning him to do something like "blowing up basketballs in North Dakota." In fact, he managed to stay near the center of the action. After the warring factions in the Balkans signed a peace treaty in Dayton, Ohio, Furlong was one of the first Americans to deploy to Bosnia, commanding a psychological-operations battalion assigned the mission of maintaining a fragile peace by using leaflet drops and radio and television propaganda to convince locals to cooperate with the foreign peacekeeping troops.

During the 1990s, psychological-operations missions were still something of a sideshow within the U.S. military. They were dismissed as a fringe component to the shooting wars, carried out by strange people who had probably failed to cut it in other, more respected military specialties like infantry or artillery. It wasn't like the heyday of military psychological operations during the Vietnam War, when Special Forces teams worked with CIA teams to carry out sustained psychological warfare against leaders in Hanoi and the broader population in North Vietnam. Robert Andrews, the former Green Beret who became Donald Rumsfeld's civilian adviser and guide through the special-operations world, had participated in these missions, trying to sow confusion with phony mail campaigns and forged documents.

The operations were sometimes far more elaborate, like when Andrews and the rest of his unit created a fake resistance movement in North Vietnam—the Sacred Sword of the Patriots League—to propagate the fiction that there was an armed opposition to the Vietnamese Communist Party north of the demilitarized zone. In addition to letters and leaflet drops, American operatives kidnapped North Vietnamese fishermen using unmarked gunboats, blindfolded them, and brought them to the island of Cu Lao Cham, off the coast of Da Nang. The phantom group had built a "headquarters" there where detainees were told about extensive guerrilla operations to undermine the government in Hanoi. Some of the fishermen were even asked to join the "resistance." After several weeks the captives were given gift bags with radios tuned to the Voice of the SSPL radio station and were returned to North Vietnam, where they could tell everyone about the shadowy organization. Between 1964 and 1968, according to *The Secret War Against Hanoi*, by Tufts University professor Richard H. Shultz Jr., more than a thousand detainees were brought to Cu Lao Cham and indoctrinated into the ways of the Sacred Sword of the Patriots League.

Andrews and his small group dreamt up other ideas, like floating a dead body off the coast of North Vietnam with fake coded messages in the dead man's pocket. North Vietnamese intelligence analysts would decipher the codes and pass the false information to their commanders, the planners figured. But the idea was shot down in Washington; Andrews never learned by whom. Washington was "that mysterious place that said 'yes' or 'no' to our great ideas. And we all cursed it."

By September 11, 2001, Michael Furlong had retired from active duty and was working for Science Applications International Corporation (SAIC), a Beltway contractor soon to be awash in money from classified U.S. government contracts. Furlong had spent years studying ways to spread pro-American messages to hostile audiences overseas, and suddenly he found himself at the center of a war to win hearts and minds in the Muslim world. In the fall of 2001 he worked with Donald Rumsfeld's staff to develop information-operations strategies— earning a Defense Department civilian medal for his work—and occasionally sat in the White House Situation Room as Bush officials flailed about in search of ways to communicate White House talking points to Muslims.

Less than two years later, SAIC got an infusion of cash when the military parceled out new contracts to try to rebuild a shattered Iraq. Furlong traveled to Baghdad to lead a $15 million project the Pentagon awarded to SAIC to create a television station, the Iraqi Media Network. The network was envisioned as a counterweight to Al Jazeera and other Arabic networks that Washington perceived as having an anti-American bias. But the project was soon beset by problems. The Iraqi employees quit after they weren't paid, and the network had technical problems reaching Iraqi homes. Within months, SAIC had burned through $80 million of Pentagon money, and the endeavor was on the verge of collapse. Furlong was removed from the project in June 2003, although former colleagues said he was hardly the only one to blame for the network's difficulties. But he could be a showboat: He insisted on driving around Baghdad in a white Hummer—still bearing Maryland dealer plates—that he had had shipped to Iraq.

Yet while his behavior alienated some colleagues, Furlong's mastery of the Pentagon's byzantine contracting system made him invaluable to defense companies. Information-operations projects cost just a small fraction of what it cost to build a tank or a fighter jet, and what Furlong knew better than most was that inside multibillion-dollar enterprises like the Pentagon, smart and ambitious people can sometimes secure millions of dollars by identifying untapped pools of money in obscure corners of the bureaucracy. In doing so, they can build small empires.

When he arrived at the Las Vegas convention in the spring of 2005, he was about to take a senior civilian job within the psychological-operations division of U.S. Special Operations Command (SOCOM). He was carrying a stack of business cards identifying him as an office-supplies salesman to deflect questions about his real business: finding small companies with the right technology to help the Pentagon conduct propaganda and intelligence-gathering campaigns in the Middle East.

Over two days, Furlong spent hours at the booth of U-Turn Media, a small Czech firm that had been developing ways to stream video to mobile phones. The team from U-Turn had figured out almost immediately that Furlong was not selling office supplies, as some of them recognized the Special Operations Command's Tampa address listed on Furlong's business card. The chance meeting with Michael Furlong, it turned out, was a windfall for a struggling company that had come to Las Vegas to drum up new business.

U-Turn was run by Jan Obrman, a Czech national whose family had fled Prague during the Soviet crackdown in the late 1960s. His childhood experiences had made Obrman staunchly pro-American and a fierce champion of spreading Western ideas of democracy throughout the world. He worked for a pro-American think tank during the 1980s and later became an executive at Radio Free Europe. The prospect of making money in the growing Internet and mobile-phone market, and the financial backing of a wealthy German investor, led him to create U-Turn Media in 2001. The company had difficulty during its early years, before smartphones turned the mobile industry into a behemoth.

Back then, U-Turn was relying on somewhat clunky technology to make money. The company signed agreements with content providers and set up a marketing campaign to drive consumer traffic to Web sites owned by their clients. From there, customers could download an icon to their mobile phone that would act as a "portal" to the Internet. But during this paleolithic era of mobile phones, U-Turn found few clients ready to take advantage of its service.

U-Turn widened its hunt for clients by teaming up with pornography companies to figure out ways to stream video porn to cell phones. One of its partnerships was with a business producing a low-budget program called *Czech My Tits*, which featured a man walking the streets of Prague, giving women five hundred Czech koruna if they exposed their breasts to the camera. U-Turn was hired to help stream the pictures and audio to mobile phones. Bill Eldridge, a former company executive, recalls that the flesh business seemed like a path to riches. "In building a business like that, you want to target either the porn industry or the intelligence world," he said. "Those are the only people who have the money to pay for that kind of stuff."

Having dabbled in porn, Obrman got his opportunity to tap the intelligence market when he ran into Furlong in Las Vegas. The two actually had met in the Balkans in the 1990s and they spent hours swapping stories about the Cold War and the bloody ethnic conflicts that came after the fall of the Berlin Wall. They shared identical views about the importance of spreading American ideals abroad, especially in the Muslim world. But Furlong also represented a tremendous business opportunity for U-Turn.

Once Furlong began his job at SOCOM, he talked to Obrman and other U-Turn executives about developing video games that people throughout the Middle East could download to their mobile phones. For SOCOM, the games could address two problems at once: that a great many people in the Muslim world disliked the United States and that the United States knew very little about who those people were. Furlong was interested in building games that could influence the user's perceptions of the United States and also collect information about who was playing the games. It was a potential intelligence bonanza: Thousands of people would be sending their mobile-phone numbers and other identifying information to U-Turn, and that information could be stored in military databases and used for complex data-mining operations carried out by the National Security Agency and other intelligence agencies. The spies wouldn't have to go hunting for information; it would come to them.

It was just one aspect of a web of programs that had escalated in the years since the September 11 attacks to feed information into sophisticated computer databases to hunt for patterns of activity that could be evidence of future terrorist plots. If large quantities of personal information could be poured into the databases, the thinking went, computer algorithms could sift through the data and make connections that human-intelligence analysts couldn't.

But the laws governing these activities were murky at best. One Special Operations Command initiative that would eventually become controversial involved collecting information about American citizens suspected of having ties to militant groups. The data was stored in computer servers in Virginia, and some military officials began to worry that they might be breaking laws that regulate how the Defense Department can collect information about citizens. Looking to move the databases offshore, officers overseeing the program for SOCOM would eventually ask Michael Furlong to house the databases at U-Turn's headquarters, in Prague, a move that would lead to a dramatic fight between Furlong and the CIA.

By the middle of 2006, U-Turn had put together a glossy, twenty-seven-page presentation for a pilot program for the Pentagon to use in countries throughout the Muslim world. The proposal's opening paragraphs emphasized the power of cell phones as a tool to reach a mass audience:

"What do a soccer mom in Atlanta, a Bedouin trader, a Chinese businessman, a U.S. military family, a Kuwaiti civil servant, a well-connected oil company executive, an Al Qaeda martyr, a peacefully devout Iranian Muslim, and a Serbian rebel all have in common with youth throughout the U.S., Asia, Europe, and the Middle East?

"Every one of these people, adults and teenagers around the world, probably has a mobile phone in his possession almost every waking minute of every day."

In the proposal, U-Turn was offering the military a menu of options to clandestinely broadcast messages around the world. The proposal offered "compelling news, political, and religious content mixed with USSOCOM's message" that could "target teenagers in high risk/ unfriendly areas." And over time the Pentagon's message could be integrated "into the lifestyle of these targets." The proposal promised that all of this could be delivered without the "Made in America" label—a "covertly branded" campaign that appeared to be led by a European entertainment company.

U-Turn won the competition for the program in August 2006, a contract worth just $250,000. But its symbolic value was far greater. The obscure telecommunications company from Prague that until recently had been peddling newscasts and soft-core pornography for mobile phones had won its first contract from one of the most secretive—and fastest-growing—corners of the military bureaucracy. As Michael Furlong's partnership with U-Turn Media was budding, his division inside U.S. Special Operations Command was in the midst of awarding large classified contracts to communications firms for propaganda campaigns in the Middle East and Central Asia. SOCOM was doling out hundreds of millions of dollars for the effort, and a rush was on. Small companies with little or no experience in the propaganda world began rebranding themselves as "strategic communications" firms to win the new business. For U-Turn, it would be the first contract of many, and the beginning of a new era for a company that had stumbled upon a patron with a seemingly limitless budget. U-Turn had found its golden goose.

THE PURVEYORS OF PROPAGANDA working at Special Operations Command in Tampa knew that for campaigns meant to "influence" opinion in the Muslim world to be effective, America's role had to be hidden. Shortly after he signed up U-Turn Media to set up a pilot program for video games and other digital offerings, Furlong convinced the firm's executives to create an offshore company that could receive Pentagon contracts but not be tied directly to the United States. By late 2006, Jan Obrman had established JD Media Transmission Systems LLC, a company incorporated in the Seychelles Islands and set up to receive money transfers from the United States through a foreign bank account.

With few restrictions about how the Pentagon spent money on clandestine programs, Furlong had nobody looking over his shoulder. He sometimes liked to call himself "the king of the gray areas," and was using every bit of contract trickery to secure deals for the U-Turn front companies to carry out the propaganda operations. Taking advantage of a law that allows firms owned by Native Americans to get a leg up when bidding on government contracts, Furlong arranged for U-Turn to partner with Wyandotte Net Tel, a firm located on a tiny speck of tribal lands in eastern Oklahoma.

The first big project that U-Turn developed for SOCOM was a "shooter" game in the style of the popular *Call of Duty* game series. The game took the player on an odyssey through the streets of Baghdad, shooting up insurgents trying to kill civilians in a wave of terrorist attacks. The goal was to reach an Iraqi police station and deliver the secret plans for an upcoming insurgent attack, plans that had been stolen from a militia group's headquarters. The title of the game was *Iraqi Hero.*

It was part of a broad Pentagon psychological-operations campaign, with the code name Native Echo, timed to the "surge" of American forces into Iraq that President Bush ordered in 2007. Native Echo's main focus was on combating the flood of foreign fighters entering Iraq from Yemen, Syria, Saudi Arabia, and parts of North Africa. *Iraqi Hero* was built in a way that it could be easily modified for any number of countries in the Muslim world. A U-Turn presentation to SOCOM listed thirteen countries where the game could be distributed after slight modifications, including Saudi Arabia, Morocco, Egypt, and Jordan. The game's graphics, featuring streets lined with mosques, old cars, and palm trees, would not need to be dramatically changed; only the dialogue would have to be altered. For example, a Lebanese version of the game would use dialogue to reflect the political situation there and would be called *Maghaweer*, named after a Lebanese commando unit.

U-Turn developed two other games for the Native Echo operation, one called *Oil Tycoon*, which allowed gamers to build oil pipelines and protect the government's oil infrastructure in the face of constant terrorist attacks, and *City Mayor*, which put players in the role of urban planner, deciding how to allocate limited resources to rebuilding a fictional city that had been destroyed by terrorists.

A team of Czech programmers at U-Turn's Prague headquarters built the games, and Furlong put the company on an accelerated timetable to finish them as quickly as possible and get them distributed in the Middle East.

U-Turn worked with SOCOM developing various ways to deliver the games. The easiest was distribution by hand, putting the games on thousands of memory cards and selling them or giving them away in the markets and bazaars. The way to get far wider distribution, however, was to post the games on Web sites and blogs frequented by gamers in the Middle East. This also allowed SOCOM to monitor how many people were downloading the games and, more important, who was doing it.

It is hard to assess the extent of SOCOM's secret gaming operations or to know exactly how many companies like U-Turn the Pentagon contracted to create propaganda targeting young people in the Muslim world. Furlong pushed the Czech company to come up with as many new initiatives as possible, and U-Turn even put together proposals for a clothing brand using popular singers and celebrities in the Middle East as pitchmen. There were even discussions about dropping large flat-screen televisions into remote villages around Central Asia and North Africa, the televisions protected by armor plates so they could not be destroyed. The televisions would have a large antenna that could receive and broadcast pro-American messages beamed from thousands of miles away.

This far-fetched idea was never approved. But as the Pentagon was expanding its propaganda initiatives around the world in late 2007, U-Turn was hired to support a new SOCOM program to run Web sites focused on Central Asia, North Africa, China, and other regions. The Trans-Regional Web Initiative hired freelance reporters to write up reports and post them on Web sites with names like *Central Asia Online*, which carried decidedly positive news about the United States and some of its authoritarian allies in Uzbekistan and elsewhere. A controversy erupted when news of the program leaked out, and SOCOM ditched initial plans to keep America's role in the Web sites hidden, choosing to place a small label at the bottom of each site that identified it as a Defense Department product. But some in Congress and the State Department believed that the Pentagon had crossed a line with the Web sites, the line separating information operations carried out as part of a military campaign and the Pentagon's more basic requirement to deliver truthful information to the American public.

In reality, however, this boundary had been blurred years earlier, and companies like U-Turn Media were the beneficiaries. Furlong traveled frequently to Prague to meet with Obrman and the U-Turn programmers, and by early 2008 U-Turn had won more than $5 million in SOCOM contracts, usually working as a subcontractor tied to a larger firm or as a partner with a Native American–owned firm. Obrman created a U.S.–based company, International Media Ventures, with the idea that having a company inside the United States would make it easier to win classified government contracts. He set up IMV's office next to other CIA and Pentagon contractors in an office park in St. Petersburg, Florida, just across Tampa Bay from the sprawling headquarters of SOCOM and U.S. Central Command, at McDill Air Force Base.

But some inside the CIA began to raise suspicions about how U-Turn/IMV had managed to win classified government contracts. What exactly was the connection between Furlong, a high-ranking civilian bureaucrat, and an obscure Czech company that had employed a small army of computer programmers to build games and Web sites for the Pentagon? The CIA's station in Prague began sending cables back to Langley raising questions about the arrangement and how easy it might be for Russian intelligence operatives to penetrate U-Turn's operation.

There was an even bigger problem. In 2007, SOCOM had quietly relocated the computer servers housing data it had collected about American citizens to U-Turn's headquarters in Prague. While military officials figured moving the servers there might bring the Pentagon in line with American eavesdropping laws, the United States had now set up a clandestine computer operation inside of the Czech Republic, an American ally, without notifying the government in Prague. This was chancy even under normal circumstances, because American officials would have to weigh the risk of the allied country's intelligence service discovering the operation, shutting it down, and extracting payback by refusing to cooperate with the CIA on other operations.

But this wasn't a normal period of diplomatic relations between the United States and the Czech Republic. The Bush administration was aggressively courting the Czech government for permission to build a tracking radar southwest of Prague as part of the White House's missile-defense program. Getting Czech approval had proven difficult, primarily because Vladimir Putin's government in Moscow had denounced the Bush administration's missile-defense plans for years and had pressured Eastern European countries to deny the United States' request to build radar stations in their countries.

The tension between the CIA and Furlong escalated. By the middle of 2008, Michael Furlong had switched jobs, moving to Lackland Air Force Base in San Antonio, Texas, the headquarters of a psychological-operations cell called the Joint Information Operations Warfare Command. But he retained oversight of U-Turn/IMV, and in June 2008 he decided at the last minute to stop in Prague to meet with company employees on his way home to Texas from Afghanistan.

The CIA's station chief and other American-embassy officials in Prague had, not long before, learned that the Pentagon had been running the secret database operation out of U-Turn's offices. The operation had been shut down because of concerns in Washington about the legality of the database, but now Furlong was sitting in the American embassy—without having been given proper clearance to travel to Prague on business—and CIA officers in Prague suspected that he might be trying to resurrect the data-mining program. They worried that the bombastic, chain-smoking man might be planning to spend weeks in the country overseeing his clandestine programs, and could derail months of diplomatic negotiations over the missile-defense pact.

What followed was a flurry of frantic calls between Prague, Washington, and San Antonio as everyone tried to figure out what to do about the Furlong situation. Everyone agreed the answer was simple: Get him out of the country as quickly as possible. Lt. General John Koziol, Furlong's boss in San Antonio, reached him in Prague and delivered a blunt message: Check out of your hotel, get to the airport, and take the first flight out of the country. Furlong was effectively kicked out of the Czech Republic. "The CIA came down on him like a ton of bricks," said one military officer who worked with Furlong in San Antonio.

Furlong's ambitions had been blunted, and he was now on the CIA's blacklist. But he figured that his patrons at the top ranks of the Defense Department would protect him, and he was already redirecting his energies to a new problem: the growing militant violence in Pakistan that was spilling across the border into Afghanistan. Furlong was determined to help American military commanders with the problem, and he was certain that the CIA wasn't up to the job. And now it was personal. After the Prague episode, he began to refer to the CIA as "my nemesis."

Just weeks after Furlong was kicked out of the Czech Republic, a plane carrying Secretary of State Condoleezza Rice and a gaggle of American diplomats touched down at the airport in Prague. That evening, at a lavish celebratory dinner, Rice clinked champagne glasses with Czech foreign minister Karel Schwarzenberg—a toast to a new missile-defense pact and a new era of warm relations between the United States and the Czech Republic.

11: THE OLD MAN'S RETURN

"You remember the first rule of retirement, George? No moonlighting, no fooling with loose ends. No private enterprise, ever."

—*John le Carré*, Smiley's People

General David McKiernan had heard enough. It had been months since the top commander in Afghanistan had been told of a plan developed by two businessmen to deliver regular reports from a network of sources throughout the country, and across the border in Pakistan. McKiernan wanted to know why the effort had stalled. He had hoped that it would provide reliable information about Pakistan, in contrast with CIA dispatches that he suspected were spoon-fed by Pakistani spies. Somewhere in the Pentagon bureaucracy, he figured, faceless gnomes were delaying things.

"Who is the communist I need to kill in order to get this contract?" McKiernan barked to his staff, after learning that the funding for the information program had still not been approved.

Sitting alongside General McKiernan that day in fall 2008 was Michael Furlong, who had been shuttling between Kabul and San Antonio hoping to start a variety of information-operations projects for the generals in Afghanistan, from mapping the tribal structure in the south to conducting polls about Afghan attitudes toward the American military. The war was getting worse by the day. The Taliban had reclaimed large swaths of territory in the southern and eastern regions of the country, assassinated Afghan government officials, and set up shadow governments in Kandahar and Helmand provinces. The 2006 peace deals in North and South Waziristan had allowed the Taliban and Haqqani Network to flourish and escalate their attacks from Pakistani villages on American outposts in Afghanistan. By the end of June 2008, the month that McKiernan took command, more American troops had died than during any other month since the war began in 2001.

When he arrived in Kabul, McKiernan was immediately convinced that he didn't have enough troops. The Iraq war continued to be the Bush administration's top priority, ensuring that the neglected conflict in Afghanistan remained what the Pentagon euphemistically called an "economy-of-force operation." McKiernan's predecessor, General Dan McNeill, had delivered a stinging indictment of the war strategy on his way out of the country, saying that American commanders needed more ground troops, helicopters, and intelligence units. During a congressional hearing, Admiral Mike Mullen, chairman of the Joint Chiefs of Staff, said, "In Afghanistan, we do what we can. In Iraq, we do what we must."

General McNeill had also blamed the government of Pakistan for not doing enough to stem the flow of fighters crossing the border into Afghanistan. Indeed, Pakistan had become a favorite target for American generals complaining about the rise in violence in the country. As far back as September 2006, Lt. General Karl Eikenberry—who preceded McNeill—tried to get the White House's attention by compiling a dossier on Pakistan's inaction in the tribal areas. He traveled to Washington with a PowerPoint presentation alleging Pakistani complicity in fostering militancy there, even citing the fact that Jalaluddin

Haqqani openly operated his madrassa in Miranshah (the same madrassa that Art Keller and CIA officers had pushed Pakistani troops to raid in the summer of 2006), less than a mile from a large Pakistani military base.

So, two years later, when the two businessmen pitched General McKiernan on their proposal to collect information inside Pakistan and feed it to the American military command in Kabul, the general was immediately intrigued. The men making the pitch—Eason Jordan, a suave former CNN executive, and Robert Young Pelton, an iconoclastic Canadian writer who had written a series of books helping travelers navigate the world's danger spots—had worked together before. During the bloodiest days of the Iraq war, Jordan and Pelton had launched IraqSlogger, a Web site devoted to fact, rumor, and on-the-ground reports by local Iraqi journalists. The site had a small but devoted following, but it struggled financially, and Pelton and Jordan had to shut it down. They wanted to replicate the project in Afghanistan and had put together a network of local stringers in Afghanistan and Pakistan for a new Web site, which they had named AfPax Insider. This time, however, they hoped to get the Pentagon to finance their new endeavor.

But General McKiernan wasn't going to pay for a startup news service. When he met with Jordan in Kabul in July 2008, he said he wanted regular reports from places where his troops couldn't go, and where the CIA wasn't giving him any reliable information. McKiernan's relationship with the agency's station chief in Kabul was dismal; the two men barely communicated. McKiernan would openly disparage the CIA during staff meetings, and within weeks of his arrival in Kabul he concluded that the spy agency had few sources in Pakistan's tribal areas who could warn American commanders about plots that were being hatched there. Just a day before he met with Jordan, Taliban gunmen had ambushed an American military outpost at Wanat, in eastern Afghanistan, killing nine soldiers and wounding twenty-seven.

In a previous meeting, McKiernan had been impressed that Jordan had given military officials a sheet of phone numbers of militant suspects in Pakistan that had been collected by his team of stringers. According to Jordan, he only gave phone numbers of Taliban "spokesmen" that were widely available to journalists. The phone numbers had been fed into a classified database maintained by military officers at Bagram Air Base, and a handful of them matched numbers that the military had already been monitoring. This raised expectations among McKiernan's staff that the team could deliver actual, real-time information. Eventually, McKiernan approved $22 million for AfPax Insider, and he ordered Michael Furlong to make sure that the money came through.

As always, Furlong had shown his ability to insinuate himself into the center of American war operations, and during the second half of 2008 he frequently attended meetings about propaganda and information-operations campaigns in Afghanistan. McKiernan would often forget his name, referring to him as "the fat sweaty guy" to other members of his staff.

But if McKiernan underestimated Furlong, he miscalculated. The general may have given little thought to the implications of approving Jordan and Pelton's information-gathering project, but putting Michael Furlong in charge of the operation set into motion one of the more bizarre episodes of the secret wars since 2001. Many of the elements that had been developing in the laboratory—the military's rivalry with the CIA, the expanding universe of government spying, the creeping privatization of war—mixed together into a volatile compound. Later, after finger-pointing and investigations, Michael Furlong would be dealt a fate worse than anything he had feared. He wasn't sent to "blow up basketballs in North Dakota." He was out of the game entirely.

For his part, an angry McKiernan would discover after approving the AfPax Insider project that even having four stars on your shoulders was no guarantee for getting what you wanted. His efforts to get funding for the project had run into obstacles, most of them set up by the CIA.

On September 5, 2008, Furlong had driven out to Langley with a group of top Defense Department officials to present the information-gathering plan to the CIA's Counterterrorism Center. Accompanying him was Brigadier-General Robert Holmes, the deputy operations officer at U.S. Central Command, and Austin Branch, a civilian official working for the Pentagon intelligence office that Donald Rumsfeld had set up several years earlier.

Because of the Prague episode just months earlier, CIA officials were already wary of Furlong, and Furlong knew well how prickly the spy agency could be when it sensed the Pentagon encroaching on its turf. At the meeting, he chose his language carefully when discussing the proposed operation. His contractors weren't "spying" or even "intelligence gathering," he said. They were merely collecting "atmospheric information" to inform commanders in Kabul and to help protect American troops. As Furlong would later describe it, "I had to come up with a euphemism for what we were doing."

Seven years after the September 11 attacks, the Pentagon had gone so deep into the spying game that an entirely new language had been created. Just as U.S. troops had been sent into countries where America was not at war, on the grounds that they were "preparing the battlefield," collecting "atmospherics" became the new catchphrase used by the military to avoid raising the hackles of the CIA. At the September meeting at Langley, Furlong tried to assure CIA officers that the operations would be coordinated with the agency's stations in Kabul and Islamabad, but the mood darkened quickly. The dozens of CIA officers who had come to listen to Furlong were immediately suspicious that the operation amounted to a back-door spying operation.

It was even worse three months later, when Furlong flew back to Afghanistan and briefed a group of CIA officers in Kabul, including the station chief, on the project. The meeting disintegrated into a shouting match, and the station chief accused Furlong of trying to gather intelligence for lethal missions inside Pakistan. "One of the CIA guys was literally spitting, and Furlong started shouting back," recalls one military officer who attended the meeting. Weeks later, a lawyer at CIA headquarters wrote a memorandum to the Pentagon, officially lodging the CIA's protest about a program the agency thought was unsupervised and potentially dangerous.

Furlong had expected the resistance, and to him it was the hidebound CIA at its worst: protecting its equities at all costs, ignoring the fact that the CIA had been unable to prevent the attacks from Pakistan that were killing American troops each day. He was convinced that the CIA had made a Faustian bargain with Pakistan. In exchange for getting access for drone flights inside Pakistan, he believed the agency was looking the other way as the ISI quietly supported the Taliban and Haqqani Network. Gathering information to protect American troops, Furlong argued to the CIA officers, was perfectly in line with the Pentagon's authorities under Title 10, no matter where it was taking place.

As the CIA tried to block approval for AfPax Insider, and military lawyers at U.S. Central Command pored over the details of the proposed operation, Furlong decided he didn't need to wait for Washington's approval. In late 2008, he arranged for the project to get $1 million in seed money from a military emergency fund and maneuvered around another thorny bureaucratic issue—the fact that neither Eason Jordan nor Robert Young Pelton was an approved government vendor. He devised a simple solution: putting the project under the control of a company he knew well, Jan Obrman's International Media Ventures, in St. Petersburg, Florida. By April 2009, Furlong had secured another $2.9 million for the project, all of it flowing through the Florida-based business. Furlong, the master at wheeling and dealing with government contracts, was taking advantage of a system that was ripe for exploitation. Congress had approved billions for the wars in Iraq and Afghanistan, but there was little congressional oversight about how the money was spent.

But Pelton and Jordan saw little of it and began to suspect that Furlong had other designs for the money that General McKiernan had ordered for AfPax Insider. Regardless, the two continued to work, and Pelton was regularly sent around Afghanistan to gather information from tribal elders, Taliban operatives, and warlords. He traveled with a team of military officers dressed as civilians, driving east for hours over washed-out roads to gather information at the Pakistan border. Pelton also took a plane in the opposite direction, to Afghanistan's border with Iran, where he met the powerful warlord of the city of Herat, Ismail Khan, to assess his support for America's war in the country.

All this time, General McKiernan's attentions were directed elsewhere. Rumors began swirling that President Barack Obama, who came into office in January 2009, was dissatisfied with the strategy in Afghanistan and planned to overhaul the war staff. In May, Secretary of Defense Robert Gates flew to Kabul to break the news to McKiernan: He was out, and President Obama had decided to replace him with Lt. General Stanley McChrystal, then the commander of Joint Special Operations Command. The leadership transition turned out to be a boon for Furlong; when he met with top members of McChrystal's staff he presented the information-gathering project as a fait accompli. During a meeting with Major General Michael Flynn, the senior intelligence officer in Afghanistan, he said that he had teams of contractors operating around Pakistan and Afghanistan, and their information reports were being "pushed" into classified military-intelligence databases.

But Jordan and Pelton's suspicions that they were being shunted to the side proved to be correct, and as they badgered Furlong for money, he began sending them e-mails about how he had found other contractors with better sources of information. In early July, Furlong returned from a trip outside Afghanistan and fired off an e-mail to Jordan and Pelton:

"The two guys who met me in Dubai last weekend are as close to the real, commercial version of Jason Bourne that I have seen. Both fluent in Dari, Pashtu and Arabic and building the networks on the ground every day," he wrote. General McKiernan was gone, Furlong said, and the new commanders in Afghanistan had little interest in paying for AfPax Insider. "Let's be honest guys," Furlong wrote, "you are asking the government to pay to start-up your service. The other guys have already made their investment in establishing their network over the past 4.5 years."

Who exactly were these mysterious new contractors, these "Jason Bournes"? Furlong didn't say in the e-mails. He spoke only of a network of former special-operations troops and CIA officers who refused to work with the spy agency because it was too risk-averse and too dependent on foreign intelligence services like the ISI.

They had formed what he called a "shadow CIA" and were willing to gather intelligence that might be used for special-operations missions. As for the person running this shadow CIA, Furlong referred to him only as "the old man."

DUANE "DEWEY" CLARRIDGE, age seventy-seven, never passed quietly into retirement. It wasn't his style; and besides, there were too many old scores to be settled. He had left the CIA amid the fallout from the Iran–Contra affair, convinced that his bosses had made him a scapegoat. He considered his indictment two years later for lying to Congress about his role in Iran–Contra as the work of a partisan witch hunt.

When President George H. W. Bush pardoned Clarridge and other Iran–Contra figures—including former defense secretary Caspar Weinberger—during the waning days of his presidency on Christmas Eve 1992, Clarridge felt some degree of vindication. He had the presidential pardon framed, and he displayed it in a hallway of his home. It was the first thing that visitors saw when they entered.

He wrote a memoir in the late 1990s, *A Spy for All Seasons*, offering vivid details about many of his Cold War exploits, and he stayed committed to Republican causes. As a private consultant in 1998, he worked with retired general Wayne Downing—the former head of Joint Special Operations Command—on a plan to insert thousands of Iraqi exiles and American commandos into Iraq to bring down Saddam Hussein's regime. The proposal had the endorsement of Ahmed Chalabi, the head of the Iraqi National Congress and a favorite of Republicans advocating a war in Iraq, but it was dismissed by the commander of U.S. Central Command as fantasy. The commander, General Anthony Zinni, referred to the Downing–Clarridge plan as "Bay of Goats."

When the United States did finally get around to overthrowing Saddam Hussein, in 2003, Clarridge raised money for various private efforts to prove, against all evidence, that the Iraqi dictator had stashes of chemical and biological weapons around the country. All the while, he remained an unflinching cheerleader for American intervention overseas. In one exchange during a 2007 interview, he angrily defended many of the CIA's most notorious operations, saying it was the duty of the United States to exert its will overseas.

"We'll intervene whenever we decide it's in our national-security interests to intervene," Clarridge told a reporter. "And if you don't like it, lump it.

"Get used to it, world, we're not going to put up with nonsense."

But he had also soured on the CIA. That same year he gave a speech in Arkansas about how much the CIA's human-intelligence operations had atrophied over the years. The spy agency couldn't get reliable information about the regimes in Iran and North Korea, he said, because it had become too dependent on spy satellites and electronic eavesdropping. He believed the problem was that nervous lawyers held too much sway at Langley and routinely scuttled proposals for risky intelligence-collection missions. He began dreaming of a new model for espionage, something smaller and leaner than the CIA and beholden to no foreign government. It would be like the Office of Strategic Services but updated for the world of the twenty-first century—a world dominated by corporations, loose international criminal and terror networks, and multinational institutions.

Private spying was not an entirely new idea. After World War II, OSS founder William Donovan was so despondent that President Truman had not named him the first director of central intelligence he decided to set up an intelligence operation of his own. During business trips to Europe he collected information about Soviet activities from American ambassadors and journalists and scouted for possible undercover agents. He showered CIA officials with ideas for covert operations. But Truman, when he learned of Donovan's activities, was furious, calling him a "prying S.O.B." In the years since, the

CIA has generally had success snuffing out other, similar efforts at private spying.

Clarridge had damaged most of his relationships at Langley in the years since his retirement. But he remained close to a fraternity of retired special-operations officers who maintained ties to active-duty commandos at Fort Bragg and at forward bases in Afghanistan and Iraq. His criticism of the CIA as bumbling and amateurish made him popular with some of them, and he turned to a small cadre of retired special-operations troops as he built up a network of agents for operations in Afghanistan and Pakistan.

Teaming up with Mike Taylor, a former Green Beret and sometime business partner who ran a private security firm based in Boston called American International Security Corporation, Clarridge put together a network of Westerners, Afghans, and Pakistanis who he believed could operate in the region without drawing suspicions about their activities. They got their first job when Clarridge was hired to assist in helping free *New York Times* reporter David Rohde, whom the Haqqani Network had kidnapped in eastern Afghanistan and brought over the border to Miranshah, the large town in North Waziristan. During the months-long ordeal, Clarridge told members of Rohde's family that his agents in the Pakistani tribal areas would be able to find out where the reporter was being held and either feed the information to the military for a rescue operation or negotiate for Rohde's release.

In the dark of night in June 2009, Rohde and his Afghan translator hopped over the wall of the compound where they were being held and found their way to a Pakistani military outpost. Clarridge's agents hadn't helped in the escape, but the exact circumstances of the dramatic episode were murky enough during the summer of 2009 that Clarridge saw an opportunity to market his role in the Rohde case to win new business. Working private kidnapping cases in Afghanistan was not a business model promising explosive growth, and Clarridge was aiming much higher. If he could get the government to hire his network, he figured, he would be back in the spying game.

That opportunity came within weeks, with American troops searching for another missing person in Afghanistan, this time a young soldier from Idaho named Bowe Bergdahl. Private Bergdahl had vanished in June 2009 under mysterious circumstances in Afghanistan's Paktika Province, and conflicting reports suggested that he had either been captured while on patrol or simply gone AWOL. When he failed to show up for morning roll call at his base, military commanders dispatched Predator drones and spy planes to scour the area.

Within hours, the planes intercepted a conversation between Taliban fighters, crackling over two handheld radios. The fighters were discussing plans to ambush the search party looking for Bergdahl:

"We are waiting for them."

"They know where he is, but they keep going to the wrong area."

"OK, set up the work for them."

"Yes, we have a lot of IEDs on the road."

"God willing, we will do it."

But the Americans didn't in fact know where Bergdahl was. He had become a prisoner of war, given the military label DUSTWUN: short for "duty status: whereabouts unknown." Furlong jumped into the operation to locate Bergdahl, and he soon found himself in Dubai meeting with members of Clarridge's team who had contacted him claiming they had information about the location of the missing soldier. Furlong was enthralled, in no small part because he had a chance to work with the legendary Dewey Clarridge, whom he affectionately called "the old man."

Even though he was still working to pry loose the original $22 million first requested by General McKiernan, Furlong had far grander ambitions for his spying operation. He had found his "Jason Bournes," and he no longer needed what he considered the pedestrian service originally pitched by Eason Jordan and Robert Young Pelton. In an e-mail marbled with spy jargon, he explained that the Clarridge men he had met in Dubai—one who went by the handle "WILLI 1"—were "wired like none I have ever seen" and have "moved an operative in close to the package" inside Pakistan. The "package" was Bowe Berg-dahl. But Furlong knew that running a covert spy network inside Pak-istan was far beyond his brief, and he was certain that his enemies at the CIA would try to kill the operation if they learned about what he was up to. He wrote that he would "need top cover to keep from get-ting in hot water w/ our nemesis," meaning the CIA.

Until Furlong could get money for the operation, Clarridge and his team were working pro bono for the military. With no system in place to get the Clarridge team's reports into the military-intelligence sys-tem, Furlong used back channels to get the dispatches to friends at U.S. Central Command and Special Operations Command in Tampa. But the ad hoc arrangement caused confusion, and soon the deputy commander of Bergdahl's unit sent an angry e-mail to Kabul asking who, exactly, were these intelligence agents running around the tribal areas of Pakistan? "I am not comfortable with this arrangement," he wrote. "Request you provide direct contact information for these 'sources' so I can get an experienced human intelligence officer and analytical team involved. Otherwise, there is huge potential for mis-takes and missed opportunities."

Through the summer of 2009, Clarridge and his team steadily expanded the scope of the information they passed to military offi-cers. A detailed dossier that Clarridge produced about the purported locations inside Pakistan of senior leaders of the Haqqani Network was fed into classified intelligence channels and used by special-operations troops to monitor the network's activities.

Clarridge was running all of this from thousands of miles away, from his modest home in the San Diego suburbs. Inside his house in Escondido, California, he had created a nerve center for the operation and kept up with his agents using a computer and a cell phone. Some special-operations officers in Tampa and in Kabul began jokingly referring to his command post as "Escondido 1." He padded around the house at all hours of the night, answering e-mails from members of his team twelve time zones ahead of him. Sometimes, he spoke to agents while lounging next to his pool.

By late September 2009, Furlong had finally secured a contract for the private spying operation, a $22 million deal overseen by Lockheed Martin. It was to last for six months, with an option for renewal. The extraordinary new arrangement established procedures for how Clarridge could get his reports—a mash-up of rumors about the whereabouts of Taliban and al Qaeda leaders, gossip at village bazaars, and some very precise information about plots being hatched against American troops in Afghanistan—into intelligence databases used by military commanders.

Clarridge acted as a clearinghouse, taking the information from the field and digesting it into analytical "situation reports." The reports were then sent by Hushmail, an encrypted commercial e-mail service, to a small team of contractors whom Furlong had arranged to sit inside a military command post in Kabul. Some of the contractors worked for International Media Ventures, which had recently undergone a management shakeup. Jan Obrman had fired most of the senior leadership and brought in a group of gray-haired retired special-operations officers to run the company. Richard Pack, the company's new CEO, had been one of the planners for the botched 1980 mission to rescue the hostages in Tehran. Robert Holmes, another member of the new executive team, was a retired Air Force general who just a year earlier had been an operations officer at U.S. Central Command and had traveled to Langley with Michael Furlong to pitch the plan for intelligence collection in Afghanistan. When the team of contractors in Kabul received the Hushmail messages from Clarridge and other intelligence teams that Furlong was overseeing at the time, they entered the reports into classified military databases.

Once the reports entered the intelligence bloodstream, it was virtually impossible to distinguish the information from the private spies from that of CIA case officers and military-intelligence operatives. Some of Clarridge's reports, according to a Pentagon investigation, contained specific longitude and latitude coordinates of militant outposts in Pakistan, and of the movement of Taliban fighters in the poppy-growing regions of southern Afghanistan. The reports sometimes led to action. Based at least partly on Clarridge's intelligence, Army Apache gunships on at least one occasion shot up Taliban fighters massing near an American base east of Kandahar, and Joint Special Operations Command fired high-altitude artillery rounds into a suspected militant compound inside Pakistan. Furlong was thrilled and would frequently brag to colleagues that the information gathered by his contractor network had embarrassed the CIA.

Dewey Clarridge lived to embarrass the agency, too, and his network was at times drawn into the internecine warfare between the military and the CIA that resembled something of a cross between a Graham Greene novel and Mad magazine's Spy vs. Spy. In one case, Clarridge's group began trying to dig up dirt to discredit Ahmed Wali Karzai, the Afghan president's half brother, the most important power broker in southern Afghanistan and one of the CIA's top informants in the country.

Karzai had been collecting millions of dollars from the agency since the beginning of the war, and by 2009 he was recruiting gunmen for a CIA-trained army of Afghans called the Kandahar Strike Force. But senior American generals, including McKiernan and McChrystal, saw "AWK" as a corrosive influence in southern Afghanistan and the man at the center of widespread corruption that was turning Afghans toward the Taliban.

Clarridge compiled a dossier of allegations against Karzai, including connections to the heroin trade, land grabs, and murder accusations, and passed it along to military commanders in Kabul. The officers used the document in a campaign to get Ahmed Wali Karzai removed from power in Kandahar, but the CIA fought back and prevailed. He stayed in his post.

Ultimately, though, Ahmed Wali Karzai couldn't escape his many enemies. He was murdered coming out of his bathroom in his palace in Kandahar. The assassin was his longtime bodyguard, who fired two bullets into his head and chest.

IN SETTING UP the private spying network, Michael Furlong had violated a Pentagon regulation that prohibits the Defense Department from hiring contractors to conduct human-spying operations. But Furlong knew that the lines separating the work of soldiers and spies had blurred so much that it was relatively easy to find justification for his work. When American officials in Kabul asked Furlong who had authorized his operation, and when Furlong's bosses back in San Antonio began to get angry calls from the CIA accusing Furlong of running a rogue spying operation, he fired back with ammunition of his own.

Just as the Defense Department was approving the Lockheed Martin contract for the private intelligence operation, U.S. Central Command issued a sweeping secret directive that expanded military spying activities throughout the Muslim world, from Saudi Arabia to Yemen to Iran to Pakistan. The directive, signed by CENTCOM commander General David Petraeus, ordered new missions to "prepare the environment" for future combat operations throughout the Middle East and to ready the military for missions that the CIA couldn't accomplish. The order gave permission for highly classified units like Task Force Orange—the human-intelligence-gathering teams connected to Joint Special Operations Command formerly called Gray Fox—as well as private contractors to "develop clandestine operational infrastructure that can be tasked to locate, identify, isolate, disrupt/destroy" extremist networks and individual leaders of terror groups.

The directive, called the Joint Unconventional Warfare Task Force Execute Order, was part of a broader initiative during the first year of the Obama administration to define the role of the American military in countries beyond declared war zones. The new administration was hoping to bring some order to the chaotic world of secret military and intelligence operations that had expanded dramatically since 2001, and to tie together some of the threads that had unspooled in the years since Donald Rumsfeld initially pushed the military to become more involved in human spying.

But if anything, the new guidelines that emerged—including General Petraeus's secret order—had the effect of reinforcing most of what had been done during the Bush administration. Special-operations officers now had even broader authorities to run spying missions across the globe. These orders became a new blueprint for the secret wars that President Obama would come to embrace.

General Petraeus's directive came as the Obama administration was ramping up its clandestine war in Yemen, and much of the order was directed at bolstering special-operations personnel and equipment around Sana'a. But when Michael Furlong read the Petraeus directive, he saw it as nothing short of an endorsement for exactly what he was already doing in Pakistan and Afghanistan. And the endorsement had come from General David Petraeus, who was perhaps the most influential general of his generation. It was, Furlong figured, like getting a blessing from the pope.

But the CIA did not consider Furlong so anointed and decided he needed to be shut down for good. On December 2, 2009, the CIA's station chief in Kabul sent a withering cable to Washington laying out a detailed case against him. The bill of particulars included allegations that Furlong was running an off-the-books spy ring and lying to his superiors about the nature of his operation. It even made reference to the Prague episode of the previous year, providing details about why Furlong left the Czech Republic in a hurry during the summer of 2008.

The station chief's memo argued that having a bunch of private contractors running around Pakistan spying for the Pentagon, without coordinating their operations with the CIA, could have disastrous consequences. What the cable didn't mention, but some senior officials believed, was that intelligence from Furlong's private spies had led directly to a drone strike on a suspected al Qaeda safe house in North Waziristan in late 2009 that killed more than a dozen Arab men, including several who were working as double agents for Pakistan's ISI. ISI leaders were furious that the agents had been killed, and they complained to the CIA. The agency, in turn, complained to the military and blamed Furlong's spying operation.

The CIA was now in open warfare with Furlong, and even his supporters could no longer protect him. The station chief's cable launched a wave of investigations into Furlong's activities. By the spring of 2010 security officers at San Antonio's Lackland Air Force Base had cut off his access to classified computer networks and barred him from his office.

He was in limbo—not charged with any crimes but not able to defend himself, because he could not get access to any of his classified

THE OLD MAN'S RETURN | 209

records. He spent nearly all of his time inside his sparsely furnished condominium, in a bland apartment complex in San Antonio, trying to prepare his defense and hiding from the television reporters who had gathered outside of his gate when news of the spying operation broke.

The Pentagon's final report on the matter pinned almost all the blame on Furlong, calling his spying operation "unauthorized" and accusing him of misleading top American commanders about the legality of the work of the contractors. But he avoided any criminal charges and quietly retired from the Defense Department.

Furlong had certainly cut corners, and his attempts to evade standard bureaucratic procedures created confusion up and down the military's chain of command. But in Furlong's view of the world, these were small matters when American troops were dying and the CIA was not helping the military win the war in Afghanistan. His spying operation was essential, he said later, "when there are lives at stake and the CIA is relying on foreign services for all its information."

And Furlong wasn't exactly a rogue operator. The entire episode was born from the frustrations of an American general in Afghanistan who didn't trust the CIA and who set Michael Furlong loose. If, as the Pentagon investigation into the operation concluded, nobody "connected the dots" about what Furlong was doing, it was because nobody wanted to.

"My bosses wanted all of this," Furlong said, smoking the fifth cigarette of a lengthy interview. "And I made it happen."

THE LOCKHEED MARTIN CONTRACT that Michael Furlong had secured expired at the end of May 2010, and the money funding Dewey Clarridge's network of agents in Pakistan and Afghanistan ran dry.

Clarridge was angry that the military had chosen not to renew the contract, and even angrier that the CIA seemed to be the reason that the operation had been shut down. He had sent hundreds of intelligence reports to military commanders in Afghanistan, and he sent a message to Kabul on May 15 that he would stop sending the reports so he could "prepare approximately 200 local personnel to cease work."

But Clarridge had no intention of dismantling his network. The very next day, he set up a password-protected Web site that would allow military officers to continue viewing his dispatches, and he leaned on some wealthy friends to help keep his network afloat. He set up a front company for his operation, the Eclipse Group, and on his Web site he posted the same types of intelligence reports he had once given to the military. There were specific reports about how Pakistan's ISI was training gunmen to launch attacks into Afghanistan, and about how Pakistani spies were secretly keeping Taliban leader Mullah Mohammed Omar under house arrest so they could later install him as their puppet in southern Afghanistan once American troops left the country. Another report speculated that Mullah Omar had suffered a heart attack and was rushed to the hospital by ISI operatives.

He dreamt up ever more exotic schemes to bring down those he thought were trying to undermine the American war effort. For instance, he was convinced that Afghan president Hamid Karzai was secretly negotiating with Iran as part of a desperate attempt to sell out the Americans and remain in power in Kabul, so Clarridge cooked up a plan to dig up hard evidence to prove long-standing rumors that Karzai was a heroin addict.

The plan was straight from the old CIA playbook of dirty tricks: He would insert an agent into the presidential palace in Kabul to collect Karzai's beard trimmings, run drug tests, and then give the proof to American commanders in Kabul, who could confront Karzai with the incriminating evidence and turn the Afghan president into a more pliable ally. He dropped the plan after the Obama administration signaled it was committed to bolstering the Karzai government, not pushing the Afghan president out of power.

Even when news of the private spying operation went public and military officials grew worried about accepting information from Clarridge's network, he found other ways to get his information to the public. Clarridge's friends sent the reports to pro-military writers like Brad Thor, a successful author of spy thrillers, who dispensed some of Clarridge's information on blog posts. He even pushed information to Oliver North, his old compatriot from the Iran–Contra days, now an on-air personality on Fox News.

It was just like the old days, when Dewey and Ollie were doing the work they thought nobody else had the guts to do.

12: THE SCALPEL'S EDGE

"We'll continue saying the bombs are ours, not yours."

—*President Ali Abdullah Saleh*

T he meeting was set up for a surrender, a symbolic gesture of peace timed to the holy month of Ramadan. The Saudi minister had even sent his personal jet to pick up the frail young man and deliver him to Jeddah, Saudi Arabia's second city built along the shores of the Red Sea. There, Prince Muhammad bin Nayef was conducting the Ramadan custom of greeting well-wishers at his home, and he gave an order to his coterie of aides that Abdullah al-Asiri be allowed to bypass normal security procedures and not be searched as he entered the palace.

Al-Asiri had contacted Prince bin Nayef, the assistant interior minister and a member of the Saudi ruling family, days earlier, announcing his intention to surrender to the Saudi spy service and provide information about the group he had joined two years earlier, an offshoot of Osama bin Laden's terror network that had recently rebranded itself al Qaeda in the Arabian Peninsula (AQAP). The group considered Prince bin Nayef its bête noire, a man committed to crushing Sunni extremism in both Saudi Arabia and Yemen, the country's impoverished neighbor to the south. In 2003, when militants in Yemen launched a twenty-month campaign of violence inside Saudi Arabia—blowing up Saudi government buildings and oil facilities, bombing residential compounds used by foreigners, and beheading Westerners—bin Nayef ordered a bloody crackdown involving arresting and torturing thousands of suspects rounded up inside the country. He posted informants inside mosques he believed had been infiltrated by extremists.

Bin Nayef's aggression against al Qaeda had made him a friend of the Bush administration, and by the summer of 2009 a new American president and his aides already considered the prince an indispensable ally. He regularly received dignitaries from Washington, including a visit in May 2009 from a veteran diplomat whom President Obama had just charged with trying to manage an acceptable end to the war in Afghanistan. But when Richard Holbrooke met the prince in Riyadh to solicit the kingdom's help with a war America was losing, the prince warned that the United States might have a far greater worry than the spiraling violence in Afghanistan. "We have a problem called Yemen," bin Nayef told Holbrooke.

The prince ticked off a list of worries to the American envoy. Yemen's tribes were more sympathetic to al Qaeda than were Afghans, and Yemen was closer to al Qaeda's targets in Saudi Arabia than was Afghanistan. Yemen was a failed state, he said, with a weak and corrupt leader in President Ali Abdullah Saleh, whose vision for the country had "shrunk to Sana'a"—keeping the capital, and his base, secure. Saleh had always managed to keep Yemen's tribes in check, he said, but the president was losing control and passing more power over to his son, who didn't have close ties to the tribes. Cash payments to Saleh's government were useless, the Saudi said, because the president and those around him move the money out of the country as soon as it arrives.

"The money ends up in Swiss bank accounts," Prince bin Nayef told Holbrooke.

Instead, the Saudi government had begun paying for development projects in areas of Yemen where al Qaeda militants had put down roots, in the hope that the projects might drain away support for extremists and "persuade Yemenis to see extremists as criminals rather than heroes." At the end of their meeting, Holbrooke promised the prince that President Obama would work with the kingdom to dismantle al Qaeda's growing network in Yemen.

It was a stroke of luck, bin Nayef figured, when Abdullah al-Asiri contacted the Saudis three months later with his offer to surrender. Al-Asiri was one of eighty-five militants associated with "deviant groups" that the Saudis had been hunting, as was the young man's older brother Ibrahim. Ibrahim had been arrested for trying to join the insurgency in Iraq in 2003, and his time in prison in Saudi Arabia had kindled in him a hatred for the kingdom and its alliance with the United States, which he likened to the relationship between master and slave. Of the two brothers, it was Ibrahim whom the Saudis considered far more dangerous; he had been trained as a bomb maker, with a sinister gift for finding creative ways to hide explosives. Conscious that the Saudis might suspect the planned "surrender" was an elaborate subterfuge for the al-Asiri brothers to take revenge against Prince bin Nayef, Ibrahim devised a bomb that could evade standard security precautions. Shortly before the younger al-Asiri boarded the Saudi royal's jet for the flight to Jeddah, Ibrahim had a bomb of pentaerythritol tetranitrate—a type of plastic explosive—implanted in Abdullah's rectum.

But for all of Ibrahim's genius as a bomb maker, his lethal plots were often undone by the incompetence of his bombers. His brother had traveled with the hidden explosive from Yemen to Jeddah and arrived without incident at Prince bin Nayef's palace. After the nervous Abdullah al-Asiri entered the room where the prince was receiving visitors, he reached into his robe to trigger the explosives but set the bomb off too early, before he was close enough to the prince. The explosion blew al-Asiri in half, leaving a smoking crater on the tiled floor and bloodstains throughout the room. Prince bin Nayef received only minor wounds from the blast.

The attack was a failure. But al Qaeda in the Arabian Peninsula had managed to carry out its first operation outside of Yemen. If the group was embarrassed by the clumsiness of its assassin, it gave no indication in a boastful message it released shortly after the attack. It was the Saudis who should be embarrassed, the statement read, because Abdullah al-Asiri's security breach was the first of its kind in Saudi Arabia's history, and the militant group was in the process of uprooting a Saudi spy network in Yemen that the royal family had set up to infiltrate AQAP.

For those in Riyadh now living in fear, and those in Washington now paying attention, the statement promised more attacks to come:

"Oh tyrants, rest assured that you will suffer, because your fortress won't be able to protect you from us.

"We will reach you soon."

THE DAY AFTER Barack Obama was sworn in as the forty-fourth president of the United States, Prince bin Nayef received a call from an old friend in Washington. The man on the other end of the phone was John Brennan, a former top CIA officer who had advised Senator Obama during the campaign and had been tapped as Obama's senior counterterrorism adviser in the White House. It wasn't the job Brennan had wanted. At the end of the presidential campaign he was assumed to be the leading candidate to take over the CIA, were Obama elected. He had the right credentials: A son of Irish immigrants, Brennan was raised in New Jersey and attended Fordham University; he had spent decades as a CIA analyst and spoke fluent Arabic. He even had the rare experience of serving as a CIA station chief in Riyadh in the 1990s, despite being an analyst, not an undercover case officer. A large man with a face that looked like it had been carved from a slab of limestone, Brennan had the appearance of a Depression-era boxer.

But his dream of taking over the CIA was thwarted during Obama's transition, when remarks he had made—seeming to endorse the brutal interrogation methods the CIA had used in secret prisons— resurfaced and were criticized by human-rights activists. Brennan had been among George Tenet's top advisers when the prison pro- gram was put in place, in 2002, and therefore was closely tethered to a program that Obama had frequently said was a dark stain on Amer- ica's record since the September 11 attacks. Fearing a lengthy and distracting confirmation battle in the Senate, Brennan withdrew his name from consideration for the CIA job.

The position in the White House may have been a consolation prize, but in a short time Brennan would turn his windowless base- ment office in the West Wing into an operations hub for the clan- destine wars that President Obama would champion as president. Obama's desire to manage aspects of the targeted-killing program directly from the White House gave Brennan a role unique in the his- tory of American government: one part executioner, one part chief confessor to the president, one part public spokesman sent out to jus- tify the Obama doctrine of killing off America's enemies in remote parts of the world.

When Brennan called bin Nayef that day in January 2009, he pledged to the man he had come to know well since his days in Ri- yadh that President Obama was just as committed to hunting and killing terrorists as President Bush had been. During the transition after Obama's election, Brennan and the other senior members of Obama's national-security team had been briefed over two days at CIA headquarters, where top agency officials ran through the list of covert-action programs on the books. The head of the Counterterrorism Center, the undercover officer with the first name Mike, told the group that President Bush had accelerated the pace of drone strikes the previous summer and that the CIA was trying to get more spies into Pakistan. During the presidential campaign, Obama had repeatedly pledged that he would focus attention on Pakistan, Afghanistan, and the hunt for Osama bin Laden—a renewed emphasis on the so-called "good war" that Bush had ignored by starting the "bad war" in Iraq. At the meetings, Brennan told Mike and Stephen Kappes, the deputy CIA director whom Obama had asked to stay in his job at Langley, that the drone killings in Pakistan were likely to continue under Obama's watch.

There was another reason that Obama, Brennan, and other senior members of the new administration would come to rely on targeted killing as an important instrument of counterterrorism. During the campaign, Obama had often spoken about how the secret detentions and interrogation techniques of the Bush era had sullied America's image, and during his first week in office he announced a plan to close the prison at Guantánamo Bay and ban all of the coercive interrogation methods used by the CIA since the September 11 attacks. The decision was immediately denounced by Dick Cheney, the former vice president, as a cynical move by a callow president playing politics at the expense of national security. If there was a major terrorist attack while Obama was president, Cheney warned, it would be Obama's fault for denying the CIA the tools it needed to keep the country safe.

Cheney's vituperative comments, coming immediately after he left the White House, were a significant breach of the standard protocol that an outgoing administration doesn't criticize the incoming president—at least in the early months. But the Cheney critique was meant as a warning shot, a signal that any evidence of Barack Obama being "weak" on national security issues would become grist for partisan attacks against the new president.

As he sat in the meetings with the new team, John Rizzo, a career CIA lawyer who had achieved a degree of infamy for his role in getting Justice Department approval for the CIA's detention-and-interrogation program, was struck by the hawkish tone of Obama's aides. "They never came out and said they would start killing people because they couldn't interrogate them, but the implication was unmistakable," Rizzo said. "Once the interrogation was gone, all that was left was the killing."

The options for interrogating prisoners weren't, as Rizzo said, "gone." But interrogation and detention had clearly become a briar patch for the new administration: Besides the decision to shut Guantánamo Bay within a year, there were also concerns among Obama's team that capturing prisoners and handing them over to foreign governments could ignite liberal criticism that the administration was outsourcing torture. At the same time, no prominent member of President Obama's own party had criticized drone strikes, and Republicans were hardly in a position to challenge the new president for fighting *too* aggressive a campaign against terrorists. The political conditions were set for an escalation of the secret wars.

The meetings over two days at Langley were the first sign that President Obama planned to rely on the CIA and Joint Special Operations Command in ways that not even George W. Bush and Dick Cheney had, as America's primary tool to conduct lethal operations. Seven years after the September 11 attacks, the wars of Iraq and Afghanistan had exhausted the American public and drained the American purse. More important, though, the tools of secret war had been calibrated and refined during that period, and Obama's team thought they saw an opportunity to wage war without the staggering costs of the big military campaigns that topple governments, require years of occupation, and catalyze radicalization throughout the Muslim world. As Brennan described the Obama administration's approach during one speech, the United States could use a "scalpel" rather than a "hammer" to carry out war beyond war zones.

Obama wasn't the first liberal Democratic president to embrace black operations. John F. Kennedy gave final approval for the Bay of Pigs operation and ramped up covert operations in Vietnam. And, for all the time that Jimmy Carter spent railing against CIA adventures as a presidential candidate, he ended up authorizing a string of covert actions during his final two years in the White House.

But Barack Obama was also the first president to enter the White House who had come of age after the Vietnam War and the roiling events of the 1960s and 1970s that had fostered cynicism among an earlier generation about the CIA and, more broadly, about the use of American power overseas. In one 2010 interview, Obama told reporter Bob Woodward that he was "probably the first president who is young enough that the Vietnam War wasn't at the core of my development," and so he grew up with "none of the baggage that arose out of the dispute of the Vietnam War." It was an answer to a question about the tensions between the military and civilians during the Vietnam era, but clearly Obama also had a view of the CIA that was generationally different from that of baby boomers like Bill Clinton.

The CIA's ascendancy during the Obama administration wasn't just about the age of the man sitting in the Oval Office, or about the nature of the threats Obama learned about each day during his intelligence briefing. It also had to do with the fact that Obama's first CIA director turned out to be, in terms of his ability to advance the spy agency's interests inside the executive branch, the most influential CIA director since William Casey during the Reagan administration.

LEON E. PANETTA SEEMED at first an extremely unlikely choice to take over the CIA. He had no professional background in intelligence or military affairs outside of a two-year Army stint in the 1960s. During his years as a Democratic congressman representing a coastal pocket of Northern California, he never served on the committees overseeing either the Pentagon or the CIA. He was outwardly warm and avuncular but also a fierce backroom negotiator and fighter who slung four-letter words around a room as frequently as he did prepositions. He had had glancing contact with the intelligence world during his time as President Clinton's chief of staff, but that had been a very different era and a very different CIA.

When Panetta took over as CIA director, he had literally no idea that the CIA was killing people around the world. By early 2009, the CIA's targeted-killing campaign using drones in Pakistan was being extensively reported in the press. And yet, incredibly, Panetta was shocked to learn during his initial briefings for the CIA job that he would be, in effect, a military commander for a secret war. "He was a total blank slate on intelligence issues when he walked into the door at Langley," said Rizzo, who had helped prepare a set of briefings for Panetta before his Senate confirmation hearings. But what he lacked in tangible experience in issues of life and death he made up for in Washington savvy. Panetta had two of the qualities the ever-paranoid CIA looked for in a director: clout and respect within the White House and a willingness to defend the CIA's turf against the agency's perceived enemies in Washington.

Both of these qualities were tested immediately, after White House officials decided to end a long-standing legal battle and declassify the internal memos authorizing the CIA's interrogation methods during the early years of the Bush administration. Panetta had already made his views on the interrogation methods known during his confirmation hearings, saying unequivocally that they were nothing short of "torture." The statement had sent shocks through parts of the CIA's clandestine service and created suspicions that the new CIA director was going to be the second coming of Stansfield Turner, an outsider that a liberal president sent out to Langley to rein in what the White House believed was a spy agency out of control.

But the very opposite happened. Panetta became a CIA champion, beloved by many at Langley but criticized by others who said that, like so many CIA directors before him, he had been co-opted by the agency's clandestine branch. Within a month of his arrival he had managed to delay the release of the interrogation memos and forced a debate inside the White House about the propriety of spilling all the details of the defunct prison program.

Panetta had by that time experienced firsthand the influence that the CIA's Directorate of Operations has over spy chiefs at Langley. Both Stephen Kappes and officers at the Counterterrorism Center warned him that releasing the memos would devastate morale inside the CTC. The warning came with an implied threat: He risked permanently losing the support of the agency's clandestine workforce before he had even figured out how to get from his office to the CIA cafeteria. Panetta had spent enough time in Washington to know the implications of what he was hearing. He risked becoming another John Deutch or Porter Goss, men who had clashed with the Directorate of Operations and found their tenure at the agency to be nasty, brutish, and short. Panetta was sold.

He was on his first overseas trip as CIA director when he learned about the White House's plans to declassify and release the interrogation memos—complying with a federal judge's order in a Freedom of Information Act lawsuit brought by the American Civil Liberties

Union. He immediately called Obama's chief of staff, Rahm Emanuel, and urged him to put off the release. The two men had known each other from the Clinton White House, and it was Emanuel who had pushed for Panetta's appointment to the CIA. Emanuel went along with Panetta's request, and in the weeks that followed, Panetta made an impassioned case at the White House for keeping the memos secret, winning Emanuel over to his side. It was a curious, almost otherworldly moment: A man who had publicly accused the CIA of breaking American law by committing acts of torture was forcefully arguing that the details of those acts be kept secret from the public.

Panetta ultimately lost the debate, and President Obama ordered that the memos be released. But it hardly mattered for the new CIA director. By insisting that the White House at least debate the issue, he had proved to the agency's rank and file that he had clout inside the new administration. More important, he had gone to the mat on an issue that was deeply important to the clandestine service. He had shown, as many inside the CIA saw it, that he was part of the team.

IT WAS ANOTHER MATTER entirely for the man who, at least on paper, was Leon Panetta's boss. Admiral Dennis Blair, who had been sent to the CIA during the Clinton administration to serve as a liaison to the Pentagon, had vaulted up the Navy's senior ranks in the years since and ended his military career as a four-star admiral in charge of the U.S. Pacific Command. The job had given him oversight of more than a third of the earth's surface, and his orders were obeyed by troops spread across hundreds of thousands of square miles. But Blair, now retired from the military, was taking over a job that remained ill defined four years after the Bush administration created the Director of National Intelligence position under pressure from Congress and the 9/11 Commission to account for the intelligence failures preceding the September 11 attacks and the Iraq war. Some had envisioned the intelligence post to be a powerful job, riding herd over a fractious collection of spy agencies housed in different departments. But Donald Rumsfeld's allies in Congress were successful in neutering the new position, and the Pentagon retained much of the intelligence community's budget. These bureaucratic knife fights meant that by the time Blair took over the post in early 2009 both the Pentagon and the CIA had ensured that he would be little more than a figurehead.

Making things worse, Blair saw right away that he was an outsider in a close-knit group of advisers who had been with President Obama through much of the grueling campaign—a group Blair referred to disparagingly as the "Long Marchers," in reference to the military retreat over thousands of miles by the Chinese Communists in 1934. His suspicions were borne out during an early scrape with Panetta. Blair began pushing for the authority to appoint the senior American spy in each country overseas, a designation that by tradition automatically went to the CIA's chief of station. It was a relatively minor issue, but Panetta and his deputy, Stephen Kappes, saw it as a threat to the CIA's authority and lobbied the White House to reject Blair's plan. With the proposal languishing at the White House during the summer of 2009, Blair decided he didn't need to wait for a White House decision and issued an order directing the change. He informed Panetta about his decision during a short, tense phone call. Panetta slammed down the phone.

"That guy is a fucking asshole," he told a group of aides gathered in his office. The very next day, a secret cable from Panetta was blasted to all CIA stations overseas. The cable carried a simple message: Ignore Blair's directive.

Not used to having his orders disobeyed, Blair complained to James Jones, Obama's national security advisor, that Panetta was being insubordinate and ought to be fired. The White House sided with the CIA.

Blair had long held a dim view of the CIA's history of covert-action programs. He believed that too many presidents, too often in American history, used the CIA as a crutch when their advisers couldn't agree on how to handle a particularly thorny foreign-policy issue. And, he thought, covert-action programs usually lasted years beyond their value to the country.

So when, during his first year in office, President Obama ordered a review of the roughly one dozen covert-action programs the CIA was carrying out at the time, from the drone strikes in Pakistan to a campaign to sabotage Iran's nuclear work, Blair hoped the process would be a chance to inspect the wiring on each program and decide whether it made any sense to continue it. Instead, the summer 2009 meetings effectively rubber-stamped all of the CIA's secret ventures. At the meetings, Stephen Kappes argued forcefully for why each program had been a success and needed to continue. By the time a "principals committee" meeting was scheduled for the fall, when President Obama's top national security advisers would make final decisions on the covert-action programs, not one of them was under consideration for cancellation.

Blair watched with frustration as the process unfolded. He approached Robert Gates, the defense secretary who had spent most of his Washington career in the CIA. Gates had seen his share of covert actions blow up, and Blair knew that Gates had clout inside the White House. Gates agreed with Blair that they should draw up a list of basic principles to guide decisions on covert-action programs. The list of six principles they cobbled together were fairly innocuous: They included a provision that covert-action programs should constantly be evaluated for transition to noncovert activities and another that the programs should not undermine "the development of stable, non-corrupt, and representative governments that respect the human rights of their citizens."

When President Obama's top advisers gathered at the White House to discuss the covert-action programs, Blair passed around the list. He and Gates had hoped to turn the meeting into a forum to discuss the general wisdom of CIA covert action, and the meeting dragged on for hours as Blair tried to force a debate about each secret program. Blair recalled that "the CIA had wanted to just push [covert-action] programs through," and with each pointed question that Blair asked, both Leon Panetta and Deputy National Security Advisor Tom Donilon grew angrier.

It wasn't just that Panetta thought that Blair was grandstanding; he thought that he was attempting to take from the CIA what the spy agency had guarded jealously since its 1947 founding—a direct line to the president for getting covert actions approved. Panetta believed that the list that Blair and Gates had assembled put unnecessary restrictions on President Obama's ability to authorize secret operations.

Blair's efforts failed, and the Obama administration approved every one of the covert-action programs that had been handed down by President Bush. The CIA had secured yet another victory, and Blair's standing inside the White House was permanently crippled.

Even as the Obama administration discussed the future of the CIA's covert-action programs, there was no thought about ending the targeted-killing efforts. Quite the opposite. In the early months of the administration, National Security Advisor James Jones led a project to compile a centralized "kill list" for lethal operations beyond declared war zones. What came to be known as the Jones Memo was an early attempt by the Obama administration to establish procedures for the conduct of a secret war that most believed would last years beyond President Obama's time in the White House. The list was maintained by the National Security Council, and as much as some officials tried to keep strict criteria about who could be added to the kill list, those criteria were sometimes eased.

At the start of the Obama administration, for instance, the CIA was not authorized to kill Baitullah Mehsud, who had emerged as the undisputed leader of the Pakistani Taliban since the days when Art Keller first heard his name while serving at one of the agency's bases in the tribal areas. The Pakistani Taliban, known inside the country as the Tehrik-i-Taliban Pakistan (TTP), was attacking Pakistani military installations and government facilities in a grisly spasm of violence. Pakistan's civilian government, which came to power after President Musharraf stepped aside, began pressing the Obama administration to kill Mehsud with an armed drone, just as the CIA had killed his predecessor, Nek Muhammad. But the answer was no. During one private meeting in early 2009, CIA deputy director Stephen Kappes told Husain Haqqani, Pakistan's ambassador to Washington, that since Mehsud and his followers had not attacked the United States, the CIA couldn't get legal approval to kill him.

Some conspiracy theorists in Pakistan had a more cynical view of why the United States was refusing to kill Mehsud: that he was in fact a secret agent of India, and the United States had promised New Delhi that Mehsud would not be harmed. But as the Pakistanis continued to press, CIA lawyers began circulating legal memos making a case that since the Pakistani Taliban sheltered al Qaeda operatives, and since it was increasingly difficult to distinguish between groups bent on attacking inside Pakistan and those focused on hitting the West, senior TTP leaders could justifiably be put on the kill list. Besides the legal rationale, some thought there could be diplomatic benefits if the CIA were to kill Pakistan's most dangerous enemy.

On a warm evening in early August 2009, a CIA drone hovering over the village of Zanghara, in South Waziristan, trained its camera on a rooftop where Baitullah Mehsud and several members of his family were taking in the night air. Mehsud, a diabetic, was receiving an intravenous insulin drip when the drone launched a missile that killed everyone on the roof. Pakistani officials cheered the killing, and some in Washington described the drone strike as a "goodwill kill."

Leon Panetta had taken to his new role as military commander, and his time at Langley would be known for the CIA's aggressive—some would come to believe reckless—campaign of targeted killings. At the end of his CIA tenure, Panetta, a devout Catholic, joked that he had "said more Hail Marys in the last two years than I have in my whole life."

Two months after Baitullah Mehsud's killing, Leon Panetta arrived at the White House with a long list of requests for CIA paramilitary operations. He sought more armed drones and approval to ask Pakistan's permission for the drones to fly over larger swaths of the tribal areas, what the CIA called "flight boxes." President Obama, at the urging of Vice President Joe Biden, had already agreed to increase the number of covert officers inside Pakistan, many of whom were operating in the country without the knowledge of the ISI.

The CIA requests to expand its drone fleet did raise eyebrows, and some officials openly questioned why a spy agency was moving so far from its primary mission of collecting and analyzing intelligence. General James Cartwright, the vice chairman of the Joint Chiefs of Staff, asked on several occasions, "Can you tell me why we are building a second Air Force?" Others thought that the CIA had become so enamored of its killer drones that it wasn't pushing its analysts to ask a basic question: To what extent might the drone strikes be creating more terrorists than they are actually killing? But by the end of the meeting in the Situation Room, President Obama had granted every one of Panetta's requests. "The CIA gets what it wants," the president said.

BUT EVEN WITH the new resources, the CIA's war in the mountains of Pakistan still consumed the bulk of the intelligence community's drones, spy satellites, and case officers. That left little for a different war, three thousand miles to the west, that President Obama's advisers were quietly expanding. The assassination attempt on Prince bin Nayef in August 2009 created a new urgency in Washington to take on the al Qaeda–affiliated group in Yemen that had announced its intentions to strike at the West.

In late 2009, there was only a small cluster of American soldiers and spies stationed inside the U.S. embassy in Sana'a. In addition to the CIA's station in the country, the Pentagon had kept a group of special-operations troops in Yemen since 2002, but the wars in Iraq and Afghanistan had for years been a higher priority than the mission in Yemen. But with the Iraq war now winding down, Joint Special Operations Command had more Navy SEALs to devote to new missions.

General David Petraeus, the commander of American forces in the Middle East, had been worried about the growing influence of al Qaeda in the Arabian Peninsula since he assumed control of U.S. Central Command the previous year. In late September 2009, Petraeus signed off on the classified order to expand American military spying in Yemen and elsewhere, the same order that Michael Furlong had used to justify his intelligence-gathering operation in Pakistan. It authorized the military to conduct a host of unconventional missions in Yemen, from broader eavesdropping activities to paying off locals for information.

Admiral William McRaven, the JSOC commander, wanted to use in Yemen the same blueprint that commandos had used in Iraq to fight al Qaeda in Mesopotamia: frequent night raids to capture al Qaeda operatives, interrogate them for intelligence, and then use the information to carry out more snatch-and-grab operations. This model, relying on what commanders called the "cycle of intelligence," was already being duplicated in Afghanistan, and McRaven thought that getting more troops into Yemen could cripple AQAP's strength before it could successfully attack the United States.

But McRaven's ambitious ideas for Yemen were rejected in Washington as unrealistic. President Saleh, of Yemen, would never allow American ground troops to set up a detention-and-interrogation center inside Yemen, let alone permit capture-and-kill operations throughout the country. The White House had already run into fierce political opposition to its plans to close the prison at Guantánamo Bay, and the president's aides hardly relished the prospect of taking on a slew of new detainees picked up in Yemen. McRaven was told he needed to figure out a different way to wage war in Yemen.

What followed was a strange, half-baked campaign: a quasisecret war undermined by sometimes absurd attempts to hide the American hand in military operations. With little precise intelligence about the whereabouts of militant leaders, and the Yemeni president's refusal since 2002 to permit armed drones, war planners were forced to rely on cruise missiles fired from Navy ships off Yemen's coast and occasional bombing runs by Marine Harrier jets. The results were unsightly, and over the next several months the American strikes in Yemen would claim more civilian casualties than senior operatives affiliated with al Qaeda in the Arabian Peninsula.

The first American strike came on December 17, 2009. The Americans had intercepted communications from a terrorist camp in Abyan province, a remote expanse of desert and coastal villages running south to the port city of Aden. AQAP was in the final stages of sending a group of suicide bombers to attack the U.S. embassy in Sana'a.

In a video teleconference a day earlier, Admiral McRaven gave a detailed briefing to White House, Pentagon, and State Department officials about his plan to hit the camp. While the CIA generally had blanket approval to carry out drone strikes in Pakistan without getting White House permission, the military required a green light from a small team in Washington—a group nicknamed the "Counterterrorism Board of Directors," with John Brennan serving as chairman. The group would decide on a plan and then take its recommendation to President Obama, who personally signed off on each strike.

Obama approved the operation. The next day, a coded message went out to a small fleet of American ships patrolling the Arabian Sea, and within hours several Tomahawk cruise missiles slammed into the desert camp in Abyan. By the end of the day, Yemen's government had put out a press release hailing the success of the operation, saying that a strike by Yemen's air force had killed "around 34" al Qaeda fighters.

The following day, President Obama called Ali Abdullah Saleh to thank him for his cooperation, even though Yemeni troops had merely been a fig leaf for the American operation. Videos taken by locals at the camp revealed missile fragments with American markings and also proved that the Tomahawk missiles had been topped with cluster bombs—weapons designed to cut a wide path of destruction by dispersing smaller munitions over a wide area. Most of the dead were civilians, and bloody images of dead women and children went viral on YouTube. During a street protest after the strike, broadcast on Al Jazeera, one al Qaeda fighter shouldering an AK-47 made a direct appeal to Yemeni troops.

"Soldiers, you should know we do not want to fight you," he said. "There is no problem between you and us. The problem is between America and its agents. Beware of taking the side of America!"

THREE WEEKS AFTER the American strike, General Petraeus arrived in Sana'a to meet with President Saleh and his advisers about the next phase of the war. There was new urgency: On Christmas Day 2009, a young Nigerian man boarded a plane in Amsterdam bound for Detroit, and sewn into his underwear was the latest diabolical creation of Ibrahim al-Asiri, the master bomb maker of Yemen. As the plane made its final descent, Umar Farouk Abdulmutallab tried to set off the bomb—made with eighty grams of plastic explosives—using a syringe filled with liquid acid. Once again, Asiri's work was undone by the incompetence of his bomb carrier. Abdulmutallab set only his leg on fire, and other passengers quickly wrestled him to the ground. The hapless terrorist was taken into custody in Detroit, and the United States only narrowly averted its first large-scale terrorist incident of the Obama administration.

While the assassination attempt on Prince bin Nayef had been the first sign of AQAP's ambitions to strike beyond Yemen, the thwarted Christmas attack proved that the group was truly committed to continuing the work begun by Osama bin Laden and his now diminished band of al Qaeda operatives hiding in Pakistan. When General Petraeus's plane touched down in Yemen's capital in early January 2010, the Obama administration had already decided to escalate the American strikes in the country.

President Saleh had long been prickly about allowing Yemen to become a playground for secret American operations, so meetings between the Yemeni president and American officials often degenerated into horse-trading sessions. Petraeus began the ninety-minute meeting by softening up the Yemeni president: He praised him for his military's successful operations against AQAP and said that he had requested that cash payments to Yemen for counterterrorism operations nearly double, from $67 million to $105 million annually.

But the wily autocrat pushed for more. Raising the subject of the recent American airstrikes, Saleh said that "mistakes were made" in the killing of civilians in Abyan. Tomahawk cruise missiles were ill suited for a fight against terrorists, and civilian casualties could be averted if only the United States would give him a dozen helicopter gunships to swoop into terrorist camps. This, Saleh said, would allow him to spare the innocent and kill the guilty. If Washington wouldn't bless this request, Saleh said, maybe General Petraeus could pressure Saudi Arabia and the United Arab Emirates to contribute six helicopters each. Petraeus countered with a request of his own: Allow American special-operations troops and spies closer to the front lines in Yemen. That way, Petraeus said, Americans could download intelligence feeds from drone aircraft and satellites and use the intelligence to hit terrorist hideouts with greater speed and precision.

Saleh flatly rejected the request and told Petraeus that the Americans must stay inside an operations center that the CIA and JSOC had recently set up just outside of the capital city. But, he said, the air war could continue. He would allow American jets and bombers to loiter offshore and come into Yemeni airspace for specific missions if intelligence emerged about the whereabouts of AQAP leaders. He said he would keep up the ruse that the United States was not at war inside Yemen.

"We'll continue saying the bombs are ours, not yours," Saleh said.

The United States was slowly getting deeper into a war inside a country that Washington had long ignored and little understood. It was a war against a band of zealots punching above their weight in a fight against the world's only superpower, and the Obama administration still had only the vaguest ideas about how much support the

militants had and where they were hiding. It was hard to differenti-
ate between what was real intelligence and what was misinformation
handed to the Americans by Yemeni sources advancing their own
agendas.

Five months after Petraeus's meeting with Saleh, American missiles blew up the car of Jaber al-Shabwani, the deputy governor of
Ma'rib province and the man President Saleh had tapped to be a liaison between the Yemeni government and the al Qaeda faction. When
al-Shabwani and his bodyguards were killed, they were on the way to
meet with AQAP operatives to discuss a truce. But al-Shabwani's political rivals had told American special-operations troops in the country a different story: that the Yemeni politician was in league with al
Qaeda. The Americans had just been used to carry out a high-tech hit
to settle a tribal grudge.

The May 2010 strike provoked outrage across Yemen, and President Saleh demanded a halt to the airstrikes. Locals in Ma'rib set an
oil pipeline ablaze, and the fire burned for days. The American war in
Yemen was on hold, indefinitely.

IN WASHINGTON, America's greatest presidents are memorialized
with grand monuments, their most famous quotations etched into
blocks of white marble. The mediocre presidents get conference
rooms in downtown hotels named for them. On April 6, 2010, Dennis Blair descended the stairs into the basement of the Willard hotel,
a warren of conference rooms named after Millard Fillmore, Zachary
Taylor, Franklin Pierce, and James Buchanan. There, he delivered
what would be his last speech as director of national intelligence.

Blair's frustrations with the job were mounting, and he knew that
support for him was dwindling both within the White House and
among Washington's national security intelligentsia. Blair had arrived

that morning determined to air his concerns about the CIA and secret operations that he believed had run amok. Though his words were couched in diplomatic language, his message was clear.

The United States, he said, too often relied on covert action in a world where secrets were hard to protect and where the hand of the American government was difficult to keep hidden.

"There are many more overt tools of national power available to attack problems in areas of the world that were previously the place where only covert action could be applicable."

He never mentioned the CIA during the speech, but it was unmistakable that his words were directed at the agency, which he had watched amass tremendous power inside the Obama administration. By going public with his concerns Blair had violated one of the Obama administration's cardinal rules: Keep fights over national security matters inside the family. Even more significant, he was challenging one of the central pillars of President Obama's foreign policy: using the CIA as an instrument of secret war. Predictably, Leon Panetta and other senior officials at the CIA were incensed when they heard about Blair's speech. Just over a month later, President Obama fired Dennis Blair.

The CIA gets what it wants.

13: THE SCRAMBLE FOR AFRICA

"This is manna from heaven!"

—*Amira*

The MV *Faina*, a Ukrainian-owned merchant ship, was hugging the coastline of Somalia as it steamed toward Mombasa, Kenya, in September 2008. But it would not reach its final port of call. As it navigated a particularly treacherous stretch of water, more than a dozen armed men swarmed the ship in motorized skiffs, taking hostage the crew of seventeen Ukrainians, three Russians, and one Latvian.

When they went down into the ship's hold, the pirates couldn't believe their luck: The ship was carrying a clandestine cargo of thirty-three Russian T-72 tanks, dozens of boxes of grenades, and an arsenal of antiaircraft guns. The pirates had no way of knowing it, but the cargo had been part of a secret effort by Kenya's government to arm militias in southern Sudan in their fight against the government in Khartoum—a violation of a UN arms embargo. The Somali pirates had become experts in setting ransoms based on the value of their cargo, and soon after the ship's capture they began demanding as much as $35 million for a safe release of the crew, the ship, and its sensitive cargo.

American Navy vessels surrounded the ship within days, and helicopters flew over the *Faina*'s deck in an attempt to assess the health of the crew. But the hostage negotiations dragged on for weeks as the Ukrainian ship owners refused to cave to the pirates' demands. Frustrated by the lack of progress, the pirates decided they wanted a new mediator for the negotiations. They scrawled a message onto a white sheet and draped it over the *Faina*'s railing.

The message was just one word long: AMIRA.

Within days, Michele "Amira" Ballarin was at the center of the tense hostage negotiations with a group of pirates holding a ship full of Russian tanks. By the time the pirates made their demand, Ballarin had already been working with a group of Somali clan elders to negotiate the ransom and end the standoff, although she would later deny that she had any financial interest in the negotiations. Her interest was purely humanitarian, she said, providing satellite phones so that pirates could communicate with Somali elders on shore and so the *Faina*'s crew could communicate with their families. But the ship's Ukrainian owners grew angry about the meddling of this strange woman from Virginia. Hers was an unwanted presence; they figured she was only driving up the price of getting their crew and cargo released. "She has to understand that offering criminals a huge amount of money, which by the way she doesn't have—she is only giving them false hope," said a company spokesman.

Ukraine's government even intervened. In early February 2009, just weeks after the Obama administration took office, Ukraine foreign minister Volodymyr Ohryzko wrote a letter to Secretary of State Hillary Clinton about the woman who, he said with a flourish, had "become an intermediary of the sea corsairs." Ballarin's actions, the Ukrainian minister went on, "incite the pirates to the groundless increase of the ransom sum," and he asked Clinton "to facilitate the exclusion of [her] from the negotiation process with the pirates."

Hillary Clinton would have had no reason to know who Michele

Ballarin was before receiving the letter from the Ukrainian minister, but plenty of other American officials did. By the time President Obama came into office, Ballarin had been given a contract with the Pentagon to gather intelligence inside Somalia, just one of the myriad projects for which she had tried to gain the approval of the United States government, with varying degrees of success.

Her efforts back in 2006 to organize a Sufi resistance to fight al Shabaab hadn't yet panned out, but she wasn't deterred. Using a number of different front companies with vague and portentous names like BlackStar, Archangel, and the Gulf Security Group, she hatched several new ventures designed to make her an indispensable partner to the American military and intelligence services. She converted a historic hotel in rural Virginia into a secure facility—with reinforced walls and encrypted locks—that she hoped the CIA or Pentagon might use to store classified information. She was unsuccessful in getting any government agencies to rent the space.

She hired a number of retired American military officers and spies, including former CIA officer Ross Newland who had left the spy agency to become a consultant, to help her get meetings with senior members of Washington's national security establishment. Working with a former Army sergeant major named Perry Davis, a stocky retired Green Beret with years of military service in Southeast Asia, Ballarin briefly considered the idea of scouting for bases on remote islands in the Philippines and Indonesia she thought could be used to train indigenous troops for clandestine counterterrorist missions, but mostly she kept her focus on Africa.

In August 2007, she wrote a letter to the CIA in which she announced herself as the president of Gulf Security Group, a company based in the United Arab Emirates with a "singular objective": hunting and killing "Al Qai'da terrorist networks, infrastructure and personnel in the Horn of Africa."

The letter went on:

"Gulf Security Group is owned and controlled by the undersigned United States citizens with no foreign interests or influence. We have deep relationships with indigenous clans and political leaders in Somalia, Kenya, Uganda and throughout the Horn of Africa, including the Islamic Courts Union, and those who control their militant and jihadist activities. These relationships will enable successful mission outcome without fingerprint, footprint or flag, and provide total deniability."

To such a breathtaking proposal, a CIA lawyer sent back a terse response. "The CIA is not interested in your unsolicited proposal and does not authorize you to undertake any activities on its behalf. I am returning your proposal," wrote John L. McPherson, the agency's associate general counsel. Ballarin's proposal to cobble together indigenous hit squads, McPherson wrote, might violate the Neutrality Act, a law that prohibits private citizens from raising private overseas armies.

As far-fetched as her offer seemed, Ballarin might just have had bad timing. Just a year earlier the CIA was still paying Erik Prince and Enrique Prado for their roles in the killing program that had been outsourced to Blackwater employees. But the agency had decided in the middle of 2006 that the Blackwater program should be shuttered, exactly because of the concerns raised in McPherson's letter about the propriety of hiring private citizens to play a part in targeted-killing operations. The CIA wasn't about to entertain a similar proposal from a mysterious woman with no track record of participating in clandestine operations.

Having been denied the opportunity to kill for the CIA, Ballarin next proposed spying for the military. In this, she had greater success. In the spring of 2008, Ballarin and Perry Davis arrived at a nondescript office building across from the Pentagon, where they had a meeting at the headquarters of the Combating Terrorism Technical Support Office. The CTTSO is a small outfit with a modest budget for giving seed money to classified military counterterrorism programs, and a contact inside the Pentagon had helped set up the meeting for Ballarin. But few inside the CTTSO office knew the first thing about the well-dressed woman standing before them. Introducing herself as the head of a company called BlackStar, Ballarin was blunt.

"I'm going to fix Somalia," she said.

Ballarin and Davis outlined a plan to set up a humanitarian food program that would be a cover to collect intelligence. Pallets of food aid would arrive by ship at a Somali port, be loaded onto trucks, and be driven to aid stations her team was planning to set up around the country. According to the plan, the Somalis who arrived at the food stations would give their names and other identifying information, and in return they would receive identification cards. The information gathered at the food stations, Ballarin told the military officials, could be fed into Pentagon databases and used both to map Somalia's complex tribal structure and, possibly, to help the United States hunt the leaders of al Shabaab.

Ballarin said she would fund much of the program out of her own pocket but was looking for both the Pentagon's blessing and additional funding. Ballarin and Davis gave few specifics about how they intended to make the operation work, but they managed to sell the plan. Shortly afterward, the Pentagon office promised BlackStar an initial sum of approximately $200,000, with a pledge for more if the program began to show promise. For the first time, Michele Ballarin had received the American government's imprimatur for clandestine work in Africa.

———

A NUMBER OF FACTORS had converged to pave Michele Ballarin's path for the intelligence-gathering operation in Somalia. The first, and most obvious, was the lack of any solid information about a country that some in Washington had vague fears about becoming a terror state in the mold of Afghanistan as it was before the September 11 attacks. The CIA was consumed by the drone war in Pakistan and supporting military operations in Iraq and Afghanistan, leaving the agency with few resources for spying inside Somalia. Besides, with the CIA still feeling burned by 2006's disastrous covert campaign with warlords there, few in Langley had much interest at the time in wading back into the Somali muck. They also weren't sure it was worth it: During his exit interview with reporters at the end of the Bush administration, CIA director Michael Hayden dismissed the al Shabaab movement as insignificant.

At the same time, however, the Pentagon was beginning a push to escalate clandestine activities throughout Africa: from the Horn, across the Arab states of the northern part of the continent, to western countries like Nigeria. The creation of U.S. Africa Command in the fall of 2008, the Pentagon's first military headquarters devoted exclusively to operations in Africa, was another sign of increased attention to the world's second-largest and second-most-populous continent, after years of relative neglect. The Pentagon had a brand new military command post in Stuttgart, Germany—but not the intelligence to support any operations.

Nor a clear idea about exactly whom to support inside Somalia. Just months after President Obama took office, the new administration announced a decision to ship forty tons of weapons and ammunition to Somalia's embattled Transitional Federal Government, the United Nations–backed government that was considered by Somalis to be as corrupt as it was weak. By 2009 the TFG already controlled little territory beyond several square miles inside Mogadishu, and President Obama's team was in a panic over the possibility that an al Shabaab offensive in the capital might push the government out of central Mogadishu. With an embargo in place prohibiting foreign weapons from flooding into Somalia, the administration had to get the UN's approval for the arms shipments. The first weapons delivery arrived in June 2009, but Somali government troops didn't keep them for long. Instead, they sold the weapons that Washington had purchased for them in Mogadishu weapons bazaars. The arms market collapsed, and a new supply of cheap weapons was made available to al Shabaab fighters. By the end of the summer, American-made M16s could be found at the bazaars for just ninety-five dollars, and a more coveted AK-47 could be purchased for just five dollars more.

Clearly, the campaign in the Horn of Africa was still being waged in a haphazard and scattershot manner, with the United States conducting an outsourced war using proxy forces and warlords. Somalia was considered a threat, but not enough of a peril to merit an American military campaign there. So the doors opened for contractors like Ballarin who offered to fill the intelligence void, just as Dewey Clarridge had done for Pakistan.

Somalia was slowly turning into a haven for all manner of clandestine operations: from the secret counterterrorism missions of Western governments to wild schemes by contractors to chase pirates. One such plan was hatched with the help of Erik Prince, former head of the beleaguered Blackwater Worldwide, who had left the United States to begin a new chapter in the United Arab Emirates. There, he said, it would be hard for the "jackals"—trial lawyers and congressional investigators—to hound him and go after his money. Besides a secret project to help the UAE build a mercenary army of Colombian soldiers, an army that Emirati officials envisioned could be dispatched to put down domestic unrest in the country and even deter attacks from Iran, Prince began working with a group of South African mercenaries to help build a counterpiracy force in northern Somalia.

The UAE had grown worried about the pirates off the Horn of Africa who were picking off ships going to and from the Persian Gulf, and Emirati officials and Prince worked to develop a new strategy for combating piracy: Instead of trying to challenge the pirates on the high seas, a new militia would carry out raids in the pirate dens on land. Never one to dodge controversy, Prince met with officials from a South African company called Saracen International, a private security firm at the time run by Lafras Luitingh, a former officer in South Africa's apartheid-era Civil Cooperation Bureau. The CCB had a brutal record of carrying out assassinations and intimidating black South Africans, and after the fall of apartheid, many of its former members became guns for hire in the myriad civil wars of the African continent. The counterpiracy operation was just the latest below-the-radar adventure for Luitingh and the South African mercenaries in a part of the world that was still very much ignored.

Besides the efforts of private companies, the military's Joint Special Operations Command began paying greater attention to fighting a stealth war against militants in Somalia. Just as he had proposed for Yemen, Admiral William McRaven at JSOC discussed with officials in Washington a plan for a full-fledged special-operations task force for Somalia, modeled after the task force in Iraq that had eviscerated the al Qaeda affiliate there: Navy SEAL snatch-and-grab and prisoner interrogations in al Shabaab–held territories to dismantle the group.

Somalia was, compared with Yemen and Pakistan, both an easier and a more difficult environment for a clandestine war. Unlike Pakistan and Yemen, there was no central government for the Americans to work with, and no local intelligence service that could penetrate al Shabaab. On the other hand, Somalia presented none of the headaches of having to ask permission before the United States carried out a targeted-killing operation. There was no Ali Abdullah Saleh or Pervez Musharraf who needed to be courted, no secret cash payments for the right to wage war inside another country. Somalia was, as one senior military officer involved in planning Horn of Africa operations put it, "a complete free-fire zone."

But the JSOC proposals found little support. The baggage of the Black Hawk Down episode still weighed down any discussion of counterterrorism operations in Somalia, and the White House ultimately rejected Admiral McRaven's ambitious proposals, insisting that each military operation inside Somalia be approved personally by the president. Obama administration lawyers even debated whether al Shabaab, which had not carried out acts of terrorism against the United States, could be a target. Was the group a threat to America or a local militia that Washington should simply ignore?

It was sometimes hard to take the group seriously. Even as it tried to blanket Mogadishu under strict sharia law, ordering that thieves have their hands chopped off and adulterers be stoned to death, al Shabaab also engaged in erratic and even comic behavior. Al Shabaab leaders would make strange pronouncements in desperate attempts to gain new recruits. They held a talent show in the vein of the television program *American Idol* and a trivia game for children between the ages of ten and seventeen where contestants were asked questions like, "In which war was our leader Sheikh Timajilic killed?" First prize was an AK-47 assault rifle. After the U.S. State Department offered cash rewards for the whereabouts of al Shabaab leaders, one top al Shabaab operative told thousands of Somalis gathered after their Friday prayers that the militant group was offering rewards of its own for information about the "hideouts" of top American officials. The person who helped lead al Shabaab to the "idiot Obama" would be rewarded with ten camels. Ten chickens and ten roosters would go to the person with information about the hideout of the "old woman Hillary Clinton."

With few options for detaining terror suspects, and little appetite for extensive ground operations in Somalia, killing sometimes was a far more appealing option than capturing. In September 2009, JSOC scored an intelligence coup: precise information on the whereabouts of Saleh Ali Saleh Nabhan, a Kenyan member of al Qaeda's East Africa cell, which had carried out the 1998 American-embassy attacks, and a man thought to be the liaison between al Qaeda and al Shabaab. The intelligence indicated that, after months of moving inside cities and towns that made American airstrikes impossible, Nabhan was set to travel in a truck convoy from Mogadishu to the seaside town of Barawa. During a videoconference connecting the White House, the Pentagon, the CIA, and JSOC headquarters at Fort Bragg, Admiral McRaven led the group through the various strike options. The option carrying the least risk was to fire Tomahawk cruise missiles from a ship off the coast, or missiles from a military plane. Alternatively, McRaven said, Navy SEALs flying in AH-6 helicopters could swoop in on the convoy, kill Nabhan, and collect enough DNA evidence at the scene to confirm his death. Finally, McRaven presented a variation on option two: Instead of killing Nabhan, the SEALs would snatch him, put him into one of the helicopters, and take him somewhere for interrogation. President Obama chose what was thought to be the least risky option: a missile strike on the convoy.

But things didn't go as planned. With JSOC making final preparations for the operation, code-named Celestial Balance, the missile-launcher malfunctioned on the plane that had been designated for the mission. With time running out and Nabhan on the move, McRaven ordered that the commandos carry out the fallback plan: The SEALs waiting on a Navy ship off the Somali coast loaded into the helicopters and headed west, into Somali airspace. The helicopters strafed the convoy, killing Nabhan and three al Shabaab operatives.

The operation was a success in Somalia, but for some involved in the mission planning, the entire episode had raised uncomfortable questions. Because Plan A had failed, the United States was forced to take the extraordinary step of using troops in one of the most hostile countries in the world. But once the troops were there, why didn't they just capture Nabhan instead of kill him? Part of the answer was that a capture mission was considered too risky. But that wasn't the only reason. Killing was the preferred course of action in Somalia, and as one person involved in the mission planning put it, "We didn't capture him because it would have been hard to find a place to put him."

THE PENTAGON had originally hired Michele Ballarin and Perry Davis to come up with the type of information that had led to Nabhan's killing. This gave Ballarin clout during her frequent trips to East Africa, where she boasted about her ties to the American government during private meetings with various Somali factions. Each trip brought new business opportunities, and as Somalia emerged as the world's epicenter of international piracy, she saw the windfall that could come from acting as an intermediary in the ransom negotiations. Ballarin's primary contact from the Pentagon office that awarded her the contract had pushed her to develop relations with the clans in Somalia with close ties to the pirate networks, and by the time the pirates displayed the AMIRA sign from the *Faina*'s hull she had designs on becoming the go-to ransom negotiator. She said publicly that her interests in negotiating were purely humanitarian, but privately Ballarin told some of her employees that taking a cut of the ransom payments could be lucrative as the scourge of piracy worsened. "She had this dream of handling all of the negotiations, and getting rich," said Bill Deininger, a former colleague. In one interview she told a reporter that her goal was to "unwind all seventeen ships and all four hundred fifty people" that Somali pirates were currently holding.

Deininger was one of a number of disgruntled former employees who became disillusioned with Ballarin and quit working for her when they thought she had failed to deliver on her many promises. Some retired military officers she had hired to work for her various companies put up some of their own money when they joined Ballarin's service, and felt burned when they didn't recoup their investment. Although the Pentagon gave her seed money for her information-gathering project in 2008, she struggled to get a steady stream of money from government contracts, and cut ties with many of her partners.

And yet she maintained the appearance of a lavish lifestyle in the rolling hills of Virginia beyond the Washington beltway. She continued to court senior American military and intelligence officials, often at the large brick mansion that she rented, which doubled as an antiques store and sat on 110 acres that was once the domain of horse farms but more recently had become part of Washington's sprawling exurbs. She entertained American and African officials in the mansion's dining room, a space decorated with antique vases, hunting prints, and a large gallery of photos of Ronald Reagan and Pope John Paul II. Bedecked in jewelry and sometimes caressing a string of prayer beads, she presided over the meetings at the head of a large antique table. At regular intervals, Perry Davis would get up and refill visitors' teacups with a sweet blend of Kenyan black tea with cardamom, cloves, and other spices.

Ballarin continued to make trips to East Africa, building up ties to factions inside Somalia united by their adherence to Sufism. And she eventually developed a catchphrase for her work inside Somalia: She was providing "organic solutions" to problems that had festered for decades, solutions that couldn't be enacted by foreign governments or what she saw as meddlesome outside groups like the United Nations. During an interview with the Voice of America she spoke about a "soft-sided" approach, eschewing violence.

"The Somalis have seen enough conflict, they've seen enough private military companies, they've seen bloodshed, they've seen enough gunpowder, they've seen enough bullets," she said. "All the ugly things that have created a generation of young people who don't know anything else. Why would anyone who cares deeply about this culture want to perpetuate that? It's not the way forward; it really isn't."

But her definition of an "organic solution" was clearly elastic. In 2009, for example, she tried to help a group of Somali hit men kill five prominent al Shabaab operatives who were gathering for a meeting in Mogadishu. All they needed, she said, were silencers for their handguns.

In her telling of the story, the details of which a former American government official confirmed, she was sitting in her suite at the Djibouti Palace Kempinski, the only five-star hotel in the tiny, impoverished nation. The hotel was hosting an international conference to select the next leaders of Somalia's anemic transitional government— a literal gathering of the clans. After negotiations in conference rooms and poolside, Sharif Sheikh Ahmed, a moderate, former commander of the Islamic Courts Union, was chosen to run the country.

In the middle of one night, a group of Somalis knocked on Ballarin's door and took her to meet a senior official of Somalia's new transitional government. There, the Somali official told her that he had been in contact with a senior al Shabaab operative who was interested in switching sides and joining the government. The informant knew about an upcoming gathering of al Shabaab leaders and was offering— with America's blessing—to kill them all.

His list of needs was short: His men would need some training with handguns, and silencers to ensure that the operation could be carried out as discreetly as possible. And the defector wanted the United States to put up money to help the widows and children of the slain al Shabaab leaders.

When Ballarin returned to the United States, she and Perry Davis contacted a small group of military officers they knew at the Pentagon. As she saw it, this was not a difficult decision, and she later recalled with a measure of anger what she told the military officials with whom she had met.

"This is manna from heaven! Take it!" she recalled telling the military men.

But the Americans balked. If JSOC was going to bless the operation, the Americans were going to do it themselves. But Ballarin thought that having Somalis—rather than American commandos or other foreign proxies—kill the top echelon of al Shabaab in one blow would be especially crippling for an indigenous terror organization.

"*This* is an organic solution," she said. "You don't dispatch SEAL teams. This is Somali-style, and this isn't pleasant stuff we're talking about."

When she recalled the episode several years later, she spoke wistfully about what might have been.

"All they wanted was silencers."

Ballarin wasn't content with playing the role of mere passive collector of intelligence. Her vision was to be at the center of a great Sufi awakening, overseeing the unification of various Sufi groups across North and East Africa in a forceful campaign against Wahhabism. When al Shabaab militants took over radio stations in Mogadishu, banning music and forcing radio programmers to introduce news reports with the sounds of canned gunfire, bleating goats, and clucking chickens, Ballarin wrote a song of resistance to the Sufis of Somalia.

The song, written in English and sung by a Brazilian pop singer, carried the rallying cry *"Sufi life they'll never defeat!"*

> Raise your voices . . . Take a stand!
> Reclaim our honor and our land
> From foreign powers and meddling hands.
> Brothers and sisters, take a stand!
> Raise your voices . . . Take a stand!
> From regional strings . . . international bans.
> Brother, come with me . . . man for man.
> Brothers and sisters . . . take a stand!

Ballarin believed that the great awakening should begin in Somalia, where she had already had contacts with Ahlu Sunna Waljama'a (ASWJ), a Sufi group that controls large swaths of territory in central Somalia. The ASWJ had a somewhat checkered history. During the Somali civil war that raged during the 1990s, the group was aligned with the same warlord who commanded the Somali gunmen fighting Army Rangers and Delta Force operatives during the Black Hawk Down episode. Before the rise of al Shabaab, the ASWJ had not wielded significant influence in Somalia's clan wars. But as al Shabaab fighters began capturing towns in southern and central Somalia, the Wahhabi gunmen made a point of destroying Sufi graves and mosques wherever they went. Bones were exhumed and left to bleach in the sun, and caretakers of graveyards were arrested or told never to return to work. Al Shabaab fighters said that the gravesites were overwrought memorials—idolatry that was banned by Islam. Sheikh Hassan Yaqub Ali, the al Shabaab spokesman in the southern port city of Kismayo, told the BBC, "It is forbidden to make graves into shrines."

The grave desecration ignited a militant strain within the largely peaceful ASWJ, and they began to mobilize into an armed group with the aim of acting as a counterweight to al Shabaab. Recognizing the potential of a Sufi armed awakening, Ballarin began encouraging Sufi leaders to develop a strategy to break al Shabaab's advance. She and Perry Davis spoke repeatedly with Sufi sheikhs and ASWJ military leaders, traveling to central Somalia to talk about their military campaign, acting like a two-person battlefield staff. Ballarin and Davis boasted to Americans that the ASWJ was like their own private militia, and that they had instructed the Sufi fighters in how to recover weapons off the battlefield and store ammunition.

Then, after months of stalemate, ragtag columns of gun-wielding ASWJ fighters moved into El Buur, an al Shabaab stronghold in central Somalia. Ballarin beams when she recalls a text message she said she received in the middle of the night from ASWJ commanders:

"We've taken El Buur!"

SITTING IN FRONT OF the television in her brick mansion in Northern Virginia in 2011, watching video feeds on Fox News of the Arab revolts across North Africa, Michele Ballarin didn't see a hopeful Arab "spring." She saw a nightmare unfolding: radical Wahhabi Islam cutting across northern Africa all the way to the west coast of the continent. In her mind, authoritarian governments in places like Egypt and Libya had been a bulwark against the spread of Wahhabism, and the fortifications were now crumbling. She was certain that Wahhabism's rich patrons in Saudi Arabia would move into the region with money to build mosques and religious schools, and that the United States was losing its only partners in a fight against radical Islam. As she saw it, Muammar Gaddafi might have been a ruthless thug and the enemy of her hero Ronald Reagan, but to her, the Libyan dictator had come to be on the side of the righteous in the age's defining struggle of good versus evil.

Like a desert sandstorm, the popular revolts spreading across the states of North Africa were in the process of burying decades of authoritarian rule. But they had also caught the CIA flat-footed, and White House officials were aware that for all of the billions of dollars that the United States spends each year to collect intelligence and forecast the world's cataclysmic events, American spy agencies were several steps behind the popular uprisings. "The CIA missed Tunisia. They missed Egypt. They missed Libya. They missed them individually, and they missed them collectively," said one senior member of the Obama administration. In the frantic weeks after the Arab revolts began, hundreds of intelligence analysts at the CIA and other American spy agencies were reassigned to divine meaning from the turmoil. It was a game of catch-up.

It was the first mass uprising of the social-media age, and the revolutions were playing out in Twitter messages and Facebook updates. It was unlike anything that officials at Langley had seen before, and historical precursors like the fall of Communism were of little help to CIA leaders as they struggled to advise the White House and State Department about which Arab dictator was likely to fall next. At one senior staff meeting, CIA director Leon Panetta pressed his aides to make sense of the blizzard of digital messages. "Isn't anyone able to capture all of these messages in one place?" he asked, clearly puzzled by the ways of the younger generation.

But the problem went deeper for the CIA, a spy agency that very quickly was coming to experience the downside of its reorientation toward counterterrorism. The CIA was founded in 1947 on the premise that presidents and policy makers needed advance warning about the dynamics shaping world events, but both President George W.

Bush and Barack Obama had decided that hunting and killing terrorists should be the agency's top priority. The agency didn't have enough
spies doing actual spying, not enough case officers on the ground in
countries like Egypt and Tunisia whose job it was to collect intelligence about ferment in the streets or about fears among foreign leaders that they might be losing their grip on power.

The CIA had allied itself with ruthless intelligence services
throughout the Middle East and North Africa, forming partnerships
with foreign spy services run by the likes of Hosni Mubarak and
Muammar Gaddafi. These partnerships had helped the CIA amass
scalps for the war on terror. CIA directors were on a first-name basis
with Moussa Koussa, the head of Gaddafi's brutal spy service, and
American and Libyan spies had worked together to hunt down men
with suspected ties to al Qaeda, capture them, and put them in Libya's notorious Abu Salim jail. After Gaddafi fell and rebels sacked
Libyan intelligence headquarters, troves of documents were found
detailing the close ties between American and Libyan intelligence.
There was even a letter to Moussa Koussa from Porter Goss, the former CIA director, thanking the Libyan spymaster for his Christmas
gift of fresh oranges.

Therein lay much of the problem: Libyan or Egyptian spies were
hardly about to be candid with American officials about the fragility
of their own governments. And they kept close watch on dissident
leaders, making it difficult for CIA case officers in cities like Cairo to
meet with opposition groups and collect intelligence about domestic
unrest in the North African states. Mike Hayden, the former CIA
director, would later admit that the agency's decision to tie itself to
authoritarian regimes in the Arab world had crippled its ability to collect political and social intelligence in those countries. As he put it,
"How much do you want to push collection on the Muslim Brotherhood in Egypt if you're going to alienate [Mubarak's intelligence chief]

Omar Suleiman and he stops being a good counterterrorism partner for you?"

Government leaders from around the world hailed the end of North Africa's calcified dictatorships. But for sleep-deprived, often neurotic officers inside the CIA's Counterterrorism Center, the events of early 2011 were hardly the cause for optimism. It wasn't just that they were watching their close foreign allies be unceremoniously pushed from power. Even more worrying was that Islamist groups that for decades had been under the heel of dictators—from Egypt's Muslim Brotherhood to radical groups in Libya that the CIA and Libyan intelligence had worked together to snuff out—were gaining political power. The whirlwind taking place in the Arab world could, the CTC feared, sow the seeds for a resurgence of al Qaeda and its affiliates.

Such was the heartening prospect of al Qaeda's leader, holed up inside the top floor of a compound in Abbottabad, Pakistan. Furiously writing letters to his subordinates during what would be the final weeks of his life, Osama bin Laden was making a case in the early months of 2011 that the Arab revolts were the realization of a vision he first laid out in the 1990s, when he founded al Qaeda. In fact, the revolts had played out nothing like he had predicted, and the governments in Egypt and Tunisia had been toppled not by al Qaeda or by those seeking a pan-Muslim caliphate but by a youthful grassroots effort using media technology to further the revolution.

But bin Laden still found hope in the chaos. He wrote gleefully to one of his deputies that Secretary of State Hillary Clinton had expressed worries that "the region will fall into the hands of the armed Islamists." What the world was witnessing in "these days of consecutive revolutions," he wrote, "is a great and glorious event" that would likely "encompass the majority of the Islamic world with the will of Allah."

14: THE UNRAVELING

"It was the Americans!
It was Blackwater!
It was another Raymond Davis!"

—*Hafiz Muhammad Saeed*

T he American spy sat for weeks inside a dark cell at Kot Lakhpat prison, on the industrial fringes of Lahore, a jail with an unsavory reputation for inmates dying under murky circumstances. He had been separated from the rest of the prisoners, held in a section of the decaying facility where the guards didn't carry weapons, a concession for his safety that American officials had managed to extract from the prison staff. The United States consulate in Lahore had negotiated another safeguard: A small team of dogs was tasting Raymond Davis's food, checking that it had not been laced with poison.

For many senior Pakistani spies, the man sitting in the jail cell seemed the first solid proof of their suspicions that the CIA had built up a small army inside Pakistan, a group of trigger-happy cowboys carrying out a range of nefarious activities. For the CIA, the disclosure of Davis's role with the agency shed an unflattering light on a post–September 11 phenomenon: how the CIA had farmed out some of its most sensitive jobs to outside contractors and others with neither the experience nor the temperament to work in the war zones of the Islamic world.

The third child of a poor bricklayer and a cook, Raymond Allen Davis grew up in a small clapboard house in the Strawberry Patch hamlet of Big Stone Gap, a town of six thousand people in Virginia coal country named for the gap in the mountains where the Powell River sluiced through. Shy and reserved, Davis was unusually strong and became a football and wrestling star at the local high school. After graduating, in 1993, he enlisted in the Army infantry and did a tour in Macedonia in 1994 as a United Nations peacekeeper. When his five-year hitch in the infantry was up, in 1998, he reenlisted, this time in the Army's 3rd Special Forces Group based at Fort Bragg. He left the Army in 2003 and, like hundreds of other retired Navy SEALs and Green Berets, was hired by Erik Prince's company, Blackwater USA, and soon found himself in Iraq working as a security guard for the CIA.

Little is known about his work for Blackwater, but by 2006 he had left the firm and, together with his wife, founded a private security company in Las Vegas. Soon he was hired by the CIA as a private contractor, what the agency calls a "Green Badge," for the color of the identification cards that contractors show to enter CIA headquarters at Langley. Like Davis, many of the contractors were hired to fill out the CIA's Global Response Staff—bodyguards who traveled to war zones to protect case officers, assess the security of potential meeting spots, even make initial contact with sources to make sure that case officers wouldn't be walking into an ambush. It was officers from the CIA's security branch who would come under withering fire the following year on the roof of the agency's base in Benghazi, Libya. The demands of the wars in Iraq and Afghanistan had so stretched the CIA's own cadre of security officers that the agency was forced to pay inflated sums to private contractors to do the security jobs. When Davis first deployed with the CIA to Pakistan in 2008, he worked from the CIA base in Peshawar, earning upward of two hundred thousand dollars per year, including benefits and expenses.

Davis had already been in jail for several weeks by mid-February 2011, and it was unlikely he would be freed anytime soon. The murder case had inflamed anti-American passions inside Pakistan, with street protests and purple newspaper editorials demanding that Pakistan's government not cave to Washington's demands for Davis's release and instead sentence him to death. The evidence at the time indicated that the men Davis had killed had carried out a string of petty thefts that day, but there was an added problem: a third man killed by the unmarked American SUV fleeing the scene.

Making matters even worse for Davis, the American had been imprisoned in Lahore, where the family of Nawaz Sharif dominated the political culture. The former president made no secret about his intentions to once again run Pakistan, making him the chief antagonist to President Asif Ali Zardari and his political machine in Islamabad, 250 miles away. As the American embassy in Islamabad leaned on Zardari's government to get Davis released from jail, the diplomats soon realized that Zardari had little influence over the police officers and judges in the city of the president's bitter rival.

But the most significant factor ensuring that Davis would languish in jail was that the Obama administration had yet to tell Pakistan's government what it already suspected, and what Raymond Davis's marksmanship in the Lahore traffic circle made clear: He wasn't just another paper-shuffling American diplomat. Davis's work in Pakistan was much darker, and involved probing an exposed nerve in the already hypersensitive relationship between the CIA and the ISI.

Ever since the Pakistani militant group Lashkar-e-Taiba, the "Army of the Pure," dispatched teams of assassins to lay siege to luxury hotels in Mumbai, India, in November 2008, killing and wounding more than five hundred people over four days of mayhem, CIA analysts had been warning that the group was seeking to raise its global profile by carrying out spectacular attacks beyond South Asia. This spurred the

CIA to assign more of its expanding cadre of operatives in Pakistan toward gathering intelligence about Lashkar's operations—a decision that put the interests of the CIA and ISI in direct conflict. It was one thing for American spies to be lurking around the tribal areas hunting for al Qaeda figures; it was quite another for the CIA to go into Pakistani cities on espionage missions against a group that the ISI considered a valuable proxy force.

Lashkar was founded in 1990 as an alliance of various groups that the Pakistani spy service had nurtured to fight the Soviet Union in Afghanistan. The group's focus turned almost immediately from Afghanistan to India, and Pakistani president Muhammad Zia-ul-Haq began sending Lashkar fighters to Kashmir to act as a counterweight to Kashmiri independence groups the president feared might push to create a separate state in the disputed mountain region claimed by both India and Pakistan. The ISI had nurtured the group for years as a useful asset against India, and the fact that its leaders operated in plain sight made a mockery of President Musharraf's "banning" of the group in 2002 after a brazen assault on the Indian parliament building in New Delhi. Lashkar's sprawling headquarters in Muridke, a Lahore suburb along the famous Grand Trunk Road, housed a radical madrassa, a market, a hospital, and even a fish farm. The compound had been built with contributions from wealthy donors in Saudi Arabia and other Persian Gulf countries, but Lashkar also ran successful fund-raising campaigns and delivered a raft of social services to the poor using an allied organization, Jamaat-ud-Dawah ("Party of Truth"), as a front.

The group's charismatic leader, Hafiz Muhammad Saeed, had been put under house arrest over the years, but in 2009 the Lahore High Court quashed all terrorism charges against the fifty-nine-year-old and set him free. A stocky man with a wild beard, Saeed preached out in the open on many Fridays, flanked by bodyguards and delivering sermons to throngs of his followers about the imperialism of the United States, India, and Israel. Even after the United States offered a $10 million reward for information linking Saeed to the Mumbai attacks, he continued to move freely in public, further cementing his legend as a Pakistani version of Robin Hood.

By the time Raymond Davis had moved into a safe house with a handful of other CIA officers and contractors in late 2010, the bulk of agency officers in Lahore were involved in collecting information about the growth of Lashkar. With many of the CIA operatives brought into the country under false cover to mask their movements, Pakistani intelligence officials could make only wild guesses about what the Americans were doing.

To get more of its spies into Pakistan, the CIA had exploited the arcane rules in place for approving visas for Americans. The State Department, the CIA, and the Pentagon all had separate channels to request visas for their personnel, and all of them landed at the desk of Husain Haqqani, Pakistan's pro-American ambassador in Washington. Haqqani, a former politician and professor at Boston University, had orders from Islamabad to be lenient in approving the visas, since many of the Americans coming to Pakistan were—at least officially— going to be administering millions of dollars in foreign aid money to Pakistan. By the time of the Lahore killings, in early 2011, so many Americans were operating inside Pakistan under both legitimate and false identities that even the U.S. embassy in Pakistan didn't have accurate records to keep track of their identities and whereabouts.

THE AMERICAN EMBASSY in Islamabad is essentially a fortress within a fortress, a pile of buildings enclosed by walls topped with razor wire and surveillance cameras and then encircled by an outer ring of walls that separate a leafy area, called the Diplomatic Enclave, from the rest of the city. If it seemed like overkill, and a bit undiplomatic, to have the U.S. government cloistered behind so much concrete and steel, the Americans at least had good reason: The previous embassy had been set on fire in 1979 by student protestors enraged over false reports that the United States was behind the occupation of the Great Mosque, in Mecca. In actuality, a radical Islamic splinter group had seized the mosque and taken hostages among the hundreds of thousands who had come to Mecca for the haj. Inside the American embassy, the work of diplomats and spies is kept largely separate, with the CIA station occupying a warren of offices in its own wing of the embassy, accessed only through doors with encrypted locks.

But after Raymond Davis was picked up by the Lahore police, the embassy became a house divided by more than mere geography. Just two days before the shootings in Lahore, the CIA had sent a new station chief to Islamabad, the latest in what had become something of a revolving door at the agency's main Pakistan outpost. His previous foreign posting had been in Russia, where the CIA had sent its most wily and capable officers during the Cold War and more recently had assigned personnel tough enough to knock heads with the SVR, the KGB's post-Soviet incarnation. Old-school and stubborn, the new chief did not come to Pakistan to be friendly with the ISI. Instead, he wanted to recruit more Pakistani agents to work for the CIA under the ISI's nose, expand electronic surveillance of ISI offices, and share little information with Pakistani intelligence officers. This hawkish approach to spycraft has long had a name within the CIA: Moscow Rules. The strategy was now being applied to Pakistan, making the new station chief feel right at home.

That hard-nosed attitude almost immediately put him at odds with the American ambassador in Islamabad, Cameron Munter. A bookish career diplomat from California with a Ph.D. in history from Johns Hopkins University, Munter had ascended the ranks of the State Department's bureaucracy focused on Europe. He then accepted several postings in Iraq and ultimately took over the American mission in Islamabad, in late 2010. The job was considered one of the State Department's most important and difficult assignments, and Munter had the burden of following Anne Patterson, an aggressive diplomat who, in the three years before Munter arrived, had cultivated close ties to officials in both the Bush and Obama administrations. She had won praise from the CIA for her unflinching support for drone strikes in the tribal areas.

Munter, though, saw things differently; he was skeptical about the long-term value of counterterrorism operations in Pakistan. Arriving in Islamabad at a time when relations between the United States and Pakistan were quickly deteriorating, Munter wondered whether the pace of the drone war might be undercutting relations with an important ally for the quick fix of killing midlevel terrorists. Munter would learn soon enough that his views about the drone program ultimately mattered little. In the Obama administration, when it came to questions about war and peace in Pakistan, it was what the CIA believed that really counted.

With Raymond Davis sitting in prison, Munter argued it was essential to go immediately to the head of the ISI, Lt. General Ahmad Shuja Pasha, to cut a deal. The United States would admit that Davis was working for the CIA, the families of the Lahore victims would be secretly compensated, and Davis would quietly be spirited out of the country, never to return again. But the CIA objected. Davis had been spying on a militant group with extensive ties to the ISI, and the CIA didn't want to own up to it. Top CIA officials worried that appealing for mercy from the ISI might doom Davis. He could be killed in prison before the Obama administration could pressure Islamabad to release Davis on the grounds that he was a foreign diplomat with immunity from local laws—even those prohibiting murder. On the day of Davis's arrest, the CIA station chief walked into Munter's office and announced that a decision had been made to stonewall the Pakistanis. Don't cut a deal, he warned, adding: Pakistan is the enemy.

The strategy meant that American officials, from top to bottom, had to obfuscate both in public and in private about what exactly Raymond Davis had been doing in the country. On February 15, more than two weeks after the shootings, President Obama offered his first comments about the Raymond Davis affair during a press conference. The matter was simple, Obama said: Davis, "our diplomat in Pakistan," should be immediately released under the "very simple principle" of diplomatic immunity. "If our diplomats are in another country," said the president, "then they are not subject to that country's local prosecution."

Calling Davis a "diplomat" was, technically, accurate. Davis had been admitted into Pakistan on a diplomatic passport, which under normal circumstances would protect him from being prosecuted in a foreign country. But after the shootings in Lahore, the Pakistanis were not exactly receptive to debating the finer points of international law. As they saw it, Davis was an American spy who had not been declared to the ISI and whom CIA officials still would not admit they controlled. Shortly before Obama's press conference, General Pasha, the ISI chief, had traveled to Washington to meet with Leon Panetta and get more information about the matter. He was nearly convinced that Davis was a CIA employee and suggested to Panetta that the two spy agencies handle the matter quietly. Sitting in Panetta's office, he posed a direct question.

Was Davis working for the CIA? Pasha asked.

No, he's not one of ours, Panetta replied.

Panetta went on to say that the matter was out of his hands, and that the issue was being handled inside State Department channels. Pasha was furious when he left CIA headquarters, and he decided to leave Raymond Davis's fate in the hands of the judges in Lahore. The United States had just lost its chance, he told others, to quickly end the dispute.

THAT THE CIA DIRECTOR would be overseeing a large clandestine network of American spies in Pakistan, and then dissemble to the ISI director about the extent of America's secret war in the country, showed just how much the relationship had unraveled since the days in 2002, when Asad Munir teamed up with the CIA in Peshawar to hunt for Osama bin Laden in western Pakistan. Things were far worse even than during the period in 2006, when the ISI allowed Art Keller and other CIA operatives to work out of Pakistani military bases in the tribal areas. Where had it gone so wrong?

While the spy agencies had had a fraught relationship since the beginning of the Afghan war, the real breach came in July 2008, when CIA officers in Islamabad paid a visit to General Ashfaq Parvez Kayani, the Pakistani army chief, to tell him that President Bush had signed off on a set of secret orders authorizing a new strategy in the drone wars. No longer would the CIA give Pakistan advance warning before launching missiles from Predator or Reaper drones in the tribal areas. From that point on, the CIA officers told Kayani, the CIA's killing campaign in Pakistan would be a unilateral war.

The decision had been made in Washington after months of wrenching debate about the growth of militancy in Pakistan's tribal areas; a CIA internal assessment had likened it to al Qaeda's safe haven in Afghanistan in the years before the September 11 attacks. The highly classified CIA paper, dated May 1, 2007, concluded that al Qaeda was at its most dangerous since 2001 because of the base of operations that militants had established in North Waziristan, South Waziristan, Bajaur, and the other tribal areas.

That assessment became the cornerstone of a yearlong discussion about the Pakistan problem. Some of the Pakistan experts in the State Department warned that expanding the CIA war in Pakistan would further stoke anti-American anger on the streets and could push the country over the brink. But officials inside the CIA's Counterterrorism Center argued for escalating the drone campaign without the ISI's blessing. Since the killing of Nek Muhammad in 2004, they said, there had been fewer than twenty-five drone strikes in Pakistan, and only three of those strikes killed militants on the CIA's list of "high-value targets." Other potential strikes had been scuttled at the last minute because of delays in getting Pakistani approval for the strikes, or because the targets seemed to have been tipped off and had fled. The targeters inside the CTC had been trying to amass evidence that members of the ISI's Directorate S—the branch with historical ties to militant groups—had alerted the militants, but there was no clear proof.

Unlike years earlier, when some CIA case officers had derided the Counterterrorism Center operatives as Philistines and "boys with toys," by 2008 the various factions within the spy agency had united around the position that the drone campaign should intensify. Since late 2005, the CIA had managed to develop more sources in the tribal areas who could provide precise information about the whereabouts of al Qaeda leaders. Moreover, defense contractor General Atomics had ramped up production of Predator and Reaper drones, allowing the CIA to propose near-constant surveillance over suspected al Qaeda compounds and training camps with the unmanned aircraft. Inside the CIA's analytics division, the Directorate of Intelligence, analysts had decided that launching unilateral operations in Pakistan would not, as Bush officials worried for years, lead to the ouster of Pakistan's secular government and a rise of Islamist rule in the country. The analysts concluded that the civilian government in Islamabad led by Asif Ali Zardari, who was elected after General Musharraf caved to demands to step down, was just strong enough to weather any surge in public anger that came from an increase in drone strikes.

The change in leadership at the Pentagon had also contributed to the Bush administration's taking a more aggressive approach in Pakistan. For all his efforts to expand his authorities to dispatch special-operations troops outside of war zones, Donald Rumsfeld had actually been cautious about carrying out too many "boots on the ground" operations inside Pakistan, fearing a public backlash that might undercut President Musharraf. But with Musharraf gone, Rumsfeld's successor, Robert Gates, believed that the United States could take more risks in the country. Gates, the former CIA director, had helped manage the CIA's covert campaign against the Soviets in Afghanistan during the 1980s and saw the benefits of a partnership with Pakistan. But he also had a jaundiced view of how Pakistan managed its security and knew Islamabad wouldn't take aggressive action against militant groups in the tribal areas if it had neither the interest nor the ability to do so. During his first trip to Afghanistan as defense secretary, Gates sat in a secure briefing room at Bagram Air Base where Rear Admiral Robert Harward, deputy commander of Joint Special Operations Command, gave a classified briefing on all of the compounds in the tribal areas where the military believed al Qaeda operatives were hiding. "Well, why don't you go in and get them?" Gates asked.

So, in July 2008, when CIA director Michael Hayden and his deputy, Stephen Kappes, came to the White House to present the agency's plan to wage a unilateral war in the mountains of Pakistan to President Bush and his war cabinet, it wasn't a hard sell to a frustrated president. "We're going to stop playing the game," Bush said. "These sons of bitches are killing Americans. I've had enough." That began what would become the blistering, years-long drone assault on the tribal areas that President Obama continued when he took office. And as the CIA's relationship with the ISI soured, Langley sent station chiefs out to Islamabad who spent far less time and energy building up goodwill with Pakistani spies than their predecessors had. Richard Blee, the former head of the CIA's bin Laden–hunting unit and a former Islamabad station chief, lamented that, at the CIA, "the 'fuck you' school took over." From 2008 on, the CIA cycled a succession of seasoned case officers through Islamabad, and each left Pakistan more embittered than the last.

One of the station chiefs, John Bennett, was a longtime clandestine officer who had run CIA operations in Somalia from the agency's station in Nairobi and more recently had run the CIA station in South Africa. An officer from the post–Church Committee generation, Bennett arrived in Pakistan with some of the same concerns about CIA targeted-killing operations shared by many of his peers, but his tenure in Pakistan gradually changed his mind. He saw the drones as the only reliable means of eviscerating al Qaeda in Pakistan, especially since most of the intelligence sharing between the CIA and ISI had withered. His relationship with the ISI turned icy when Bennett began to examine the Pakistani agency's role in ginning up domestic opposition to the drone campaign, and by the time he left Islamabad, in 2010, he had a cynical view of the ISI. To his colleagues, he would recall his time in Pakistan and dealing with the ISI as "years of his life [he'd] never get back." Bennett's successor as station chief, who dug even deeper into what he saw as an ISI propaganda campaign to foment anger about the drone strikes, had to leave the country in haste when his identity was revealed in the Pakistani press. The CIA suspected the leak came from the ISI, retaliating because General Pasha was named as a defendant in a New York lawsuit brought by victims of the 2008 Mumbai attacks.

Even many of the operations that at first blush seemed likely to signal a new era of goodwill between the CIA and the ISI ended in recriminations and finger-pointing. In January 2010, during Bennett's tenure as CIA station chief, a clandestine American team of CIA officers and special-operations troops working in Karachi traced a cell phone to a house in Baldia Town, a slum in the western part of the sprawling city. The CIA did not conduct unilateral operations inside large Pakistani cities, so the Americans notified the ISI about the intelligence. Pakistani troops and policemen launched a surprise raid on the house.

Although the CIA didn't know in advance, hiding inside the house was Mullah Abdul Ghani Baradar, a man considered to be the Afghan Taliban's military commander and the second in command to Mullah Mohammed Omar. Only after suspects in the house were arrested and questioned did the CIA learn that Baradar was among the detainees. The ISI took him to a detention facility in an industrial section of Islamabad and refused the CIA access to him. "At that point, things got really complicated," said one former CIA officer.

Was the entire episode a setup? Rumors had circulated inside Pakistan that Baradar wanted to cut a deal with the Americans and bring the Taliban to the negotiating table in Afghanistan. Had the ISI somehow engineered the entire arrest, feeding intelligence to the CIA so that Baradar could be taken off the street and the nascent peace talks spoiled? Had ISI played the CIA? Months later, senior CIA officials at Langley still couldn't answer those questions.

THE CIA'S STRONG SUSPICION that the ISI continued to play a double game with the Afghan Taliban was a constant weight on the spying relationship, and yet there were some joint operations that produced an intelligence windfall. In June 2010, eight months before the world had heard the name Raymond Davis, the two spy agencies ramped up a surveillance operation monitoring the cell phones of a group of Arabs suspected of giving logistical support to al Qaeda leaders hiding in Pakistan. But the operation was only "joint" up to a point: The CIA did not tell the Pakistanis that one of the cell-phone numbers belonged to Abu Ahmed al-Kuwaiti, the alias of a man whom captured al Qaeda operatives had identified to the CIA years earlier as a personal courier for Osama bin Laden. Since first learning about al-Kuwaiti, the trail to the courier had led down multiple blind alleys, and it wasn't until 2007 that the CIA got a tip from a foreign intelligence service that his real name was Ibrahim Saeed Ahmed. This was hardly an uncommon name in the Muslim world, but the new information allowed the National Security Agency to gradually pinpoint a cell-phone number used by the courier and feed it to the CIA for the cell-phone monitoring operation.

It was that summer in 2010 when a call came into al-Kuwaiti's tapped cell phone. The caller was a friend of al-Kuwaiti's, contacting him from a country in the Persian Gulf region, and the American snoops were listening.

"We've missed you. Where have you been?" asked the man.

Al-Kuwaiti's response was vague but tantalizing.

"I'm back with the people I was with before," he said.

The coded message seemed to be significant: It suggested that al-Kuwaiti was again working with al Qaeda, and possibly even had a direct line to Osama bin Laden. Using geo-location technology to pinpoint where al-Kuwaiti was using his cell phone, the NSA homed in on an area around Peshawar. That made some sense if al-Kuwaiti was traveling back and forth to the tribal areas, where the bulk of al Qaeda's top leadership was thought to be hiding, although by then a small group of analysts inside the CIA suspected that bin Laden may be hiding somewhere else, perhaps even in the settled areas of Pakistan. It was a hunch, informed to some degree by sheer process of elimination: The CIA had spent years focused on the tribal areas without as much as a sliver of new evidence that the al Qaeda leader was hiding there. At some point, it made sense to start looking elsewhere.

The hunch proved to be right. Two months after the cell-phone call, a Pakistani man working for the CIA spotted al-Kuwaiti in Peshawar behind the wheel of a white Suzuki Potohar truck with a spare tire attached to the rear gate. He followed al-Kuwaiti out of the city—but not west into the tribal areas and the wild mountains. Instead, the truck drove more than 120 miles east, to a quiet hamlet north of Islamabad that is home to Pakistan's premier military-training academy and is a popular haven for retired officers who while away their days hitting golf balls on one of Pakistan's best golf courses. There, in Abbottabad, the Suzuki pulled into a sprawling compound encircled by concrete walls twelve feet high. Rising above the walls were the upper floors of a large house—the top floor distinguished from the others because it had only small, opaque slits for windows. The house had neither a phone line nor an Internet connection. Whoever lived inside was trying to stay detached from the outside world.

In the months that followed, Leon Panetta pushed the agency's Counterterrorism Center to consider a number of exotic schemes to determine who might be hiding in the house, some of them reminiscent of the period before the agency had a fleet of Predators and considered using hot-air balloons to spy on bin Laden's training camps in Afghanistan. CTC officers brought a giant telephoto lens into Panetta's office, the largest lens available, and proposed stationing it in the mountains several miles away. A safe house that the CIA had quietly set up not far from the large compound did not have a line-of-sight view into the house, so the telephoto lens was useless from that vantage point. For weeks on end, spy satellites took thousands of photographs of the house during passes over Pakistan, but the eyes in the sky produced no definitive proof that bin Laden was hiding there.

The CIA watched, and waited, for a shred of hard proof that might bring the near decade-long manhunt to an end.

WITH THE CIA PURSUING its most promising bin Laden lead since the terrorist leader escaped his lair at Tora Bora, in Afghanistan, and fled across the border into Pakistan in 2001, it was more than a bit inconvenient that one of its undercover officers was sitting in a jail in Lahore facing a double murder charge. Pakistan's Islamist parties organized street protests and threatened violent riots if Raymond Davis was not tried and eventually hanged for his crimes. American diplomats in Lahore regularly visited Davis, but the Obama administration continued to stonewall Pakistan's government about the nature of Davis's work in the country. And the episode claimed another victim.

On February 6, the grieving widow of one of Davis's victims swallowed a lethal amount of rat poison and was rushed to the hospital in Faisalabad, where doctors pumped her stomach. The woman, Shumaila Faheem, was certain that the United States and Pakistan would quietly broker a deal to release her husband's killer from prison, a view she expressed to her doctors from her hospital bed. "They are already treating my husband's murderer like a VIP in police custody and I am sure they will let him go because of international pressure," she said. "The man murdered my husband and I demand justice. I don't care if he is American. He must not be allowed to get away with this." She died shortly afterward and instantly became a martyr for the groups inside Pakistan who had turned the Davis affair into a cause célèbre.

The furor over the Davis incident was quickly escalating, threatening to shut down most CIA operations in the country and possibly even derail the intelligence-gathering operation in Abbottabad. But the CIA stood firm and sent top officials to Islamabad who told Ambassador Munter to stick to the strategy. Force the Pakistanis to release Davis and threaten them with dire consequences if they don't comply. Dial up the pain, and they will come around.

But Munter had decided by then that the CIA's strategy had not worked, and he and several other American officials began devising a new plan. After discussions among White House, State Department, and CIA officials in Washington, Munter approached General Pasha, the ISI chief, and came clean. Davis was with the CIA, he said, and the United States needed to get him out of the country as quickly as possible.

Pasha wasn't about to let the Americans off so easily. He was still fuming that Panetta had lied to him, and he was going to let the Americans squirm by letting Davis sit in jail while he considered—on his own timetable—the best way to resolve the situation.

More than a week later, Pasha came back to Munter with his response. It was a purely Pakistani solution, one based on an ancient tradition that would allow the matter to be settled outside the unpredictable court system. Pasha had devised the plan with a number of Pakistani officials, including Ambassador Haqqani in Washington. The reckoning for Davis's actions would come in the form of "blood money," or *diyat*, a custom under sharia law that compensates the families of victims for their dead relatives. The matter would be handled quietly, the CIA would make the secret payments, and Davis would be released from jail.

The ISI took over. Pasha ordered ISI operatives in Lahore to meet the families of the three men killed during the January episode and negotiate a settlement. Some of the relatives initially resisted, but the ISI negotiators were not about to let the talks collapse. After weeks of

discussions, the parties agreed on a total of two hundred million rupees, approximately $2.34 million, to offer "forgiveness" to the jailed
CIA officer.

Only a small group of Obama administration officials knew of the
talks, and as they dragged on the clock was ticking toward a ruling by
Lahore's High Court about whether Davis would be granted diplomatic immunity, a ruling the CIA expected to go against the United
States and worried might set a precedent for future cases in Pakistan.

Raymond Davis remained in the dark about all of this. When he
arrived for his court appearance on March 16, he was fully expecting
to hear that the trial would proceed and the judge would issue a new
court date. He was escorted into the courtroom, his arms handcuffed
in front of him, and locked inside an iron cage next to the judge's
bench. In the back of the courtroom sat General Pasha, Pakistan's
spymaster, who took out his cell phone and began sending out a
stream of nervous text messages to Ambassador Munter, updating
him about the court proceedings. Pasha was one of the most powerful
men in Pakistan, and yet the ISI had little control over the mercurial
courts in Lahore, and he wasn't entirely sure that things would proceed according to plan.

The first part of the hearing went as everyone expected. The judge,
saying that the case would go ahead, noted that his ruling on diplomatic immunity would come in a matter of days. Pakistani reporters
frantically began filing their stories about how this seemed a blow to
the American case, and that it appeared that Davis would not be released from jail anytime soon. But then the judge ordered all the reporters out of the courtroom, and from the back General Pasha
watched his secret plan unfold.

Through a side entrance, eighteen relatives of the three victims
walked into the room, and the judge announced that a civil court had
switched to a sharia court. Each of the family members approached

Davis, some of them with tears in their eyes or sobbing outright, and announced that he or she forgave him. Pasha sent another text message to Munter: The matter was settled. Davis was a free man. In a Lahore courtroom, the laws of God had trumped the laws of man.

The drama had played out entirely in Urdu, and throughout the proceeding a baffled Raymond Davis sat silently inside the steel cage. It was even more jarring when ISI operatives whisked Davis out of the courthouse through a back entrance and pushed him into a waiting car that sped to the Lahore airport.

The move had been choreographed to get Davis out of the country as quickly as possible. But American officials, including Munter, waiting for Davis at the airport began to worry. Davis had, after all, already shot dead two men he believed were threatening him. If he thought he was being taken away to be killed, he might try to make an escape, even try to kill the ISI operatives inside the car. Sure enough, when the car arrived at the airport and pulled up to the plane ready to take Davis out of Pakistan, the CIA operative was in a daze. It appeared to the Americans waiting for him that Davis was only realizing then that he was safe.

Raymond Davis got on the plane and flew west, over the mountains and into Afghanistan, where he was handed over to CIA officers in Kabul. For the first time since late January, he was able to tell his story about the killings in Lahore, his arrest, and his incarceration—without the fear of Pakistani spies listening in.

He tried to settle back into his life in the United States, but in the end Raymond Davis couldn't stay out of jail. On October 1, 2011, just seven months after his abrupt departure from Pakistan, Davis was eyeing a parking spot in front of a bagel shop in Highlands Ranch, Colorado, a suburb of Denver. So was Jeff Maes, a fifty-year-old minister who was driving with his wife and two young daughters. When Maes beat Davis to the spot, Davis stopped his car behind Maes's parked vehicle and shouted profanities through his open window. Then he jumped out of his car and confronted Maes, telling the minister that he had been waiting for the parking spot.

"Relax," Maes said, "and quit being stupid."

Davis struck Maes in the face, knocking him to the pavement. Maes testified that when he stood up from the fall, Davis continued to hit him. Davis was eventually arrested on charges of third-degree assault and disorderly conduct, but the charges were upgraded to felony assault when Maes's injuries turned out to be worse than originally thought. The minister's wife, later recalling the episode, said she had never in her life seen a man so full of rage.

THE DAVIS AFFAIR HAD led Langley to order dozens of covert officers out of Pakistan in the hope of lowering the temperature in the CIA–ISI relationship. Ambassador Munter issued a public statement shortly after the bizarre court proceeding, saying he was "grateful for the generosity of the families" and expressing regret for the entire incident and the "suffering it caused."

But the secret deal only fanned the anger in Pakistan, and anti-American protests flared in major cities, including Islamabad, Karachi, and Lahore. Demonstrators set tires ablaze, clashed with Pakistani riot police, and brandished placards with slogans such as I AM RAYMOND DAVIS, GIVE ME A BREAK, I AM JUST A CIA HIT MAN.

He had become a bogeyman in Pakistan, an American assassin lurking in the subconscious of a deeply insecure nation. He was the subject of wild conspiracy theories, and his name was regularly heard at anti-American rallies. After the CIA scaled back operations in Pakistan, one Pakistani newspaper even cited the withdrawal of the secret American army as the reason why there had been a reduction of terrorist violence in Pakistan in recent months.

On a steamy summer night the following year, Hafiz Muhammad Saeed—the head of Lashkar-e-Taiba and the reason Raymond Davis and his team had been sent to Lahore in the first place—stood on the back of a flatbed truck and spoke to thousands of cheering supporters less than a mile from Pakistan's parliament building in Islamabad. A $10 million American bounty still hung over Saeed's head, part of a broader squeeze on Lashkar-e-Taiba's finances. But there he was, out in the open and whipping the crowd into a fury with a pledge to "rid Pakistan of American slavery." The rally was the culmination of a march from Lahore to Islamabad that Saeed had ordered to protest American involvement in Pakistan. The night before the march reached the capital, six Pakistani troops had been killed by gunmen riding motorcycles not far from where the marchers were spending the night, leading to speculation that Saeed had ordered the attack.

But Saeed insisted that night that he was not to blame for the deaths. The killers had been foreigners, he told the crowd, a group of assassins with a secret agenda to destabilize Pakistan and steal its nuclear arsenal. With a dramatic flourish, he said he knew exactly who had killed the six men.

"It was the Americans!" he shouted to loud approvals.

"It was Blackwater!" and the cheers grew even louder.

He saved the biggest applause line for last:

"It was another Raymond Davis!"

15: THE DOCTOR AND THE SHEIKH

"I don't want to be the ambassador."

—*CIA station chief in Islamabad*

D r. Shakil Afridi had already been working for the CIA for more than a year when his American handler gave him a new set of instructions. It was January 2011, the month of Raymond Davis's arrest, and the Pakistani surgeon had just gone through the lengthy protocol the CIA had put in place for him to meet his American contact. Two men would pick him up at a designated spot—sometimes a Shell gas station, sometimes a crowded outdoor market—body-search him, and order him to lie down in the backseat of their car with a blanket covering him. That day the car zigzagged through the streets of Islamabad until stopping to let Afridi out. There, an American woman he knew only as Sue was waiting for him in a Toyota Land Cruiser.

Sue told the doctor that he should prepare to launch a vaccination campaign aimed at inoculating women between the ages of fifteen and forty-five against hepatitis B. She instructed that he should begin in two towns in Kashmir—Bagh and Muzaffarabad—and in the region of Khyber Pakhtunkhwa, focusing on the pastoral garrison town of Abbottabad. The campaign should take six months, she said, carried out in three phases. Afridi made quick calculations about the cost of the campaign, factoring in the large markup he always included when he was giving his price for a CIA operation. He would need 5.3 million rupees, he told Sue, about fifty-five thousand dollars.

Afridi by then had become comfortable with the Americans, and he knew that the CIA wasn't about to start quibbling over money. He was exactly what the Americans were desperate for—an agent who could move easily through cities and villages in Pakistan without raising the suspicions of either militants or Pakistan's intelligence service. He was the perfect spy, and the Americans paid handsomely for that.

Sue was just the latest in a succession of CIA officers who had been assigned to work with Afridi since 2009, when the doctor with a checkered history was first approached by the Americans. Then in his late forties, he had risen from humble origins to become Pakistan's top doctor for Khyber Agency in the tribal areas, despite being dogged by allegations that he regularly accepted kickbacks from medical suppliers, ordered unnecessary surgical procedures, and sold hospital medicines on the black market.

Few doubted his dedication to improving health conditions in one of the world's poorest regions, but Afridi was also a fast talker who enjoyed telling bawdy jokes to female colleagues and was a bit too eager to push the boundaries of medical ethics to make extra money. The allegations against him eventually came to the attention of Mangal Bagh, a former bus driver turned warlord and drug runner in Khyber Agency, who was the leader of an obscure group called Lashkar-e-Islam. Bagh's fighters regularly received medical treatment from Afridi. The warlord summoned Afridi to his house and demanded that the doctor pay a fine of one million rupees, about ten thousand dollars, for his transgressions. When Afridi refused, Bagh kidnapped him and detained him for a week until he paid.

Afridi was attending a medical workshop in Peshawar in November 2009 when, according to an account he later gave to Pakistani investigators, a man approached him claiming to be the Pakistan country director for Save the Children, the international charity. The man, Mike McGrath, took an immediate interest in Afridi's work and invited him to Islamabad so the two could talk further over dinner. Whether or not Afridi suspected there was an ulterior motive is unclear, but when he arrived in the Pakistani capital on the appointed day he attended a dinner at McGrath's house in a posh section of Islamabad. There, he said, he met a tall blond woman in her late thirties whom he would later describe as having "British looks." She called herself Kate, and she became Dr. Shakil Afridi's first CIA handler.

Save the Children has denied that neither McGrath nor any of its employees do any work for the CIA. American officials also dispute that Save the Children was ever used for spying, saying that if the CIA were to use large international charities to help recruit agents it would put all aid workers at risk of reprisals. Nevertheless, when a Pakistani investigative report of Afridi's work for the CIA and his meeting with McGrath became public in Pakistan, officials in Islamabad moved to shutter all of the group's operations inside the country.

What American officials don't dispute, however, is that midway through the last decade the CIA began sending officers into Pakistan undercover in a number of professions that might allow the spies to move freely through the country. During the "surge" of CIA officers into Pakistan beginning in 2005 and 2006, when Art Keller was deployed to the tribal areas, American spies arrived in Pakistan in a desperate search for clues about Osama bin Laden and stretched the normally accepted rules of international spycraft.

After the Church Committee revelations of the 1970s, the CIA implemented a policy of not recruiting American journalists, clergy, or Peace Corps volunteers to spy for the agency, all of which had been routine up to that time. But senior CIA leaders said these post-Church rules were not cast in stone. Testifying before the Senate Intelligence Committee in 1996, CIA director John Deutch said there might be instances of "extreme threat to the nation" when the CIA might need to abandon the policy. Under certain circumstances, Deutch said, "I believe it is unreasonable to foreclose the witting use of any likely source of information." The CIA never restricted itself from recruiting foreign journalists or foreign aid workers, but American officials have long understood the dangers of using humanitarian workers as spies. Still, the CIA would carry out all manner of activities in the years after the September 11 attacks—from making detainees endure near drowning in secret prisons to killing militant suspects with armed drones—using the justification that the operations were necessary to keep the country safe. Expanding the categories of who can be recruited to spy was just another tactic of a CIA in the midst of an enduring war.

During the two years after Dr. Afridi's first meeting with the tall, blond CIA officer, the Pakistani doctor would conduct a number of public health campaigns as a ruse to gather intelligence on militant activity in the tribal areas. Vaccination campaigns were considered a good front for spying: DNA information could be collected from the needles used on children and analyzed for leads on the whereabouts of al Qaeda operatives for whom the CIA already had DNA information. In that time, Afridi conducted half a dozen vaccination campaigns around Khyber Agency, and the CIA paid him eight million rupees. According to his account, every few months he was passed off to a new CIA handler, from "Kate" to "Toni" to "Sara" and finally to "Sue," who assumed his case in December 2010. He was given a laptop computer and a secure transmitter to communicate with the CIA, and he was alerted to the Americans trying to reach him when the transmitter sent out a beeping sound.

ONE MONTH into the vaccination campaign in Abbottabad, Sue told Dr. Afridi to focus his activities in Bilal Town, an upper-middle-class neighborhood not far from the headquarters of Pakistan's premier military academy, the country's equivalent of West Point. The hepatitis-B program was already being carried out in a slipshod manner, ignoring established protocols that dictate a careful, neighborhood-by-neighborhood strategy for vaccination campaigns. Afridi hadn't even bought enough injections to ensure that everyone in his target population of fifteen-to-forty-five-year-old women received the multiple injections required to be vaccinated. Some local officials had even refused to cooperate with Afridi under the assumption that he didn't have permission for his work. Shaheena Mamraiz, a public health officer in Abbottabad, said she was taken aback by Afridi's aggressiveness when he burst into her office in March 2011 wearing a black business suit and telling her the details of his planned vaccination campaign. It was only after urgings from her supervisor that she agreed to cooperate with Afridi.

Of course, the details of exactly who in the greater Abbottabad area would be vaccinated were irrelevant to Afridi's CIA handlers. By spring 2011, a small cluster of officers inside the Counterterrorism Center at Langley and at the CIA station in Islamabad were interested only in Bilal Town and, more specifically, the large walled compound on Pathan Street that American spy satellites had spent months watching. Afridi's CIA handlers never told the doctor whom they suspected was hiding in the house. Whether Osama bin Laden and his entourage were living there was still a matter of intense speculation, and American officials hoped that getting inside the house might settle the matter. With the vaccination campaign as a cover, the CIA wanted Afridi to get one of his staff inside the compound and get what American soldiers and spies still didn't have after nearly a decade of frantic searching: hard evidence of where Osama bin Laden was hiding.

But neither Afridi nor any member of his staff was able to provide that. On the day Dr. Afridi vaccinated residents of Pathan Street, the only people to refuse the hepatitis-B vaccinations lived in the mysterious compound, the ones who rarely ventured beyond the house and burned their trash rather than send it out for collection. Afridi was told that two reclusive brothers from Waziristan, along with their families, occupied the house and that the men had no interest in meeting anyone from the neighborhood. After investigating further, a female health worker on Afridi's team managed to get the cell-phone number of one of the "brothers" who lived in the house. She called the number using Dr. Afridi's phone and spoke to a man who said he was away from the house and that she should call again in the evening.

The vaccination team never got into the compound, and Afridi decided that pressing the matter might arouse suspicions and prompt the people in the compound to alter their procedures or even flee. Having completed the work in Bilal Town, Dr. Afridi went to Islamabad with his empty vaccination kits to where Sue and her Toyota Land Cruiser were waiting for him at a designated spot. He told her everything he knew about the people in the compound. He handed her the vaccination kits, and she handed him 5.3 million rupees in cash.

FROM A MAKESHIFT BASE in eastern Afghanistan, four American helicopters lifted off, banked east against a moonless sky, and brought dozens of heavily armed young men into battle in a country where the United States had not declared war. The group of Navy SEALs had prepared for a bloody firefight with fiercely loyal men defending Osama bin Laden, or even with Pakistani troops: A decade of secret American operations inside Pakistan had so frayed relations between two putative allies that a pitched battle between American and Pakistani troops in the middle-class hamlet of Abbottabad was a risk that the SEALs contemplated as they touched down inside bin Laden's walled compound.

There had been ominous signs of disaster as the helicopters reached their destination. One of the helicopters got caught in a wind vortex and was forced into a hard landing after its tail clipped the wall of the compound, a snafu with echoes of the failed 1980 mission to rescue the American hostages in Iran. But once the SEALs penetrated the house on Pathan Street with C-4 explosives and made their way up the stairs, bin Laden's end came swiftly. The Americans saw the al Qaeda leader at the top of the stairs on the third floor, peering out of his room, and one of the commandos shot him in the right side of his face. He fell back into his bedroom and lay twitching on the floor in a pool of blood. The SEALs took pictures of bin Laden's corpse, put it into a body bag, and dragged it down the stairs and out the door.

Less than forty minutes after the helicopters arrived in Abbottabad, history's most expensive and exasperating manhunt had been brought to an end. The SEALs destroyed the downed helicopter to prevent the Pakistanis from gaining access to the classified navigation equipment inside, with only the helicopter's severed tail surviving the planned destruction. They piled into the functioning Blackhawk and a Chinook helicopter that had been waiting in reserve. They flew west, back into Afghanistan, carrying bin Laden and dozens of computer hard drives, cell phones, and thumb drives that had been scattered around the compound.

The details of the bin Laden raid did not trickle out into Pakistan until later that day. As they did, Asad Munir sat mesmerized in front of the television in his living room. He was convinced there was more to the story. The former ISI station chief in Peshawar, the man who spoke reverentially about his days working with the CIA in the months after the September 11 attacks, was certain that the CIA would never carry out a military operation in the middle of his country without the help of Pakistani soldiers or spies. "How could they?" he recalled thinking. "The CIA doesn't have any troops."

But that night, the CIA did have troops.

In the months before the mission was launched, as spy satellites peering down from space took pictures of the house on Pathan Street and Dr. Afridi and his team tried to get inside the compound, U.S. military and intelligence officials presented the White House with a number of attack options. The option considered least risky, using a B-2 stealth bomber to slip past Pakistani radar and raze the compound, was ruled out because it would have provided the Obama administration no definitive proof that bin Laden had been killed in the operation. Pakistani authorities would cordon off the area and sift through the rubble, and the only details that the United States would learn would be those things that the ISI chose to tell.

President Obama instead chose the riskier option, sending the SEALs deep into Pakistan to kill bin Laden. Besides the obvious perils of such an operation, officials worried about sending American ground troops so far into Pakistan. Until then, the only combat missions the American military had carried out on Pakistani soil had been in the tribal areas. The missions took place within miles of the Afghan border, allowing for a quick escape back into Afghanistan if something went wrong.

There was also the question with which American leaders had been grappling for years: Under what authority could the United

States send troops into a country with which America was not at war? It was the question that Donald Rumsfeld asked in the days after the September 11 attacks, when he looked with envy at the CIA's ability to go to war anywhere around the globe. In the years since, lawyers and policy makers had steadily chipped away at the wall separating the work of soldiers and spies. The rivalries between the Pentagon and CIA during the early part of the decade gave way to a détente and a new arrangement in which special-operations troops on combat or spying missions were "sheep-dipped": temporarily turned into CIA operatives.

So as President Obama made the final decisions about the bin Laden operation, a decade of evolution in the way America wages war gave him more options than had existed for previous American presidents. It would be an American military mission, carried out by teams of Navy SEALs. But the entire team was "sheep-dipped" for the mission, put under the CIA's Title 50 authority for launching covert actions. President Obama put CIA director Leon Panetta in charge of the operation.

From the moment that the Blackhawk helicopters took off from the base in Jalalabad, Afghanistan, through the tense minutes when the SEALs moved up the dark staircase in the house on Pathan Street, to the final moments when the helicopters rose into the sky carrying bin Laden's dead body, Panetta relayed updates from the mission to rapt Obama administration officials jammed into the White House Situation Room. The liberal Democratic congressman from California, a man who learned only shortly before arriving at Langley that much of his job would require delivering death sentences to America's enemies around the world, had the controls of the killing machine. As the operation unfolded, Panetta kept one hand in his pocket, fingering a string of rosary beads.

The suffocating tension inside the White House Situation Room

lifted only after all the SEALs had piled into the helicopters and escaped Pakistani airspace without forcing a confrontation with the
Pakistani air force. But back in Abbottabad, the wreckage from one of
the Blackhawks was still burning and several dead bodies lay on the
floor of the house where the SEALs had done their violent work.

Somebody was going to have to tell the Pakistanis what had just
happened.

The task fell to Admiral Mike Mullen, the chairman of the Joint
Chiefs of Staff, who had been something of a troubleshooter as the
United States and Pakistan lurched from one crisis to the next. The
son of a Hollywood press agent and a man who from an early age saw
the value of cultivating personal relationships, Mullen had developed
a close rapport with General Kayani—the former head of the ISI who
had become army chief—during endless dinners at Kayani's house in
Islamabad. The two men would talk late into the night about Pakistan's precarious security in a region dominated by India, China, and
Russia, with Kayani chain-smoking through each dinner course. Mullen had spent the flights to Islamabad reading *Freedom at Midnight*,
the 1975 classic about India's independence from the British Empire
and the India–Pakistan partition. One member of Mullen's traveling
entourage noticed that, from behind, the two men even looked alike—
roughly the same height, same hair color, same slightly rumpled khaki
uniform, similar lumbering gait—distinguished only by the cigarette
smoke that rose from the Pakistani general.

Speaking from a phone outside the Situation Room, Mullen called
Kayani and informed him of what had just happened.

Kayani already knew the basics. Hours earlier, he had taken a call
from one of his aides, who told him about vague reports that a helicopter had crashed in Abbottabad. Kayani's first thought was that
Pakistan was under attack from India, and he immediately ordered

his air-force commanders to scramble F-16 jets to repel the invasion. But the concerns about an Indian attack soon receded, and by the time Mullen called Kayani, the Pakistani general knew that Americans had been in his country.

During a tense phone call, Mullen said that American troops had been in the compound in Abbottabad and had killed bin Laden. There was a downed American helicopter at the scene. Then Mullen raised a subject that Obama officials had been debating since bin Laden's death had been confirmed: Should President Obama make a public announcement that night or wait until the following day? Dawn had already broken in Islamabad, and Kayani told Mullen that President Obama should make an announcement as soon as possible, if only to explain why there was a burning American military helicopter in central Pakistan. After a few more minutes, the conversation was over and the two men hung up.

Kayani, whose position as head of the Pakistani military made him the most powerful figure in the country, was facing the most acute crisis of his long career. Within days, Pakistan's top generals would excoriate him for allowing the United States to violate Pakistani sovereignty, but during the phone call with Mullen he had struck a conciliatory tone, because bin Laden had just been killed less than a mile from Pakistan's premier military academy. Lashing out at Mullen that night, it seemed to Kayani, might feed America's suspicions about Pakistan's government harboring terrorists and lead to a permanent break between the United States and Pakistan. A proud man who had reached the pinnacle of his military career, Kayani faced an unsavory choice. He could either appear complicit in hiding Osama bin Laden or incompetent for being unable to stop the world's most hunted man from taking refuge in the middle of his country. He chose the latter.

290 | THE WAY OF THE KNIFE

IN TRUTH, any fading embers of productive relations between the United States and Pakistan had largely been extinguished by the time bin Laden was killed. The Raymond Davis episode had poisoned Leon Panetta's relationship with General Pasha, the ISI chief, and the already small number of Obama officials pushing for better relations between Washington and Islamabad dwindled even further. Ambassador Cameron Munter was reporting daily back to Washington about the negative impact of the armed-drone campaign, and Admiral Mullen generally agreed with Munter that the CIA seemed to be conducting a war in a vacuum, oblivious to the ramifications that the drone strikes were having on America's relations with Pakistan's government.

The CIA had approval from the White House to carry out missile strikes in Pakistan even when CIA targeters weren't certain about exactly who it was they were killing. Under the rules of so-called signature strikes, decisions about whether to fire missiles from drones could be made based on patterns of activity deemed suspicious. The bar for lethal action had again been lowered.

For instance, if a group of young "military-aged males" were observed moving in and out of a suspected militant training camp and were thought to be carrying weapons, they could be considered legitimate targets. American officials admit it is somewhat difficult to judge a person's age from thousands of feet in the air, and in Pakistan's tribal areas a "military-aged male" could be as young as fifteen or sixteen. Using such broad definitions to determine who was a "combatant" and therefore a legitimate target allowed Obama administration officials to claim that the drone strikes in Pakistan had not killed any civilians. It was something of a trick of logic: In an area of known militant activity, all military-aged males were considered to be enemy fighters. Therefore, anyone who was killed in a drone strike there was categorized as a combatant, unless there was explicit intelligence that posthumously proved him to be innocent.

The perils of this approach were laid bare on March 17, 2011, just two days after Raymond Davis was released from prison under the "blood money" arrangement and spirited out of the country. CIA drones attacked a tribal council meeting in the village of Datta Khel, in North Waziristan, killing dozens of men. Ambassador Munter and some at the Pentagon thought the timing of the strike was disastrous, and some American officials suspected that the massive strike was the CIA venting its anger about the Davis episode. Munter thought that General Pasha, the ISI chief, had gone out on a limb to help end the Raymond Davis affair and that the Datta Khel strike could be perceived as a deliberate thumb in the eye. More important, however, many American officials believed that the strike had been botched, and that dozens of people died who shouldn't have.

Other American officials came to the CIA's defense, saying that the tribal meeting was in fact a meeting of senior militants, and therefore a legitimate target. But the drone strike unleashed a furious response in Pakistan. General Kayani issued a rare public statement, saying the operation was carried out "with complete disregard to human life," and street protests in Lahore, Karachi, and Peshawar forced the temporary closure of American consulates in those cities.

Munter wasn't opposed to the drone program, but he believed that the CIA was being reckless and that his position as ambassador was becoming untenable. His relationship with the CIA station chief in Islamabad, already strained because of their disagreements over the handling of the Raymond Davis case, deteriorated even further when Munter demanded that the CIA notify him before each missile strike

and give him the chance to call off the operation. During one screaming match between the two men, Munter tried to make sure the station chief knew who was in charge, only to be reminded of who really
held the power in Pakistan.

"You're not the ambassador!" Munter shouted.

"You're right, and I don't want to be the ambassador," the CIA station chief replied.

This turf battle spread to Washington, and a month after bin Laden
was killed President Obama's top advisers were openly fighting in a
National Security Council meeting over who really was in charge in
Pakistan. At the June 2011 meeting, Munter, who participated via
secure video link, began making his case that he should have veto
power over specific drone strikes. Using soccer terminology, he said
he should get a "red card" to scuttle proposed strikes.

Leon Panetta cut Munter off midsentence, telling him that the CIA
had the authority to do what it wanted in Pakistan. It didn't need to
get the ambassador's approval for anything.

"I don't work for you," Panetta told Munter, according to several
people who attended the meeting.

But Secretary of State Hillary Clinton came to Munter's defense.
She turned to Panetta and told him that he was wrong to assume
he could steamroll the ambassador and launch strikes against his
approval.

"No, Hillary," Panetta said, "it's you who are flat wrong."

There was a stunned silence, and National Security Advisor Tom
Donilon tried to regain control of the meeting by quieting the squabbling aides. In the weeks that followed the meeting, Donilon brokered
a compromise of sorts: Munter would be allowed to object to specific drone strikes, but the CIA could still press its case to the White
House and get approval for strikes even over the ambassador's objec-

tions. The ambassador was given, at best, a "yellow card." Obama's CIA had won another battle.

In the months that followed, Munter increasingly found himself isolated. Even Admiral Mullen, once the administration's most prominent advocate of maintaining at least barely functional relations with Islamabad, began to take a darker view toward Pakistan after the bin Laden raid. Not only did Mullen have his suspicions that someone senior in the Pakistani military or ISI may have been hiding Osama bin Laden; he had also become aware of an astonishing piece of intelligence. American spies had telephone intercepts that seemed to prove that the killing of Syed Saleem Shahzad, a Pakistani journalist who had been investigating links between the ISI and Pakistani militant groups, had been ordered by Pakistani spies. Shahzad had been beaten to death and tossed into an irrigation canal eighty miles south of Islamabad. According to classified assessments by American spy agencies, the killing had been an order from the highest ranks of the ISI, from General Ahmad Shuja Pasha himself.

Not long afterward, a separate intelligence tip warned that two suspicious fertilizer trucks were navigating the NATO supply routes from Pakistan into Afghanistan. The tip was vague and warned only that the trucks might be used as bombs and driven into Afghanistan for an attack against an American base. U.S. military officials in Afghanistan called General Kayani in Pakistan to alert him, and Kayani promised that the trucks would be stopped before they reached the Afghan border.

But the Pakistanis did not act. The trucks sat in North Waziristan for two months, as operatives from the Haqqani Network turned them into suicide bombs powerful enough to kill hundreds of people. American intelligence about the location of the trucks remained murky, but Admiral Mullen was certain that, given the ISI's history of contacts with the Haqqanis, Pakistani spies would be able to put a stop to any attack. By September 9, 2011, the trucks were moving toward Afghanistan, and the top American commander in the region, General John Allen, urged General Kayani to stop the trucks during a trip to Islamabad. Kayani told Allen he would "make a phone call" to prevent any imminent assault, an offer that raised eyebrows because it seemed to indicate a particularly close relationship between the Haqqanis and Pakistan's security apparatus.

Then, on the eve of the tenth anniversary of the attacks on the World Trade Center and the Pentagon, one of the trucks pulled up next to the outer wall of a U.S. military base in Wardak Province, in eastern Afghanistan. The driver detonated the explosives inside the vehicle and the blast ripped open the wall to the base. The explosion wounded more than seventy American Marines inside the base, and spiraling shrapnel killed an eight-year-old Afghan girl standing half a mile away.

The attack infuriated Mullen and convinced him that General Kayani had no sincere interest in curbing his military's ties to militant groups like the Haqqanis. Other top American officials had been convinced of this years earlier, but Mullen had believed that Kayani was a different breed of Pakistani general, a man who saw the ISI's ties to the Taliban, the Haqqani Network, and Lashkar-e-Taiba as nothing more than a suicide pact. But the Wardak bombing was, for Mullen, proof that Pakistan was playing a crooked and deadly game.

Days after the bombing—and immediately after the Haqqani Network launched another brazen attack, this time on the American-embassy compound in Kabul—Admiral Mullen went to Capitol Hill to give his final congressional testimony as chairman of the Joint Chiefs of Staff. He came to deliver a blunt message, one that State Department officials had been unsuccessful in trying to soften in the hours before he appeared before the Senate Armed Services Committee.

Pakistani spies were directing the insurgency inside of Afghanistan, Mullen told the congressional panel, and had blood on their hands from the deaths of American troops and Afghan civilians. "The Haqqani Network," Mullen said, "acts as a veritable arm of Pakistan's Inter-Services Intelligence agency."

Even after a tumultuous decade of American relations with Pakistan, no top American official up to that point had made such a direct accusation in public. The statement carried even more power because it came from Admiral Michael Mullen, whom Pakistani officials considered to be one of their few remaining allies in Washington. The generals in Pakistan were stung by Mullen's comments, no one more than his old friend General Ashfaq Parvez Kayani.

The relationship was dead; the two men didn't speak again after Mullen's testimony. Each man felt he had been betrayed by the other.

DAYS AFTER Osama bin Laden was killed, Dr. Shakil Afridi received an urgent call from Sue, his CIA handler. The fallout from the American operation was still roiling Pakistan, and Afridi had not heard from anyone in the CIA since the Navy SEALs stormed the house in Abbottabad. As the details of the operation began trickling out, Afridi finally understood why he had been in Abbottabad, why the CIA had asked him to focus his work on Bilal Town, and why there had been so much interest in the house on Pathan Street. Sue told Afridi to come immediately to Islamabad—and meet her at one of their regular rendezvous spots.

It's not safe for you to stay in Pakistan, she told the doctor when they met. The ISI was already hunting for anyone who might have helped the Americans find bin Laden, and it was just a matter of time before his work for the CIA was discovered. She told him to get on a bus and head west, across the border into Afghanistan. She handed him a telephone number and told him to call the number once he reached the bus station in Kabul. From there, he would receive further instructions.

He never went. Afridi assumed that since the CIA had never told him that he was involved in the bin Laden hunt, he would be safe in his own country and not be caught up in the dragnet that Pakistani security services had set up after the Abbottabad raid. It was a gross miscalculation. By the end of May, Dr. Afridi had been arrested by the ISI and imprisoned.

After years of tumult between the Central Intelligence Agency and Pakistan's Directorate for Inter-Services Intelligence, after the double dealing by both sides, and after the recriminations when a CIA contractor killed two people in Lahore and drew back the curtain on the new front of America's secret war in Pakistan, the case of Dr. Shakil Afridi showed just how far things had plummeted for the United States and Pakistan. The ISI had arrested a key CIA source, a man who played a role in the effort to track down the world's most wanted terrorist, and put him in a jail cell in Peshawar.

Of course, no country looks kindly upon one of its citizens when he is caught working for a foreign spy service. But, bizarrely, Afridi was not charged with treason or espionage, nor was he even charged under Pakistani law. Instead, he found himself in a court in Peshawar for violating the obscure British-era Frontier Crimes Regulations that govern Pakistan's tribal areas. Afridi had joined a "conspiracy to wage war against the state," the court found, because of his ties to Lashkar-e-Islam, the militant group run by the bus driver–cum–drug lord who had kidnapped him in 2008. Because Afridi had given medical treatment to Bagh's fighters, and because of what the court described as "his love for Mangal Bagh," Dr. Afridi was sentenced to thirty-three years in prison.

When the sentence was handed down, Lashkar-e-Islam issued a public statement vehemently denying any ties with "such a shameless man."

Afridi was no friend of the group, the statement said, because of his history of overcharging his patients.

16: FIRE FROM THE SKY

"Everything is backwards."

—*W. George Jameson*

O ne morning in late summer 2011, days before he took over as director of the Central Intelligence Agency, General David Petraeus paid a visit to Michael Hayden, the Bush administration's third
and final CIA director. The two men had ascended the ranks of the
military during the same era but had chosen very different paths and
had never been particularly close. Hayden had been a military-
intelligence specialist and ran the ultrasecret National Security
Agency in the years before he took over at Langley. Petraeus had spent
a career in combat units, running the wars in Iraq and Afghanistan
and leading U.S. Central Command. He had emerged as one of American history's most lauded generals.

The men shared a cordial breakfast at Hayden's house, and Hayden
offered advice to Petraeus about managing the tribal dynamics at
Langley. As Hayden had learned, the case officers and analysts could
be devoted yet prickly, didn't salute smartly, and sometimes had little
tolerance for the chain of command. Midway through breakfast the
discussion turned serious, and Hayden offered a warning to Petraeus.

The CIA had changed, perhaps permanently, he said, and there
was a real danger that the spy agency could turn into no more than a
smaller, more secretive version of the Pentagon.

"Never before has the CIA looked more like the OSS," Hayden said, referring to William Donovan's band of cloak-and-dagger men. After a decade of secret war, Hayden said, man hunting and targeted-killing operations were consuming the CIA, and if that continued, the agency might one day be incapable of carrying out what was supposed to be its primary mission: spying.

"The CIA is not the OSS," Hayden continued. "It's the nation's global intelligence service. And you've got to discipline yourself to carve out time to do something else besides counterterrorism."

Hayden, of course, had done more than his part to accelerate this transformation. A spy agency that on September 11, 2001, had been decried as bumbling and risk-averse had, under the watchful eye of four successive CIA directors, gone on a killing spree. During the long, hot summer in Pakistan in the months after Osama bin Laden's death, the CIA killed a string of al Qaeda operatives, including Atiyah Abd al-Rahman, who had been bin Laden's tether to the outside world during his time in hiding in Abbottabad. Some in Washington likened President Obama to Michael Corleone during the final minutes of *The Godfather*, coolly ordering lieutenants to dispatch his enemies in a calculated burst of violence.

Thirty-five years earlier, after the toxic details about the CIA's efforts to kill foreign leaders seeped into public view, President Gerald Ford ordered a ban on assassinations that he hoped would prevent future presidents from being too easily seduced by black operations. But in the decade since the September 11 attacks, legions of U.S. government lawyers had written detailed opinions about why the targeted-killing operations carried out by the CIA and Joint Special Operations Command far from declared war zones didn't violate President Ford's assassination ban. Just as lawyers for President Bush had redefined torture to permit extreme interrogations by the CIA and the military, so had lawyers for President Obama given America's secret agencies latitude to carry out extensive killing operations.

One of them was Harold Koh, who had come to Washington from Yale Law School, where he had been the school's dean. He had been a fierce critic from the left of the Bush administration's war on terror and had decried the CIA's interrogation methods—including waterboarding—as illegal torture. But when he joined the government as the State Department's top lawyer, he found himself spending hours poring over volumes of secret intelligence in order to pass judgment over whether men should live or die. In speeches, he offered a muscular defense of the Obama administration's targeted-killing operations, saying that in a time of war the American government was under no obligation to give suspects normal due process before putting them on a kill list.

Still, in moments of public reflection, he spoke of the psychological burdens of spending so much time reading the biographies of the young men the United States was debating whether or not to kill. "As the dean of Yale Law School I spent many, many hours looking at the résumés of young twenty-year-olds, students in their twenties, trying to figure out which ones should be admitted," he said during one speech. "I now spend a comparable amount of time studying the résumés of terrorists, same age. Reading about how they were recruited. Their first mission. Their second mission. Often I know their background as intimately as I knew my students'."

In the midst of the surge of drone attacks, President Obama ordered a reshuffling of his national-security team. The result was something of a grace note at the end of a decade during which the work of soldiers and spies had become largely indistinguishable. Leon Panetta, who as CIA director had made the spy agency more like the military, was taking over the Pentagon. General Petraeus, the four-star general who had signed secret orders in 2009 to expand military spying operations throughout the Middle East, would run the CIA.

In his fourteen months at Langley, before ignominiously resigning over an extramarital affair with his biographer, Petraeus accelerated the trends that Hayden had warned him about. He pushed the White House for money to expand the CIA's drone fleet, and he told members of Congress that, under his watch, the CIA was carrying out more covert-action operations than at any point in its history. Within weeks of arriving at Langley, Petraeus even ordered an operation that, up to that point, no CIA director had ever done before: the targeted killing of an American citizen.

BY THE TIME PETRAEUS took over the CIA, an owlish, bespectacled preacher with a bushy black beard and a message of rage had ascended to the top of America's kill list, the list coordinated in the basement office of John Brennan, the White House counterterrorism adviser. With bin Laden dead and the punishing campaign of drone strikes thinning al Qaeda's ranks in Pakistan, counterterrorism officials in Washington began to devote more attention to the threat from Yemen and al Qaeda in the Arabian Peninsula. That meant hunting down and killing Anwar al-Awlaki.

Al-Awlaki had taken a strange path to being designated as an enemy of the United States. Born in New Mexico in 1971, he spent his early years in the United States while his father, Nasser al-Awlaki, a prominent Yemeni who would go on to serve as President Saleh's minister of agriculture, studied agricultural economics at New Mexico State University. Nasser moved the family back to Yemen seven years later, where Anwar lived until returning to the United States for college in the early 1990s.

At Colorado State University, Anwar won the presidency of the school's Muslim Student Association but was not comfortable with the rigidly conservative strand of Islam—with its prohibitions on sex and alcohol—that some of his fellow students practiced. He stayed in Colorado after graduation, and to his father's chagrin he began preaching at a mosque in Fort Collins. Nasser had wanted his son to enter a more lucrative profession, but within a few years Anwar had moved to San Diego to take a position as an imam at a mosque at the edge of the city.

His views gradually grew more conservative, and he preached about living a life of purity. But in his private life he sometimes strayed from his own teachings; he was picked up multiple times by the San Diego police for soliciting prostitutes. More significantly, in 1999 the FBI began investigating al-Awlaki's ties to militant suspects in the San Diego area, suspicions that rose partly from his work for a small Islamic charity. He would even come into contact with two future September 11 hijackers, Khalid al-Mihdhar and Nawaf al-Hazmi, who both prayed at his mosque and attended conferences with the cleric.

But the FBI inquiries into his work unearthed no criminal activity, and by the time of the September 11 attacks al-Awlaki had resettled in Northern Virginia, where he was preaching at a large mosque in the suburbs of Washington, D.C. He infused his sermons with references to pop culture and American history, and he soon got his first taste of media stardom when he began getting calls from reporters to help explain the basics of Islam to American newspaper readers. He was even considered something of a voice of moderation—participating in an online chat for *The Washington Post* about Ramadan and attending a Pentagon prayer breakfast. "We came here to build, not to destroy," he said during one sermon, calling himself and other imams in America "the bridge between Americans and one billion Muslims worldwide."

But his message would soon turn darker. After a police crackdown on Muslim charities and other Muslim-owned institutions in 2002, al-Awlaki lashed out publicly about how the Bush administration's war against terrorism had become a war against Muslims. Shortly afterward, he moved to London, where he enthralled young Muslims who attended his fiery sermons and those who listened to his lectures on CD recordings, which he sold in a boxed set. But even as his fame grew, he had trouble supporting himself in the United Kingdom, and in 2004, he returned to Yemen, where he used Internet chat rooms and eventually YouTube to transmit his sermons globally.

The fact that his sermons were delivered in English limited his influence in the Muslim world, but his virulent anti-American rhetoric spurred a sliver of his followers to action. One of them was Umar Farouk Abdulmutallab, the young Nigerian student who would try to set off a bomb hidden in his underwear while on an airplane descending into Detroit on Christmas Day 2009. Months before, Abdulmutallab had written an essay about his reasons for wanting to wage jihad and sent it to al-Awlaki. As American investigators began piecing together the failed Christmas Day plot, they began to get a better understanding of the role al-Awlaki played within al Qaeda in the Arabian Peninsula. The thirty-eight-year-old American man who had once spoken about being America's "bridge" to the Muslim world was not merely an inspirational prophet for the digital age, a peddler of Internet hatred; he had put deeds to words and had begun helping the terror group plot a wave of terror against the United States.

John Brennan, who maintained close ties to Saudi intelligence officials and had already been running much of America's clandestine war in Yemen from the White House, believed that it was al-Awlaki who was principally responsible for a shift in the al Qaeda affiliate's strategy. While the group had long thought globally, it had acted locally by focusing its attacks on targets inside Saudi Arabia. But when bin Laden and his followers in Pakistan were under siege, AQAP saw the opportunity to pick up the mantle as America's chief tormenter. Brennan believed that al-Awlaki was pushing the group increasingly in this direction.

This may or may not have been the case, but inside the National Security Council, officials began debating an extraordinary matter: whether to authorize the secret killing of al-Awlaki, an American citizen, without capturing him or bringing him to trial. Harold Koh and other government lawyers began studying the raw intelligence about al-Awlaki's role inside the Yemeni militant group, and within months of Abdulmutallab's failed attempt to blow up the jetliner, the Justice Department's Office of Legal Counsel had produced a classified memo giving the Obama administration approval to kill the renegade American cleric. Because al-Awlaki had a senior position inside al Qaeda in the Arabian Peninsula and had declared war on the United States, the memo argued, he no longer had a Constitutional right to due process.

And yet the United States hadn't a clue where al-Awlaki or any other top AQAP operatives were hiding. Joint Special Operations Command had just begun ramping up its efforts to collect intelligence in Yemen, and the Obama administration was almost entirely dependent on the spies that Yemeni president Ali Abdullah Saleh and Saudi Arabia's intelligence service had planted around the country. And after the botched American strike in May 2010 that accidently killed a deputy governor in Yemen, Saleh had put even more restrictions on American activities there, and the clandestine war had ground to a halt.

SLOWLY, HOWEVER, THE STRONGMAN in Yemen began to lose his grip. President Saleh had maintained power for decades by expertly manipulating the various factions inside the country, often pitting them against each other in a fashion that one Bush administration official had likened to "dancing in the snake pit." But by early 2011, Yemen had become caught up in the street revolts spreading across the Arab world, and a government that once could barely control territory beyond the capital now couldn't even keep order there. Then, during an attack on the presidential palace in June, a barrage of rockets struck the room where President Saleh was hiding and knocked him to the floor. He suffered from internal bleeding in his skull, and the fires from the attack burned 40 percent of his body. Saleh's bodyguards put the wounded leader on an emergency flight to Saudi Arabia, where he spent hours in surgery. He survived, but his days as president were over. Ali Abdullah Saleh was no longer around to dictate what the United States could and could not do in his country.

The CIA and JSOC had used the yearlong pause in the American air war in Yemen after Deputy Governor Jaber al-Shabwani's death to build up a network of human spies and a web of electronic eavesdropping around Yemen. At the National Security Agency, at Fort Meade, Maryland, more analysts were assigned to monitor cell phones in Yemen and to penetrate computer networks in the hope of intercepting e-mail traffic. And, very quietly, the CIA began to build a drone base in the southern desert of Saudi Arabia to serve as a hub for the al Qaeda hunt in Yemen. Saudi Arabia had given permission to the CIA to build the base on the condition that the kingdom's role be masked. Said one American official involved in the decision to build the base, "The Saudis didn't want their face on the operation."

Until the CIA base was ready, Yemen was still JSOC's war. In May 2011, the Pentagon began sending armed drones over Yemen, flown from Ethiopia and Camp Lemonnier, in Djibouti, the hardscrabble former French Foreign Legion base where a small group of American Marines and special-operations troops had operated since 2002. The buzzing of the drones became a regular sound in some of Yemen's most remote expanses of desert, and a cat-and-mouse game between the jihadis and the killer machines began.

One Yemeni journalist, after spending two weeks with AQAP leaders, described the security procedures the group enacted to avoid being hit from the air. If a Yemeni jet fighter was approaching, they remained in place because, as the militants told the reporter, "The Yemeni planes always miss their targets." But if an American drone began buzzing overhead, they did the opposite. They shut off their cell phones, hopped into trucks, and began moving, because the drones "can't bomb moving targets." The militants had figured out one of the weaknesses of the drones, a problem created by flying the planes by satellite. Because drone pilots were separated from their airplanes by thousands of miles, what the pilots saw on their screens in the United States was sometimes several seconds behind what the drone was watching. The problem, known as latency, had for years made it difficult for targeting officers at the CIA and the Pentagon to figure out where to aim the missile fired from the drone, which explains some of the civilian casualties and missed targets of the drone wars.

Being in a moving truck allowed al-Awlaki to narrowly escape death in May 2011, just days after the commando raid in Pakistan that killed bin Laden. A human source spying for the Americans provided information that al-Awlaki was riding in a truck in Shabwa province, and the JSOC team sent drones and Marine Harrier jets to the area. But the first American missile missed al-Awlaki's truck, and when clouds moved into the area and obscured the view of the planes, al-Awlaki was able to jump into another truck and drive in the opposite direction. The American planes continued to follow the first truck, and a missile strike killed two local al Qaeda operatives in the vehicle. Al-Awlaki took refuge in a cave. According to Yemen scholar Gregory

Johnsen, al-Awlaki later told his friends that the incident "increased my certainty that no human being will die until they complete their livelihood and appointed time."

At the White House, President Obama and John Brennan were growing frustrated that JSOC kept missing al-Awlaki and other top leaders. A year and a half since Obama had expanded American clandestine activities in Yemen, no senior AQAP leaders had been killed and a number of strikes had been carried out with faulty intelligence. More civilians had been killed than militant leaders. Flying armed drones over Yemen was an improvement over cruise missiles, but Djibouti's government would not allow the United States to launch any lethal missions from Camp Lemonnier without first getting its approval. JSOC leaders bristled at the restrictions.

The CIA operated under no similar restrictions, and by September 2011 the drone base that the spy agency had built in the Saudi desert was completed and ready for use. David Petraeus, who by now was CIA director, ordered some of the agency's fleet of Predator and Reaper aircraft from Pakistan to Saudi Arabia. Spy agencies also repositioned satellites and reconfigured data networks to allow the drones to communicate with pilots back in the United States, and they carried out the other technological work required to open a new front in the drone war.

And the CIA had something beyond drone aircraft parked close to Yemen's border: a source within al Qaeda in the Arabian Peninsula who began providing regular information about al-Awlaki's movements. The CIA had already collected intelligence about AQAP's structure, and had managed to get an early warning about the group's glossy Internet publication, *Inspire*, each time before it was published. AQAP had used the magazine, written in English, to raise its profile and to incite would-be jihadis in the United States or the United Kingdom to wage war close to home. Major Nidal Hassan—an Army psychiatrist who killed thirteen people in a crowded military facility at Fort Hood, Texas, in November 2009—was a reader of *Inspire*. So was Faisal Shahzad, a junior financial analyst living in Connecticut who seven months later tried to detonate a van full of explosives in the middle of Times Square. One *Inspire* article, written by the magazine's Pakistani-American publisher, Samir Khan, carried the title "Making a Bomb in the Kitchen of Your Mom."

Each time they learned about an upcoming issue of *Inspire*, Obama officials debated whether to sabotage the magazine before it went online or insert messages into the text that might embarrass AQAP and set off alarms inside the group that a Saudi or American mole might have penetrated its ranks. But they decided against it, in part because they worried that anyone suspected of helping them might be executed. But there was a second reason. Since *Inspire* could be read online in the United States, any efforts by the CIA to manipulate its content might violate laws prohibiting the agency from carrying out propaganda operations against Americans. These same concerns had led the CIA to mostly abandon its propaganda operations since the advent of the Internet, when Americans sitting in front of laptop computers could read news and information that had been written thousands of miles away. The vacuum had allowed the Pentagon, and people like Michael Furlong, to fill the void with a new kind of information warfare tailored for the digital age.

Impressed by the CIA's record of targeted killings in Pakistan, White House officials took the hunt for Anwar al-Awlaki away from the Pentagon and gave it to the CIA. On September 30, a fleet of American drones took off from the base in Saudi Arabia, crossed into Yemen, and began tracking a group of men riding in a convoy across al Jawf province, an expanse of desert near the Saudi border once renowned for breeding Arabian horses. The men had stopped to eat breakfast when, according to witnesses, they spotted the drones and rushed back to their cars. But the drones had locked onto their target, and what followed was a carefully orchestrated symphony of destruction. Two Predator drones pointed lasers on the cars, a tactic that improved the accuracy of the missile strikes, and a Reaper drone fired missiles that delivered a direct hit. Every man riding in the convoy was killed, including American citizens Anwar al-Awlaki and Samir Khan, a diabolical propagandist and the creative force behind *Inspire*.

ABDULRAHMAN AL-AWLAKI—the imam's skinny sixteen-year-old Denver-born son—had slipped out of the kitchen window in his family's house in Sana'a two weeks earlier. It was the only home he had known since he moved to Yemen as a young boy, after his father had become famous in the United States and the United Kingdom for his inflammatory sermons. In the years since, his father became the Obama administration's most hunted man and fled Sana'a for the relative security of Yemen's remote provinces, but Abdulrahman mostly lived the life of a normal adolescent. He entered high school with an interest in sports and music, and he kept his Facebook page regularly updated.

In the middle of September 2011, he decided he needed to find his father, wherever he was hiding. Before sneaking out of the house, he left a note for his relatives:

"I am sorry for leaving," he wrote, "I'm going to find my father."

He went to Shabwa province, the region of Yemen where Anwar al-Awlaki was thought to be hiding and where American jets and drones had narrowly missed him the previous May. What Abdulrahman did not know was that his father had already fled Shabwa for al Jawf. He wandered about, having little idea about what to do next. Then, he heard the news about the missile strike that had killed his father, and he called his family back in Sana'a. He told them he was coming home.

He didn't return to Sana'a immediately. On October 14, two weeks after CIA drones killed his father, Abdulrahman al-Awlaki was sitting with friends at an open-air restaurant near Azzan, a town in Shabwa province. From a distance, faint at first, came the familiar buzzing sound. Then, missiles tore through the air and hit the restaurant. Within seconds, nearly a dozen dead bodies were strewn in the dirt. One of them was Abdulrahman al-Awlaki. Hours after the news of his death was reported, the teenager's Facebook page was turned into a memorial.

American officials have never discussed the operation publicly, but they acknowledge in private that Abdulrahman al-Awlaki was killed by mistake. The teenager had not been on any target list. The intended target of the drone strike was Ibrahim al-Banna, an Egyptian leader of AQAP. American officials had gotten information that al-Banna was eating at the restaurant at the time of the strike, but the intelligence turned out to be wrong. Al-Banna was nowhere near the location of the missile strike. Abdulrahman al-Awlaki was in the wrong place at the wrong time.

Although the strike remains classified, several American officials said that the drones that killed the boy were not, like those that killed his father, operated by the CIA. Instead, Abdulrahman al-Awlaki was a victim of the parallel drone program run by the Pentagon's Joint Special Operations Command, which had continued even after the CIA joined the manhunt in Yemen. The CIA and the Pentagon had converged on the killing grounds of one of the world's poorest and most desolate countries, running two distinct drone wars. The CIA maintained one target list, and JSOC kept another. Both were in Yemen carrying out nearly the exact same mission. Ten years after

Donald Rumsfeld first tried to wrest control of the new war from American spies, the Pentaton and CIA were conducting the same secret missions at the ends of the earth.

Two months after his son and grandson were killed, Dr. Nasser al-Awlaki mourned their deaths in a video eulogy he posted on You-Tube. Dr. al-Awlaki spoke for nearly seven minutes in clear, deliberate English. Loyal Muslims must keep his son Anwar's message alive, he said, and spread it to all those who had not yet been touched by his words. He pledged, ominously and without further detail, that his son's "blood did not and will not go in vain."

Dr. al-Awlaki described America as a "state gone mad," enthralled with a strategy of assassinations in the darkest corners of the world. The attacks had become so routine, he said, that the strikes that killed his son and grandson went almost unnoticed inside the United States. This was partly right. On the day Anwar al-Awlaki was killed, President Obama made brief mention of his death during a speech, calling it "another significant milestone in the broader effort to defeat al Qaeda and its affiliates." But by the next day, the killing of the firebrand preacher—an American citizen whose death had been authorized by a secret Justice Department memo—received no mention on network nightly news broadcasts. Two weeks later, barely any attention was paid to the killing of Abdulrahman al-Awlaki, the skinny American teenager.

THE DRONE STRIKES REMAINED a secret, at least officially. The Obama administration has gone to court to fend off challenges over the release of documents related to CIA and JSOC drones and the secret legal opinions buttressing the operations. In late September 2012, a panel of three judges sat in front of a wall of green marble in a federal courtroom in Washington and listened to oral arguments in a case brought by the American Civil Liberties Union demanding that the CIA hand over documents about the targeted-killing program. A lawyer representing the CIA refused to acknowledge that the CIA had anything to do with drones, even under cross-examination from skeptical judges who questioned him about public statements by former CIA director Leon Panetta. In one case, Panetta had joked to a group of American troops stationed in Naples, Italy, that, although as secretary of defense he had "a helluva lot more weapons available . . . than . . . at CIA," the "Predators [weren't] that bad."

At one point in the court proceeding, an exasperated Judge Merrick Garland pointed out the absurdity of the CIA's position, in light of the fact that both President Obama and White House counterterrorism adviser John Brennan had spoken publicly about drones. "If the CIA is the emperor," he told the CIA's lawyer, "you're asking us to say that the emperor has clothes even when the emperor's bosses say he doesn't."

But for all the secrecy, drone warfare has been institutionalized, ensuring that the missions of the CIA and the Pentagon continue to bleed together as the two organizations fight for more resources to wage secret war. Sometimes, as in Yemen, the two agencies run parallel and competing drone operations. Other times, they carve up the world and each take charge of different parts of the remote-controlled war—the CIA in Pakistan, for instance, and the Pentagon running the drone war in Libya.

It was July 2004 when the 9/11 Commission concluded that the CIA should give up its paramilitary functions. It made little sense, the commission concluded, for the CIA and the Pentagon to both be in the business of waging clandestine wars. "Whether the price is measured in either money or people," the commission's final report stated, "the United States cannot afford to build two separate capabilities for carrying out secret military operations, secretly operating standoff missiles, and secretly training foreign military or paramilitary forces."

The Bush administration rejected this recommendation, and in the years since, the United States has moved in the exact opposite direction. The CIA and the Pentagon now each jealously guard different parts of the shadow war's architecture—a drone base in Saudi Arabia, a former French Foreign Legion base in Djibouti, and other remote outposts—and are loath to relinquish any control as politicians embrace targeted-killing operations as the future of American warfare. Meanwhile, the Pentagon continues its push into human spying. The Defense Intelligence Agency is hoping to build a new cadre of undercover spies, hundreds of them, for spying missions in Africa, the Middle East, and Asia. "Everything is backwards," said W. George Jameson, a lawyer who spent thirty-three years at the CIA. "You've got an intelligence agency fighting a war and a military organization trying to gather on-the-ground intelligence."

Throughout the grueling presidential election season of 2012, President Obama frequently alluded to targeted killings as a sign of his toughness, speaking with braggadocio reminiscent of President Bush during the early days after the September 11 attacks. Once, a reporter asked him about accusations made by Republican presidential candidates that his foreign policy amounted to a strategy of appeasement. "Ask Osama bin Laden and the twenty-two out of thirty al Qaeda leaders who've been taken off the field whether I engage in appeasement," Obama shot back. "Or whoever is left out there, ask them about that."

For all their policy differences during the 2012 presidential campaign, Obama and Governor Mitt Romney found nothing to disagree about when it came to targeted killings, and Romney said that if elected president he would continue the campaign of drone strikes that Obama had escalated. Fearing such a prospect, Obama officials raced during the final weeks before the election to implement clear rules in the event they were no longer holding the levers in the drone wars. The effort to codify the procedures of targeted killings revealed just how much the secret operations remained something of an ad hoc effort. Fundamental questions about who can be killed, where they can be killed, and when they can be killed still had not been answered. The pressure to answer those questions eased on November 6, 2012, when a decisive election ensured that President Obama would remain in office for another four years. The effort to bring clarity to the secret wars flagged.

A nation fatigued by the long, bloody, and costly wars in Iraq and Afghanistan seemed, by the end of President Obama's first term, little concerned about the government's escalation of clandestine warfare. Quite the contrary. According to one poll conducted for Amy Zegart, of Stanford University, the country had, to a remarkable degree, become increasingly hawkish on counterterrorism matters. A large majority—69 percent of respondents—said they supported the American government secretly assassinating terrorists.

Targeted killings have made the CIA the indispensable agency for the Obama administration and have even improved the agency's image on other matters. According to the same poll, 69 percent of respondents expressed confidence that American spy agencies had accurate information about what was happening inside Iran and North Korea. This was more than 20 points higher than a similar poll had found in 2005, when the CIA was being slammed for the botched assessments about Iraq's weapons programs. Interestingly, the 2012 poll was conducted just months after North Korean dictator Kim Jong Il died—and CIA officials hadn't learned of his death until it was announced several days later on North Korean television.

But gradually, the risks and opportunity costs of a muscle-bound

CIA are becoming evident. After the CIA was surprised during the first weeks of the Arab Spring, the agency reassigned dozens of case officers and analysts to study what was happening in the Middle East and North Africa. And once again, the Obama administration also turned to CIA officers to play the role of soldiers rather than spies. As the revolution in Libya escalated into open civil war, the CIA sent paramilitary officers and private contractors to the country to establish contact with rebel groups and help ensure that the tons of machine guns and antiaircraft weapons flowing into Libya were channeled to the right rebel leaders. President Obama insisted that no American ground troops be used in the war to drive Gaddafi from power, relying instead on the formula that his administration had come to trust: drones, clandestine officers, and a cadre of contractors that had been empowered to use the Libyan rebels as a proxy army.

But the CIA had precious little real intelligence about the rebel groups, and some of the rebels that the United States had empowered in Libya turned against their patrons.

Just after 10 P.M. on the evening of September 11, 2012, a small CIA base in Libya received a frantic call from the American diplomatic compound just a mile away, in a different part of Benghazi, the port city on the Mediterranean Sea in eastern Libya where the American government had established a beachhead after Muammar Gaddafi's fall. The diplomatic compound was coming under fire, the State Department officer at the other end of the line said, and attackers carrying AK-47s were beginning to stream through the facility's main gate. Already the mob had taken gasoline cans and set one of the buildings on the compound ablaze.

The operatives at the CIA base, who had come to Benghazi to try to prevent Gaddafi's arsenal of shoulder-fired missiles from getting into the hands of the militant groups that had splintered off from the rebels now in charge in Libya, gathered their weapons and drove in a two-car convoy to the diplomatic compound. They had failed to convince a group of Libyan militia fighters to join them in the rescue effort, and when they arrived at the compound a fire was raging. J. Christopher Stevens, the American ambassador to Libya, was trapped inside one of the buildings. The building's ceiling had collapsed, and the CIA team was unable to reach Stevens, who suffocated from the intense smoke. Circling overhead, a military drone that had been diverted from a separate mission was beaming video of the firefight into the headquarters of U.S. Africa Command in Germany. But the Predator was unarmed and incapable of providing any help to the badly outnumbered team of Americans.

Unable to hold their positions any longer, the CIA operatives and State Department security officers evacuated the diplomatic compound and drove to the CIA base a mile away. But not long after they arrived, the CIA base came under a barrage of fire from AK-47s and rocket-propelled grenades. It wasn't until 5 A.M. when a group of American reinforcements arrived from Tripoli and joined the CIA operatives on the roof of the base. By then the attackers were preparing to stage another assault, and mortar shells began exploding on the roof. CIA operatives Tyrone Woods and Glen Doherty, both former Navy SEALs, were killed. By dawn the Americans had evacuated the CIA base and were driving to the airport, the Predator keeping watch over the convoy from the sky. All American personnel, together with the bodies of the four people killed during the assault, were flown to Tripoli. U.S. operations in Benghazi, which had been the CIA's primary base for gathering intelligence in Libya, were shut down.

THE ATTACK HAD, quite literally, blinded the CIA inside Libya. And, with the agency's decade-long pivot toward paramilitary operations, there is concern among the ranks of both current and former spies that the agency might be blind in too many other places as well, for a different reason. The CIA's closed society has fundamentally changed, and a generation of CIA officers is now socialized in war. Just as a generation earlier Ross Newland and his training class had been told that the spy agency should eschew killing at all costs, many CIA officers who joined the agency since September 11, 2001, have experienced *only* man hunting and killing. This new generation has felt more of the adrenaline rush of being at the front lines than the patient, "gentle" work of intelligence gathering and espionage. The latter can be tedious, even boring, and as one former top CIA officer put it, "How are you going to keep these people on the farm now that they've seen the bright lights of the city?"

Some senior CIA officials speak with pride about how the drone strikes in Pakistan have decimated al Qaeda, forcing the dwindling band of Osama bin Laden's followers to find new places to hide—in Yemen or North Africa or Somalia or some other ungoverned part of the world. Many believe that the drone program is the most effective covert-action program in CIA history.

But in the killing years since 2001, some of those who were present at the creation of the CIA's drone program—and who cheered the lethal authorities the spy agency was handed after the September 11 attacks—had become deeply ambivalent. Ross Newland still praises a weapon that allows the United States to wage war without carpet-bombing enemy territories or indiscriminately lobbing artillery shells into remote villages in Pakistan, but he thinks that the CIA should have given up Predators and Reapers years ago. The allure of killing people by remote control, he said, is like "catnip," and drones have made the CIA the villain in countries like Pakistan, where it should be the spy agency's job to nurture relationships for the purpose of gathering intelligence. The Predator, Newland said, "ends up hurting the CIA. This just is not an intelligence mission."

Richard Blee played an even more critical role at the dawn of the drone age. As head of the CIA's Alec Station, the unit inside the Counterterrorist Center with the specific mission of finding Osama bin Laden, Blee was among a small group of counterterrorism zealots who chafed at the restrictions placed on the spy agency in the years before the September 11 attacks. Together with his boss, J. Cofer Black, Blee pushed for the CIA to be given lethal authority to kill bin Laden and his minions. During the summer of 2001, he stood in the middle of California's Mojave Desert, watching as missiles fired from a Predator destroyed a mockup of bin Laden's Tarnak Farms training camp. Weeks later he watched in agony as thousands died on September 11, wondering whether he and his colleagues could have pushed harder to prevent the attacks. On his desk, he still keeps a piece of rubble from the destroyed replica of Tarnak Farms.

He has left the CIA, and in the years since his retirement he has been burdened by doubts about the wisdom of the CIA's targeted-killing mission. As the bar for carrying out lethal action lowered, and the agency was given permission to launch missiles in Pakistan when American spies weren't even certain whom they were killing—so-called signature strikes—he grew dismayed. What had originally been conceived as a device the United States might use selectively was being abused, Blee thought.

"In the early days, for our consciences we wanted to know who we were killing before anyone pulled the trigger," Blee said. "Now, we're lighting these people up all over the place."

The pistons of the killing machine, he said, operate entirely without friction. "Every drone strike is an execution," Blee said. "And if we are going to hand down death sentences, there ought to be some public accountability and some public discussion about the whole thing."

He paused. "And it should be a debate that Americans can understand."

ABOUT AN HOUR OUTSIDE of Las Vegas, after the stucco houses of the city's suburbs have disappeared and the landscape has turned into low creosote shrubs and spiky Joshua trees, the highway swings to the west and descends into a valley. A cluster of low, beige buildings appears in the distance, and above them a small plane resembling an insect flies slow, lazy circles in the sky. It rises over a cluster of hills to the right of the highway, turns to the left, and touches down on a runway carved out of the desert sand.

The town of Indian Springs, Nevada, elevation 3,123 feet, can be seen in a three-minute drive. It is mostly a collection of RV parks and mobile homes, served by two gas stations, a motel, and Auntie Moe's Trading Post. A billboard above the post office advertises the nearest chain amenities: DENNY'S, SUBWAY, MOTEL 6 — 1 HOUR AHEAD. The small casino where Curt Hawes and his team had a celebratory breakfast in February 2001, after making history by firing the first missile from a Predator, still sits at the edge of town. But like the rest of Indian Springs, it's mostly empty; thanks to a new bypass road, it is no longer a stop for tourists on their way to Death Valley from Las Vegas.

The lonely town has reaped none of the benefits of the robust growth taking place just across the highway, behind miles of fencing and guard posts, where armed soldiers deny entry to the curious. It was in the middle of the last decade that Indian Springs Air Force Auxiliary Field was renamed Creech Air Force Base, and the ramshackle, windswept base where the early Predator test pilots tinkered with a new way of war began its transformation into ground zero for American killing operations overseas. Sitting on twenty-three hundred acres of desert, Creech is now so busy that the Air Force is hoping to expand the base by buying land from local businesses, a move that could render Indian Springs even more of a ghost town.

Both the Pentagon and CIA fly drone missions out of Creech, and military personnel and civilian contractors involved in the drone program still commute to the base from the Las Vegas suburbs, pulling shifts in long, sand-colored trailers lined up into neat rows. Sometimes they fly training missions at Creech, navigating the Predators and Reapers near the base, honing their deadly skills by tracking civilian cars and trucks driving along lonely roads. But mostly the pilots are fighting a war thousands of miles away—in Afghanistan, in Pakistan, in Yemen, and across the great desert expanse of North Africa. In the weeks after the September 2012 attack on the American diplomatic compound in Libya, the skies above Benghazi filled with the buzzing sound of American drones, sent there to track down the perpetrators of the attack.

At the edge of the Nevada base, washed-out red cement barriers carry a proud message:

CREECH AFB: HOME OF THE HUNTERS

EPILOGUE: A SPY IN LEISURE WORLD

"This is where the business is going."

—*Dewey Clarridge*

Dewey Clarridge fell down. A year after the Pentagon shuttered his private spying operation, Clarridge stumbled in his house near San Diego and broke several bones. The accident put him in the hospital, where he was more ornery than usual, and forced him to relocate to the East Coast to be closer to his family. The seventy-nine-year-old former CIA officer—the founder of the agency's Counterterrorist Center, one of the principal public villains of the Iran–Contra scandal, and the man who once bragged about coming up with the idea of mining the harbors of Nicaragua while he was drinking gin—moved to Leisure World.

He rented an apartment in one of the high-rise towers that dominates Leisure World's leafy campus, twenty-five miles from Washington, D.C., a retirement village trying to reel in baby boomers by marketing itself as "The Destination for the Ageless Generation." A Yankee Republican born during the Depression, Clarridge was hardly a boomer and generally detested much of what the generation had come to represent.

I drove out to meet him in June 2012, unsure of what kind of a reception I would get. I had written a good deal about Clarridge, and much of it I knew he didn't like. But he greeted me warmly when I pulled up to the Italian restaurant on the retirement village's property, where Clarridge appeared to be the only customer and had taken a table to enjoy the late afternoon sun. He looked like any other retiree. He was dressed in a salmon-colored shirt, unbuttoned at the top to allow the gold chain around his neck to peek out. He wore sneakers and white socks and somehow was tanner than he had been when living in San Diego. He told me he had adjusted to his new surroundings but complained that his cats were less than pleased. "Everyone here has dogs. Those little dogs."

It was a bit ironic that Clarridge was now living just miles from the CIA, an agency he viewed largely with scorn, but he didn't seem to miss California or lament his move back to the East Coast.

"This is where the business is going," he said.

By "the business" he meant the private intelligence business. And he was right. The drive out of Washington to the exurban retirement village cut through the gleaming glass towers and sprawling office parks of Northern Virginia that, over the past decade, had sprouted almost from nothing. America's defense and intelligence industries, once spread throughout the country in places like Southern California and the Midwest, had gradually consolidated and relocated to the Washington area. The companies chose to move closer to what they called "the customer": the Pentagon, the CIA, the National Security Agency, and other intelligence services. Government contractors large and small now form a ring around the capital like an army laying siege to a medieval town.

The private military and intelligence business was booming. By 2012, the global battlefield had stretched America's secret army beyond its capacities. The CIA and other intelligence services had outsourced some of their most essential missions to private contractors, who were being hired for espionage missions and to carry out intelligence analysis. They were hired to support CIA drone operations: from sitting in ground-control stations in Nevada to loading missiles and bombs onto the drones at classified bases in Afghanistan and Pakistan.

Jeffrey Smith, a former general counsel for the CIA and now partner in a prestigious Washington law firm, represents some of the companies that have won black contracts for doing military or intelligence work. It is stunning, Smith told me, how much the American government has outsourced the basic functions of spycraft to private contractors (many of the companies led by former CIA officers and special-operations troops), who promise they can do a better job than federal employees. Erik Prince sold off Blackwater and moved to the United Arab Emirates, but other companies took its place, companies that do a far better job staying out of the headlines than Blackwater did. As the American way of war has moved away from clashes between tank columns, outside the declared war zones and into the shadows, a cottage industry has materialized to become an indispensable part of a new military-intelligence complex.

Smith sometimes bristles at the relentlessly negative portrayal of private contractors, but he also sees the potential for trouble if the needs of the mission conflict with a company's profit imperative. "There's an inevitable tension as to where the contractor's loyalties lie," he said. "Do they lie with the flag? Or do they lie with the bottom line?"

By the middle of 2012, Michele Ballarin was still trying hard to win another long-term government contract for her work in Africa, and she saw opportunity in the chaos that was spreading across the northern part of the continent. After radical Islamists took over a vast stretch of desert in northern Mali, and after it became clear that Washington once again was struggling to get intelligence about a country it had

326 | THE WAY OF THE KNIFE

long ignored, Ballarin told me she was making contacts with Tuareg rebels in the eastern part of Mali and was hatching a plan to drive Islamists out of the country. She didn't elaborate.

Her planning wasn't limited to Africa. Ballarin was looking for investors for a new project to build a fleet of seaplanes modeled after the original Grumman G-21 Goose, planes that she thought the American military could use to land troops in remote locations that didn't have working airstrips. She was even scouting business opportunities in Cuba that might make her rich once Fidel Castro finally died and Communism in Cuba came to an end.

That summer day in 2012, it seemed very unlikely that Dewey Clarridge would ever again dip his cup into the stream of government money going to intelligence contractors. His operation with Michael Furlong had concluded ignominiously, and Furlong had quietly been forced into retirement. Clarridge was still angry about how the episode ended. As he saw it, it was yet another example of bureaucrats in Washington protecting their turf at the expense of soldiers in the field, who desperately needed the intelligence he could provide, if only to avoid relying on the CIA. But he said he was determined to stay in the game. He told me he still kept his network of informants in Afghanistan and Pakistan, some of whom could be maintained on a shoestring budget. If Washington was too foolish to make use of his people, he said, maybe another friendly government might be more enlightened.

He lit a cigar and turned philosophical.

"I think the Treaty of Westphalia is over," he said. He was talking about the seventeenth-century peace accords in Europe that ended the Thirty Years' War, three bloody decades of fighting among kings and emperors who sometimes used mercenaries as cannon fodder for the major battles. The Treaty of Westphalia, most historians agree, led to the birth of modern nations, standing armies, and national identities.

"Nation states no longer have a monopoly on military force," he said. It was corporations and private interests, he said, that would be the future of America's wars. "Just look at our own system. The only thing that isn't outsourced is the guy shooting the gun."

It was a rare moment when Dewey Clarridge was actually understating a situation. At times since the attacks of September 11, 2001, the United States had even outsourced the trigger pulling. Whether it was Erik Prince, Enrique Prado, and Blackwater hired by the CIA to hunt terrorists, or hired muscle like Raymond Davis driving through the streets of Lahore with a Glock semiautomatic in his glove box, or private soldiers dodging mortars during an all-night firefight on the roof of a CIA base in Benghazi, the chaotic first years of America's shadow war had seen the United States willing to farm out government's most elemental function: protecting the state.

It was getting late, and I got up to leave. Clarridge decided to stay and finish his cigar. We shook hands, and I walked to my car. Driving away, I glanced back at Dewey, sitting alone at the table of the retirement home's empty restaurant. A thin trail of cigar smoke curled up into the dying light.

ACKNOWLEDGMENTS

Writing a book involves making hundreds of decisions, and with a first book it's very difficult to know how many of those decisions are good ones. I am extraordinarily lucky that one of the first decisions I made was among the best, which was to hire Adam Ahmad to be my research assistant. From our first meeting, over coffee in Chicago, where he was finishing his master's, I could tell that Adam was bright, curious, and dedicated. He proved to be all those things and so much more. He was an absolutely integral part of the book during all of its phases. He researched documents, wrote background papers, organized endnotes, and in several cases managed to track down an Urdu speaker to translate documents and recordings neither of us could understand. When I arrived at the Woodrow Wilson International Center for Scholars, Jessica Schulberg joined the project and provided research help every bit as valuable as Adam's. Jessica has a particular interest in Africa, and her ability to unearth information about Somalia and North Africa was awe inspiring. She is a clear thinker and is wise beyond her years. During the course of writing this book, I have come to value not only Adam and Jessica's guidance but also their friendship. They both have long and bright careers ahead of them, whatever paths they choose.

It was my great fortune to spend fifteen months at the Wilson Center, the best research institution in Washington. The Wilson Center gave me a professional home, fascinating and supportive colleagues, and access to a vast library run by a crack team. Thanks to Jane Harman and Michael Van Dusen for accepting me as a Public Policy Scholar and for running such a terrific operation. A very special thanks to Robert Litwak for being a constant source of insight and humor as I went through the painful process of writing the first draft of this book.

It is my great honor to be a reporter for the *New York Times*, and I am grateful to Jill Abramson, Dean Baquet, and David Leonhardt for allowing me to take a leave from the paper to work on this project. When he was my boss in Washington, Dean encouraged me to examine the unexplored aspects of the secret wars—to write the stories that others weren't writing. Some of the issues I wrote about for the newspaper during that period are explored in greater depth in this book. My friends and colleagues Helene Cooper, Scott Shane, and Eric Schmitt gave me encouragement and guidance throughout this process, and Scott and Eric took on a great deal of extra work while I was on book leave. I can't thank them enough. In addition to those three, the national-security team in the Washington bureau is a collection of the best reporters—and most entertaining people—anywhere in journalism. Particular thanks to Peter Baker, Elisabeth Bumiller, Michael Gordon, Bill Hamilton, Mark Landler, Eric Lichtblau, Eric Lipton, Steve Myers, Jim Risen, David Sanger, Charlie Savage, and Thom Shanker. I am very lucky to work with them and the entire Washington bureau. Thanks also to Phil Taubman and Douglas Jehl, two former bosses at the paper with vast experience in intelligence reporting, who helped me greatly as I was beginning to cover a new beat.

This book would never have happened without Scott Moyers, who in his previous incarnation as a literary agent urged me to look deeper into the themes that I was writing about in my articles for the *New York Times*. Then, after Scott became the publisher of The Penguin

Press, I was lucky enough to get him as my book editor. He sees the big picture and pushed me to write as expansively as possible about the changing nature of American war and its impact. I appreciate the time he gave me to make sure the reporting for this book was right, and he provided a steady hand during the editing process. He proved that great book editing is possible even under very tight deadline pressures. Thanks also to Ann Godoff, the president and editor in chief at Penguin Press, for taking a leap on this project and for ensuring that the book could be published swiftly, at a time when these issues need far more public discussion. Mally Anderson at Penguin Press ensured that the various pieces of the book met their deadlines, and I'm very grateful to her for patiently guiding me through what was a very mysterious process. It was good having her calm voice at the other end of the phone.

Rebecca Corbett, a friend and editor at the *New York Times*, probably has no idea how much better this book is as a result of her guidance, patience, and savvy. She pored over several drafts of the book, pushing me to dig deeper in the reporting and explain myself better in the writing. She has a keen eye for detail and for making characters come to life. Our lunches at The Bottom Line not only helped me organize my reporting but also helped enormously in constructing the book's narrative. The discussion was much better than the food.

My agent, Andrew Wylie, has been a confidant since the earliest stages of writing the proposal for this book, and I am grateful to him for taking me on as a client. He's a true professional, and he gave particularly wise counsel during a nerve-racking day in New York as I had to make a decision about publishers: He told me to go with my gut. "Stop worrying," he said. "Life's too short." He was right.

My *New York Times* colleague Declan Walsh, in Islamabad, was kind enough to put me up during my time in Pakistan. Besides being a terrific reporter and a source of immense wisdom about what may be the world's most complicated country, Declan runs what is no doubt Pakistan's finest guesthouse. Thank you to everyone at the Islamabad bureau for making my reporting trip to Pakistan so productive.

I am in great debt to my friends who cover national-security issues for other news organizations. The work that they do to shed light on dark corners has informed this book immensely. Particular thanks to Greg Miller, Joby Warrick, Peter Finn, Julie Tate, and Dana Priest, of the *Washington Post*; Adam Goldman, Matt Apuzzo, and Kimberly Dozier, of the Associated Press; and Siobhan Gorman, Julian Barnes, and Adam Entous of the *Wall Street Journal*. We all may compete fiercely against each other, and curse each other when we are forced to match a competitor's story at 10 P.M., but in the end we're all on the same side.

The debt that I owe to my family is one that I can't possibly begin to repay. My parents, Joseph and Jeanne Mazzetti, taught me to be curious and to be humble. But most of all they taught me to be honest, and I hope they are as proud of me as I am of them. My sisters, Elise and Kate, are the two best friends someone could have, and they—along with their husbands, Sudeep and Chris—are role models for me in the way that they live their lives and raise their families.

The single person who has contributed the most to this book is Lindsay, my wonderful wife. From our very first discussion about the possibility of me writing a book, while walking in Riverside Park in New York, Lindsay's support was unwavering. She read and edited drafts of the book, offered suggestions, endured my insomnia, and provided encouragement during the times that I thought I was taking on more than I could handle. I couldn't possibly have done this without her, and I love her very much.

And to Max, my son. Max was born when I was in the early stages of this project, and he has changed my life in ways I'm just beginning to understand. I can't wait until he is old enough to read this book. I cherish the memories of the mornings we spent together during the first few months, and of the smiles he delivered when I came home at the end of particularly frustrating days of book writing. They put things in perspective. There is a great deal of pain and heartache in the world, but it is a far better place with Max in it.

A NOTE ON SOURCES

It is a great challenge to write an account of an ongoing war that, at least officially, remains a secret. This book is the result of hundreds of interviews in the United States and overseas, both during my years as a national-security reporter and during my book leave from the *New York Times*. I tried as much as possible to convince the people whom I interviewed to speak for the record, and those who agreed are cited by name both in the main text of the book and in the endnotes. I also conducted scores of interviews on "background," where I allowed sources to speak anonymously in exchange for their accounts of American military and intelligence operations, the vast majority of which remain classified. Although this is hardly ideal, I believe it is a necessary evil to ensure that trusted sources are able to speak candidly.

Using anonymous sources is always a risk, and as a national-security reporter I have learned that some sources can be trusted far more than others. For this book I have relied heavily on people whose information I have come to trust over the years. To the extent I am able, I have used the endnotes to give more information about who provided specific information, even if I did not use their names. On some occasions, usually because material is particularly sensitive, I presented information that does not have designated endnotes. In these instances I made sure that I could verify the information from multiple sources. When I recount conversations between two or more people, I have used quotation marks around the dialogue only when I am confident that my sources have provided an accurate recollection of the conversation.

I have tried as much as possible to draw on open source material and declassified government documents. In this effort, I have been helped by the work of several different organizations. The National Security Archive, at George Washington University, works tirelessly to get government documents declassified under the Freedom of Information Act, and I am enormously grateful for their efforts. The SITE Intelligence Group is the best resource for monitoring the writings and public statements of militant groups in Pakistan, Somalia, Yemen, and other countries, and I have drawn extensively on SITE's work. A large number of the U.S. government documents cited in this book were first made public by WikiLeaks, the antisecrecy organization. The WikiLeaks database has become an important resource for journalists and historians trying to better understand the inner workings of American government.

I am deeply indebted to the many people in several different countries who gave up countless hours of their time to let me interview them. They trusted me to tell their stories, and this is their book as much as it is mine.

Mark Mazzetti
Washington, D.C.
December 2012

NOTES

PROLOGUE: THE WAR BEYOND

2   *"Is he understanding everything?":* Raymond Davis interrogation by Lahore police comes from cell-phone video taken during the questioning. The video can be seen at www.youtube.com/watch?v=o10sPS6QPXk.

3   *An assortment of bizarre paraphernalia:* Mark Mazzetti et al., "American Held in Pakistan Worked With CIA," *The New York Times* (February 21, 2011).

4   *"our diplomat in Pakistan":* Press conference by President Barack Obama, February 15, 2011.

4   *Moscow Rules:* Author interview with two American officials.

7   *trouble for the alliance:* The officer's thoughts about the OSS quoted in Douglas Waller, *Wild Bill Donovan: The Spymaster Who Created the OSS and Modern American Espionage* (New York: Free Press, 2011): 188–189.

7   *twisted and burning:* Details of Sir Richard Dearlove's trip to CIA headquarters come from Ross Newland, a former top CIA official who was standing next to Dearlove during the Predator strike.

CHAPTER 1: PERMISSION TO KILL

9   *"You are there to kill terrorists":* Secret cable from American ambassador to Pakistan Wendy Chamberlin, to State Department, September 14, 2001. The cable was declassified and later released by the National Security Archive.

9   *license to kill:* The CIA presentation in the White House Situation Room was described by one participant in the meeting and a second former American official with direct knowledge of what transpired during the meeting.

11   *"Usama Bin Lane":* Jose A. Rodriguez Jr., *Hard Measures: How Aggressive CIA Actions After 9/11 Saved Lives* (New York: Threshold Editions, 2012): 75.

12   *to kill off as many al Qaeda operatives as possible:* George J. Tenet, *At the Center of the Storm* (New York: HarperCollins, 2007): 165.

12   *"have flies walking across their eyeballs":* Cofer Black interview, *60 Minutes,* May 13, 2012.

12   *"the flies-on-the-eyeballs guy":* Bob Woodward, *Bush at War* (New York: Simon & Schuster, 2002): 52.

13   *who should be captured:* This idea is explored in greater depth in Philip

Zelikow, "Codes of Conduct for a Twilight War," *Houston Law Review* (April 16, 2012).

13 *"we don't do policy from [Langley] . . .":* "Intelligence Policy," National Commission on Terrorism Attacks Upon the United States, 9/11 Commission Staff Statement No. 7 (2004).

15 **take a job at the State Department:** Black and Pavitt were barely speaking to each other. By early 2002, according to several former CIA officials, Black's popularity at the White House led the CTC chief to ignore his bosses at Langley and frequently say, "I work for the president." After Black's time at the State Department, he took a senior management job at Blackwater USA.

15 *"out on Business":* Rodriguez Jr., 20.

16 **He was removed from the job:** David Wise, "A Not So Secret Mission," *Los Angeles Times* (August 26, 2007).

17 **prisoners presumably would be there:** David Johnston, and Mark Mazzetti, "A Window into CIA's Embrace of Secret Jails," *The New York Times* (August 12, 2009).

18 **They dug up a handful of bodies:** Details of the Zhawar Kili exploitation operation come from Navy SEAL history of mission, July 2002. The history is titled "The Zhawar Kili Cave Complex: Task Force K-Bar and the Exploitation of AQ008, Paktika Province, Afghanistan."

18 **two teams stormed the compounds simultaneously:** Specifics of the Hazar Qadam operation come from U.S. Special Operations Command's internal history of the raid, as well as interviews with members of the special-operations task force based in Kandahar.

20 **an entirely new organization:** Donald H. Rumsfeld memorandum to George Tenet, "JIFT-CT." September 26, 2001.

20 *"If the war does not":* Donald H. Rumsfeld, "Memorandum for the President," September 30, 2001.

21 **with gun barrels pointed forward:** Details of Mullah Khairkhwa's pursuit and capture come from a U.S. Special Operations Command classified history, as well as interviews with members of the special-operations task force based in Kandahar.

23 **one of the island prison's first inmates:** Memorandum for Commander, United States Southern Command, March 6, 2008, "Recommendation for Continued Detention Under DoD Control for Guantánamo Detainee, ISN US9AF-000579DP(S)." Available at http://projects.nytimes.com/guantanamo/detainees/579-khirullah-said-wali-khairkhwa.

CHAPTER 2: A MARRIAGE AMONG SPIES

25 *"Pakistan has always seen":* Mahmud Ahmed to Richard Armitage, "Deputy Secretary Armitage's Meeting with Pakistan Intel Chief Mahmud: You're Either with Us or You're Not," State Department cable, September 12, 2001. This document and several others cited in this chapter were declassified and released on September 11, 2011, by the National Security Archive.

26 *"to save the planet":* Donald Rumsfeld to George W. Bush, "Memorandum for the President: My Visits to Saudi Arabia, Oman, Egypt, Uzbekistan, and Turkey," (October 6, 2001).

28 *"Usama bin Ladin":* U.S. embassy in Islamabad cable to U.S. Secretary of State, "Usama bin Ladin: Pakistan seems to be leaning against being helpful," State Department cable, December 18, 1998.

28 *"I cannot understand why you Americans":* John R. Schmidt, *The Unraveling: Pakistan in the Age of Jihad* (New York: Farrar, Straus and Giroux, 2011): 109.

28 *"is the future of Afghanistan":* Author interview with Shaukat Qadir.

28 *the embassy car waiting for him:* Author interview with Porter Goss.

29 *"deep introspection" in Islamabad:* Secret State Department cable detailing meeting between Richard Armitage and Mahmud Ahmed, "Deputy Secretary Armitage's Meeting with Pakistan Intel Chief Mahmud," September 12, 2001.

29 *all the intelligence it had about al Qaeda:* U.S. Secretary of State cable to U.S. embassy in Islamabad, "Deputy Secretary Armitage's Meeting with General Mahmud: Actions and Support Expected of Pakistan in Fight Against Terrorism," September 13, 2001.

30 *the northern province of Sindh:* Pervez Musharraf, *In the Line of Fire* (New York: Simon & Schuster, 2006): 206.

30 *a crushed, impoverished outcast:* Ibid., 202.

31 *"if and when the government":* Pervez Musharraf, Translated text of speech, September 19, 2001.

32 *"Afghanistan will revert to warlordism":* U.S. embassy in Islamabad cable to U.S. Secretary of State, "Mahmud Plans 2nd Mission to Afghanistan," State Department cable, September 24, 2001.

32 *"You want to please the Americans":* John F. Burns, "Adding Demands, Afghan Leaders Show Little Willingness to Give Up Bin Laden," *The New York Times* (September 19, 2001).

32 *after years of mistrust:* George J. Tenet, *At the Center of the Storm* (New York: HarperCollins, 2007): 140–141.

33 *Grenier was dead wrong:* Henry A. Crumpton, *The Art of Intelligence: Lessons from a Life in the CIA's Clandestine Service* (New York: Penguin Press, 2012): 194.

33 *"Every pillar of the Taliban regime will be destroyed":* U.S. Secretary of State cable to U.S. embassy in Islamabad, "Message to Taliban," State Department cable, October 5, 2001.

34 *turned our stalled relationship around:* Colin L. Powell to President George W. Bush, "Memorandum to the President: Your Meeting with Pakistan President Musharraf," November 5, 2001.

34 *stay in Afghanistan for years:* Author interview with General Ehsan ul Haq.

34 *Pakistan's embassies in Washington:* A description of the ISI cables comes from a former senior Pakistani official who had read the ISI analysis.

35 *"a very short-term affair":* Author interview with Asad Durrani.

35 **on level ground with the Americans:** Account of the conversation comes from author interview with Ehsan ul Haq.

36 *nothing productive came from the meeting:* Ibid.

36–37 *"range after range":* Churchill's dispatches were later compiled in his first book, Winston Churchill, *The Story of the Malakand Field Force: An Episode of Frontier War* (New York: W. W. Norton, 1989).

37 *"an inconvenient fact":* Mark Mazzetti and David Rohde, "Amid U.S. Policy Disputes, Qaeda Grows in Pakistan," *The New York Times* (June 30, 2008).

38 **The hunt for bin Laden:** Christina Lamb, "Bin Laden Hunt in Pakistan Is 'Pointless'," *London Sunday Times* (January 23, 2005).

38 *the suspicions had dissolved:* Author interview with Asad Munir.

40 *dripping wet in his swimsuit:* Ibid.

40 *informing on al Qaeda for Britain's MI6:* The information al-Jaza'iri had been a British agent came from the dossier of information compiled about his background by interrogations at Guantánamo Bay. The dossier was part of a number of documents made public by the group WikiLeaks, and is available at www.guardian.co.uk/world/guantanamo-files/PK9AG-001452DP.

CHAPTER 3: CLOAK-AND-DAGGER MEN

44 *assassination attempts:* "National Security Act of 1947," United States Congress, July 26, 1947. NSA 1947 was codified in 50 U.S.C, Chapter 15, Subchapter I § 403-4a. President Truman's views on the CIA are described in Tim Weiner, *Legacy of Ashes: The History of the CIA* (Maine: Anchor, 2008): 3.

45 *the largest and most complex:* Richard H. Schultz Jr., *The Secret War Against Hanoi* (New York: HarperCollins, 1999): 337.

45 **The war ended before any kidnappings:** Douglas Waller, *Wild Bill Donovan: The Spymaster Who Created the OSS and Modern American Espionage* (New York: Free Press, 2011): 316.

46 *the principal focus of its hearings:* L. Britt Snider, *The Agency and the Hill: CIA's Relationship with Congress 1946–2004* (CreateSpace, 2008): 275.

46 *"once the capability":* United States Senate, "Final Report of the Select Committee to Study Governmental Operations with Respect to Intelligence Activities," April 26, 1976.

46 *"avert a nuclear holocaust or save a civilization":* Ibid.

47 **London School of Economics:** Author interview with Ross Newland.

47 *in an attempt to kill Castro:* T. Rees Shapiro, "Nestor D. Sanchez, 83; CIA Official Led Latin American Division," *Washington Post* (January 26, 2011).

50 *each shadowy front of the Cold War:* Duane R. Clarridge with Digby Diehl, *A Spy for All Seasons* (New York: Scribner, 1997): 23–39.

50 **Dewey Marone and Dax Preston LeBaron:** Ibid., 26.

50 *infuriated State Department diplomats:* CNN interview with Duane Clarridge and kept by the National Security Archive, 1999.

50 ***"shallow and devious":*** Richard N. Gardner, *Mission Italy: On the Front Lines of the Cold War* (Maryland: Rowman & Littlefield, 2005): 291.

51 ***a covert war in Central America:*** Clarridge with Diehl, 197.

51 ***than the CIA had to spend:*** Ibid., 234.

52 ***CIA covert-action programs:*** Richard A. Best Jr., "Covert Action: Legislative Background and Possible Policy Questions," *Congressional Research Service* (December 27, 2011). The restrictions that came to be known as the "Casey Accords" were signed in 1986. But the horse was already out of the barn, as the accords came several months after President Reagan signed a secret finding authorizing the secret transfer of missiles to Iran.

54 ***authority to "neutralize":*** Robert Chesney, "Military-Intelligence Convergence and the Law of the Title 10/Title 50 Debate," *Journal of National Security Law and Policy* (2012). This is an excellent study on the laws buttressing the work of the CIA and the Pentagon and how the work of soldiers and spies has increasingly blurred in the years since the September 11 attacks.

54 ***"Do you know what":*** Joseph Persico, *Casey: From the OSS to the CIA* (New York: Penguin, 1995): 429.

55 ***the training of Lebanese hit men:*** Timothy Naftali, *Blind Spot: The Secret History of American Counterterrorism* (New York: Basic Books, 2005): 152.

55 ***"fighting terrorism with terrorism.":*** Ibid., 150.

55 ***the new threat:*** Vincent Cannistraro, an operations officers, said that "Casey came to the CIA believing that the evil Soviet Union was behind all terrorism in the world." By this logic, Cannistraro said during an interview, Moscow could dial up and ratchet back terrorist attacks whenever it chose to.

55 ***destroyed any hope that terrorism:*** Naftali, 180. Naftali quotes future Counterterrorism Center deputy Fred Turco describing Casey's views about the terrorism violence.

55 ***an expansive new war:*** Casey had been getting pressure from the White House to "do something" about terrorism, and told Clarridge to come up with a new covert strategy for the CIA. And as usual, Clarridge wanted as much running room as he could get. He pushed for new legal authorities that would allow him to build two teams that could hunt terrorists globally and kill them if doing so might prevent an imminent attack. One of the teams would be made up of foreigners who could move easily in the bazaars and crowded streets of Middle Eastern cities, and the second would be made up of Americans. Members of the teams were chosen based on proficiency in foreign languages, facility with weapons, and other specialized skills. One was a mercenary who had fought in the African civil wars. Another was a former Navy SEAL. See Steve Coll, *Ghost Wars: The Secret History of the CIA, Afghanistan and Bin Laden, from the Soviet Invasion to September 10, 2001* (New York: Penguin Press, 2005): 139–140; see also Clarridge with Diehl, *A Spy for All Seasons* (New York: Scribner, 1997): 325 and 327.

57 *to penetrate the Abu Nidal organization and Hezbollah:* Naftali, 183.

57 *"The wheels had fallen off for Reagan":* Ibid., 199–200.

58 *cut by 22 percent:* Author interview with senior American intelligence official.

59 *trying to get a meeting with the president:* R. James Woolsey public remarks at George Mason University, September 13, 2012.

59 *"ordered, planned, or participated":* Intelligence Oversight Board, "Report on the Guatemala Review," June 28, 1996.

60 *"Going back to the history":* Author interview with Dennis Blair.

61 *"What's the president":* Ibid.

CHAPTER 4: RUMSFELD'S SPIES

63 *"We seem to have created":* Frank C. Carlucci, "Memorandum to the Deputy Under Secretary for Policy Richard Stillwell," Washington, D.C., May 26, 1982, declassified in 2001 via Freedom of Information Act Request by the National Security Archive. Jeffrey T. Richelson and Barbara Elias of the National Security Archive compiled other declassified documents used in this chapter. Also invaluable to this chapter, Robert Chesney, "Military-Intelligence Convergence and the Law of the Title 10/Title 50 Debate," *Journal of National Security Law and Policy* (2012).

63 *"Given the nature of our world":* Donald H. Rumsfeld, "SECRET Memo to Joint Chiefs Chairman General Richard Meyers," October 17, 2001.

64 *without harming the captives:* Author interview with Robert Andrews. Also, Rowan Scarborough, *Rumsfeld's War: The Untold Story of America's Anti-Terrorist Commander* (District of Columbia: Regnery, 2004): 8–10.

64 *"We had to clear":* Author interview with Thomas O'Connell.

65 *since the days of the OSS:* Richard H. Shultz Jr., *The Secret War Against Hanoi: Kennedy's and Johnson's Use of Spies, Saboteurs, and Covert Warriors in North Vietnam* (New York: HarperCollins, 1999): ix.

66 *how the military would fight:* Author interview with Robert Andrews.

67 *"little birds in a nest":* Donald H. Rumsfeld, *Known and Unknown: A Memoir* (New York: Sentinel, 2011): 392.

69 *relying on American newspaper reports:* Mark Bowden, *Guests of the Ayatollah: The Iran Hostage Crisis: The First Battle in America's War with Militant Islam* (New York: Grove Press, 2006): 122. The CIA's one success before the operation was a lucky break, when a CIA officer on a plane out of Tehran happened to be sitting next to a Pakistani cook who had recently been working inside the American-embassy compound. The cook gave the Americans the crucial piece of information that all of the hostages were being held in the same location, inside the chancery building.

69 *"reliable human observers":* Lt. Gen. Philip C. Gast, "Memorandum for Director, Defense Intelligence Agency," Washington, D.C., December 10, 1980.

70 **"I'll be damned":** Steven Emerson, *Secret Warriors: Inside the Covert Military Operations of the Reagan Era* (New York: Putnam, 1988): 39.

70 **soldiers shouldn't also be spies:** The most significant of these operations was a secret Navy unit called Task Force 157. Using a fleet of electronic eavesdropping ships disguised as luxury yachts, Task Force 157 spies positioned themselves at the opening of the Panama Canal, inside the Strait of Gibraltar, and other maritime "choke points" to keep track of Soviet ships. The Pentagon never discussed the group's work in public, and when in 1973 the deputy chief of naval operations testified before Congress, he made only one oblique reference to how the "Navy's human intelligence collection program is expanding operations in sensitive areas." When he was the CIA's station chief in Istanbul, Dewey Clarridge worked with Task Force 157 spies who were monitoring shipping traffic on the Bosporus. For the best treatment of Task Force 157, see Jeffrey T. Richelson, "Truth Conquers All Chains: The U.S. Army Intelligence Support Activity, 1981–1989," *International Journal of Intelligence and Counterintelligence* 12, no. 2 (1999).

70 **"Also I heard":** Ibid., 171.

71 **to whomever might be watching from the sky:** Ibid., 172.

71 **the mission into Laos:** Emerson, 78.

71 **whether local sources:** Ibid., 79.

72 **front companies used:** Seymour H. Hersh, "Who's In Charge Here?" *The New York Times* (November 22, 1987).

72 **a Rolls-Royce, a hot-air balloon:** Emerson, 81.

73 **"We should have learned":** Frank C. Carlucci, "Memorandum to the Deputy Under Secretary for Policy Richard Stillwell."

73 **"Our intelligence about Grenada":** Quoted in Tim Weiner, *Legacy of Ashes: The History of the CIA* (New York: Doubleday, 2007): 454.

74 **"Mr. Casey, what you say":** Duane R. Clarridge with Digby Diehl, *A Spy for All Seasons: My Life in the CIA* (New York: Scribner, 2002): 229.

75 **"If I had known":** Author interview with Robert Andrews.

76 **to send its officers anywhere in the world:** Although any government agency technically can carry out a covert action, these activities have generally been accepted to be the preserve of the CIA because the spy agency was seen as more capable of carrying out missions officially denied by the U.S. government.

77 **"ongoing" or "anticipated" hostilities:** Jennifer D. Kibbe, "The Rise of the Shadow Warriors," *Foreign Affairs* (March/April 2004).

77 **"We had the ability to finish":** Bradley Graham, *By His Own Rules: The Ambitions, Successes, and Ultimate Failures of Donald Rumsfeld* (New York: Public Affairs, 2009): 584.

79 **"If we're at war":** Author interview with Thomas O'Connell.

80 **making use of groups like Delta Force:** Graham, 585.

80 **You don't need to put your troops:** Ibid.

81 *the CIA had the authorities:* Thomas W. O'Connell, "9/11 Commission Recommendation for Consolidated Paramilitary Activities," August 30, 2004.

81 *the CIA was set up to grade its own work:* Stephen A. Cambone, "Memorandum for Secretary of Defense," September 30, 2004.

82 *meant for only him to see:* Author interview with Edward Gnehm.

CHAPTER 5: THE ANGRY BIRD

86 *but insisted that they fire weapons:* The deployment of American troops to Yemen was authorized in an "Execute Order" signed by Donald Rumsfeld and Joint Chiefs chairman General Richard Myers. The EXORD is discussed in a classified CENTCOM chronology of operations September 11, 2001–July 10, 2002, obtained by the author.

87 *the first place outside of Afghanistan:* Account of meeting with Saleh comes from former senior American official.

87 *al-Harethi was always careful:* James Bamford, "He's in the Backseat!" *The Atlantic* (April 2006).

87 *the surveillance net got its first big catch:* Rowan Scarborough, *Rumsfeld's War: The Untold Story of America's Anti-Terrorist Commander* (Washington, D.C.: Regnery, 2004): 25 and Michael Smith, *Killer Elite* (Great Britain: Weidenfeld and Nicolson, 2006): 237.

87 *the CIA was now authorized:* Bamford, "He's in the Backseat!"

87 *found at the scene:* "U.S. Missile Strike Kills al Qaeda Chief," *CNN World* (November 5, 2002).

88 *"bloody struggle":* "Intelligence Policy," National Commission on Terrorism Attacks Upon the United States, 9/11 Commission Staff Statement No. 7 (2004).

88 *he would have refused a direct order:* Ibid. The commission's staff statement states only that "a former CTC chief" told the commission he would have refused the order to kill bin Laden. A member of the commission staff identified the CTC chief as Geoff O'Connell.

89 *"You know":* "The 9-11 Commission Report: National Commission on Terrorist Attacks Upon the United States," (2004).

89 *insufficient for White House approval:* Author interview with Richard Clarke.

90 *various options for spying:* Ibid., and author interview with former senior CIA official.

91 *a crude e-mail link:* Public remarks by R. James Woolsey at George Mason University, September 13, 2012.

91 *the CIA's war in Afghanistan during the 1980s:* Ibid.

91 *the photo was upside down:* Author interview with Curt Hawes.

92 *whom al Qaeda would end up killing:* See Henry Crumpton, *The Art of Intelligence,* and Steve Coll, *Ghost Wars: The Secret History of the CIA, Af-*

ghanistan, and Bin Laden, from the Soviet Invasion to September 10, 2001 to get fuller accounts of Blee's trip to Afghanistan in 1999. In both books he is identified only as "Rich."

92 *the direction of clandestine operations:* James Risen, "David H. Blee, 83, CIA Spy Who Revised Defector Policy," *The New York Times* (August 17, 2000).

92 *"There's no POW issue here":* Author interview with Richard Clarke.

93 *a satellite company with transponder space to rent:* Author interview with White House official during the Clinton administration.

93 *Sandy Berger and his staff:* Crumpton, *The Art of Intelligence*, 154.

94 *an abandoned church building:* Author interview with Curt Hawes.

95 *hit a target tank in its path:* Richard Whittle, "Predator's Big Safari," Mitchell Institute for Airpower Studies, Paper 7 (August 2011).

95 *as he controlled the Predator joystick and fired a missile:* Author interview with Curt Hawes.

96 *spinning the turret thirty degrees:* Air Force Press Release, February 27, 2001. Available at www.fas.org/irp/program/collect/docs/man-ipc-predator-010228.htm.

98 *"the United States is very clearly":* Jane Mayer, "The Predator War," *The New Yorker*, October 26, 2009.

98 *no authority to fire a Hellfire missile:* National Commission on Terrorist Attacks Upon the United States, "9-11 Commission Report," (2004).

100 *the spy agency was now hawking images:* Author interview with Ross Newland.

101 *he demanded that American spies:* Author interview with former senior American official.

CHAPTER 6: A TRUE PASHTUN

103 *He asked one of his lieutenants:* Zahid Hussain, *The Scorpion's Tail* (New York: Free Press, 2010): 73.

104 *just like the Soviets had years earlier:* Shaukat Qadir, "Understanding the Insurgency in FATA." Available at http://shaukatqadir.info/pdfs/FATA.pdf.

104 *the illiterate youth:* Muhammad I. Khan, "Nek Muhammad Wazir," *The Herald* (September 16, 2005).

104 *even when his commanders:* Syed Saleem Shahzad, "The Legacy of Nek Mohammed," *Asia Times Online* (July 20, 2004).

105 *American firebases across the border:* Christine C. Fair and Seth Jones, "Pakistan's War Within," *Survival* 51, no. 6 (December 2009–January 2010): 168.

105 *not only his clothes but his pillow covers:* Ibid., 169.

106 *some parents refused to accept:* Hussain, *The Scorpion's Tail*, 71.

106 *The crowd cheered wildly:* "Making Deals with the Militants," part 4 of *Return of the Taliban*, PBS *Frontline*, October 3, 2006.

107 *"Whatever happened":* Ibid.

107 *"That should make it clear":* Iqbal Khattak, "I Did Not Surrender to the Military," *Friday Times* (April 30–May 6, 2004).

107 *"If [Pakistani troops]":* Author interview with Asad Munir.

108 *"There is no al Qaeda here":* Dilawar K. Wazir, "Top Militant Vows to Continue Jihad," *Dawn* (April 26, 2004).

108 *"Nek Muhammad really pissed off":* Author interview with former CIA station chief in Islamabad.

109 *mountain camps where Kashmiri:* Author interview with senior American intelligence official.

110 HE LIVED AND DIED LIKE A TRUE PASHTUN: Hussain, *The Scorpion's Tail*, 73.

111 *preventing the simmering dispute:* Syed Shoaib Hasan, "Rise of Pakistan's Quiet Man," *BBC News* (June 17, 2009).

111 *where he would shop for suits and ties:* Author interview with former CIA official.

112 *"the price of Soviet presence in Afghanistan":* Major Ashfaq Parvez Kayani, "Strengths and Weaknesses of the Afghan Resistance Movement." Thesis paper for Kayani's Masters of Military Art and Science at the Command and General Staff, Fort Leavenworth, 1988.

113 *years more of bloody conflict:* The final passage from Kayani's thesis, a section under the heading "Political Settlement," is particularly illuminating if you were to consider substituting "Americans" for "Soviets," and "Washington" for "Moscow": "It is not likely that the Soviets will be willing to negotiate about Afghanistan itself but their presence there could be a bargaining chip or a point of leverage to bargain for concessions in some other areas as part of a package deal. If that happens, the central problem for Moscow will be the inability of the Afghan regime to survive in the absence of Soviet troops. Logically the Soviets will trade for concessions which ensure the continuation of their influence in the Afghan government. The most that they could be expected to accommodate is the ARM sharing power with the Kabul regime but as a weaker partner."

CHAPTER 7: CONVERGENCE

115 *There was about to be:* Four former CIA officers described the events surrounding the al Qaeda meeting and planning for a military operation in Pakistan.

115 *riding around the mountain villages:* Peter L. Bergen, *Manhunt: The Ten-Year Search for Bin Laden—from 9/11 to Abbottabad* (New York: Crown, 2012): 160.

116 *"This is a really bad idea, Stan":* Author interview with former CIA station chief in Islamabad.

118 *had used the technique:* Memorandum for John Rizzo from Stephen Bradbury, May 30, 2005.

118 *"unauthorized, improvised, inhumane":* CIA Inspector General, "Special

Review: Counterterrorism Detention and Interrogation Activities (September 2001–October 2003)," May 7, 2004, 102.

119 **The waterboards were bought locally:** David Johnston and Mark Mazzetti, "A Window into CIA's Embrace of Secret Jails," *The New York Times* (August 12, 2009).

119 **The entertainment was taken away:** Ibid.

120 **were the political winds to shift:** Author interview with senior Bush administration official.

120 **"the U.S. government will not stand behind them":** CIA Inspector General, "Special Review: Counterterrorism Detention and Interrogation Activities (September 2001–October 2003)," 101.

120 **the plans had been temporarily shelved:** Author interview with two retired CIA officers.

122 **he had played a leading role:** Henry A. Crumpton, *The Art of Intelligence: Lessons from a Life in the CIA's Clandestine Service* (New York: Penguin, 2012): 173.

123 **to sell programs back to the government:** Details about Blackwater's role in the assassination program comes from three former CIA officials. See also Adam Ciralsky, "Tycoon, Contractor, Soldier, Spy," *Vanity Fair* (January 2010).

123 **"the nation has relied on mercenaries":** Author interview with two former senior CIA officials.

123 **"paying for all sorts of intelligence activities":** Ciralsky.

124 **lobbying their former agencies:** Author interview with two former CIA officials.

124 **"Deniability is built in":** Enrique Prado e-mail, dated October 2007, released during investigation by Senate Armed Services Committee.

124 **the CIA had first proposed:** Ciralsky.

124 **"We were building":** Ibid.

127 **vacuumed out of the shredder:** Jose A. Rodriguez Jr., *Hard Measures: How Aggressive CIA Actions After 9/11 Saved Lives* (New York: Threshold Editions, 2012): 194.

127 **the CIA trying to cover its back:** Details about the exchange between Hadley and Goss come from two former CIA officials and one White House official during the Bush administration.

127 **criminally liable for participating:** Three CIA officers who attended the meeting with Andrew Card described the scene in the conference room.

129 **reaching nearly $8 billion in 2007:** Dana Priest and Ann Scott Tyson, "Bin Laden Trail 'Stone Cold,'" *The Washington Post* (September 10, 2006). See also, Wayne Downing, "Special Operations Forces Assessment," (Memorandum for Secretary of Defense, Chairman Joint Chiefs of Staff, November 9, 2005).

130 **"Neither was easy to understand":** Stanley A. McChrystal, "It Takes a Network," *Foreign Policy* (March/April 2011).

130 *extracted from thumb drives:* Dana Priest and William M. Arkin, "'Top Secret America': A Look at the Military's Joint Special Operations Command," *The Washington Post* (September 2, 2011).

131 *sustained operations:* Downing.

131 *"The future fight," it read:* Ibid.

131 *risky spying missions inside Iran:* Author interview with two former senior Pentagon officials and a retired CIA officer.

132 *who was in charge of each front:* Details about CIA and Pentagon negotiations come from two former CIA officers and Robert Andrews interviewed by author.

134 *missed Patek but killed several others:* Information about the missile strike in the Philippines comes from four current and former CIA officers.

134 *give away the precise coordinates:* Author interview with senior military officer who participated in the surveillance missions.

135 *officials took only hours:* Information about the Damadola operation in 2006 comes from two former CIA officers.

CHAPTER 8: A WAR BY PROXY

137 *payment for their services:* Author interview with CIA, State Department, and congressional officials. See also, Mark Mazzetti, "Efforts by CIA Fail in Somalia, Officials Charge," *The New York Times* (June 8, 2006).

138 *"cultivating supporters":* Director of National Intelligence, "Trends in Global Terrorism: Implications for the United States," (declassified key judgments of the National Intelligence Estimate, April 2006).

139 *"People made relationships":* Robert Worth, "Is Yemen the Next Afghanistan?" *The New York Times* (July 6, 2010).

139 *al Qaeda in the Arabian Peninsula:* The Interpol notice is cited in Bill Roggio, "Al Qaeda Jailbreak in Yemen," *Long War Journal* (February 8, 2006).

139 *punishments like stoning adulterers:* David H. Shinn, "Al Qaeda in East Africa and the Horn," *The Journal of Conflict Studies* 27, no. 1 (2007).

140 *a weak and corrupt organization:* Bronwyn Bruton, "Somalia: A New Approach," *Council on Foreign Relations*, Council Special Report no. 52 (March 2010): 7.

140 *reopen some of its previously shuttered stations:* Author interview with three former senior CIA officials.

140 *found themselves being extorted:* Clint Watts, Jacob Shapiro, and Vahid Brown, "Al-Qa'ida's (Mis)Adventures in the Horn of Africa," Harmony Project Combating Terrorism Center at West Point, July 2, 2007, 19–21.

142 *the CIA was running guns:* Author interview with State Department and congressional officials described Nairobi cables.

142 *"positive U.S. steps":* Cables from the American embassy in Tanzania to State Department, "CT in Horn of Africa: Results and Recommendations from May 23–24 RSI," July 3, 2006.

144 *amassed a small fortune:* "Miscellaneous Monongalia County, West Virginia Obituaries: Edward Robert Golden," Genealogybuff.com. Also, Edgar Simpson, "Candidates Promise to Liven Last Days Before Election," *The Charleston Gazette* (October 26, 1986).

145 *cutting up a piece of cardboard:* United Press International, "Braille Playboy Criticized," September 27, 1986. Also, "Debate with Stand-In Short in Fayetteville," *The Charleston Gazette* (August 19, 1986).

145 *"It symbolizes a gentler way":* Ellen Gamerman, "To know if you're anybody, check the list: In Washington, the snobby old Green Book is relished as a throwback to less-tacky times," *The Baltimore Sun* (October 22, 1997).

146 *the transformation of Michele into Amira began:* Author interview with Michele Ballarin.

147 *"He has appointed his chief":* The e-mails were first reported by Patrick Smith in the September 8, 2006, issue of respected newsletter *Africa Confidential.* More e-mail excerpts were included in a September 10, 2006, story in *The Observer* of the United Kingdom.

147 *the French debacle in Indochina in 1954:* Ibid.

147 *A better bet, he said, was the Pentagon:* Ibid.

147 *free to spend the day at the beach:* Author interview with Bronwyn Bruton.

148 *it would try to ensure:* Details of Abizaid's visit to Addis Ababa comes from an American official stationed at the embassy at the time.

149 *ten thousand people displaced by the floods:* United Nations Office for the Coordination of Humanitarian Affairs, "OCHA Situation Report No. 1: Dire Dawa Floods – Ethiopia occurred on August 06, 2006," August 7, 2006.

149 *senior ICU operatives:* Details about the clandestine shipments into Dire Dawa come from two former military officials involved in the operation. The same officials described the makeup of Task Force 88.

150 *a small fishing village:* Michael R. Gordon and Mark Mazzetti, "U.S. Used Base in Ethiopia to Hunt Al Qaeda," *The New York Times* (February 23, 2007).

151 *kill his father:* Human Rights Watch, "So Much to Fear: War Crimes and the Devastation of Somalia," December 8, 2008. See also Bronwyn Bruton, "Somalia: A New Approach," 9.

CHAPTER 9: THE BASE

154 *"The ideal person":* Information in this chapter about Art Keller's experiences in North and South Waziristan come from author interviews with Keller.

154 *"Eighteen months later":* Author interview with Arthur Keller.

157 *he held a grenade up:* Amir Latif, "Pakistan's Most Wanted," *Islam Online* (January 29, 2008).

160 *the wrong photograph:* Lisa Myers, "U.S. Posts Wrong Photo of 'al-Qaida Operative,'" *MSNBC* (January 26, 2006).

162 *the uncomfortable position:* Conflicts were also erupting between CIA of-

ficers in Afghanistan and those in Pakistan, battles that reflected the animosities between the two countries on both sides of a porous border. For much of 2005, the station chief in Kabul, Greg, had been writing reports about spasms of violence in Afghanistan and blaming Pakistan's inability to control the militants crossing into Afghanistan from the tribal areas. CIA officers in Kabul were also receiving alarming reports about Pakistan's complicity in the attacks from Amrullah Saleh, the director of Afghanistan's spy service, a former fighter with the Northern Alliance who despised Pakistan and its historical ties to the Taliban. Greg had a particularly close relationship with President Hamid Karzai, and Karzai believed he even owed Greg his life. In 2001, when Greg was part of a Special Forces team inserted into Afghanistan at the beginning of the American invasion, he saved Karzai from being blown up by a Taliban bomb. The CIA station chief in Islamabad, Sean, thought the tight relationship between Greg and Karzai had warped CIA analysis in Afghanistan, and accused Greg of "going native" by accepting conspiracy theories spun by Afghan intelligence about Pakistan's meddling in Afghanistan. Sean also believed that secret missions into Pakistan's tribal areas by both JSOC and a CIA-trained Afghan militias, which the agency had named Counterterrorism Pursuit Teams, were an unnecessary risk and threatened to get the CIA kicked out of Pakistan. The tribalism got so bad that Porter Goss intervened, calling both Sean and Greg to a meeting at the U.S. Central Command headquarters in Qatar in July as a way to get the two men in the same room and dampen tensions between the dueling CIA outposts.

163 **had converted to Islam:** Greg Miller, "At CIA, a Convert to Islam Leads the Terrorist Hunt," *The Washington Post* (March 24, 2012).

164 **nineteen thousand of them children:** Earthquake Engineering Research Institute, "EERI Special Earthquake Report," February 2006.

164 **"angels of mercy":** Trip report by Joint Chiefs chairman General Peter Pace, March 30, 2006.

166 **"We actually began to develop":** Author interview with Michael Hayden.

166 **an uneventful arrest:** Jose A. Rodriguez Jr., *Hard Measures: How Aggressive CIA Actions After 9/11 Saved American Lives* (New York: Threshold Editions, 2012): 8.

167 **a mission bedeviled:** Hayden's description of hunting the courier network as a "bank shot" is in Peter L. Bergen, *Manhunt: The Ten-Year Search for Bin Laden—from 9/11 to Abbottabad* (New York: Crown, 2012): 104.

167 **information that the CIA:** Bergen, 100.

168 **critical proxies for its defense against India:** Author interviews with five current and former American intelligence officials and one Pakistani official.

169 **phone calls between Pakistani spies and Haqqani:** In 2008, shortly after the National Security Agency intercepted communications that linked ISI operatives to a bombing of the Indian embassy in Kabul carried out by the Haqqani Network, Pakistan's president, Asif Ali Zardari, pledged that the

ISI would be "handled." He assured American officials that, unlike his pre-decessor, he had no policy of using the ISI to cultivate ties to terror groups. "We don't hunt with the house and run with the hare, which is what Mush-arraf was doing," he said.

169 *"strategic asset":* David E. Sanger, *The Inheritance: The World Obama Con-fronts and the Challenges to American Power* (New York: Crown, 2009): 248.

171 *allow American troops to withdraw:* Mark Mazzetti and David Rohde, "Amidst U.S. Policy Disputes, Qaeda Grows in Pakistan," *The New York Times* (June 30, 2008).

172 *American financial support to Pakistan would continue:* Ibid.

172 *incursions from the tribal areas into Afghanistan:* Ibid.

173 *a CIA drone killed Khalid Habib:* Pir Zubair Shah, "US Strike Is Said to Kill Qaeda Figure in Pakistan," *The New York Times* (October 17, 2008).

CHAPTER 10: GAMES WITHOUT FRONTIERS

175 *"A Mighty Wurlitzer":* Frank Wisner, quoted in Richard H. Schulz, *The Se-cret War Against Hanoi: Kennedy's and Johnson's Use of Spies, Saboteurs, and Covert Warriors in North Vietnam* (New York: HarperCollins, 1999): 129. Original citation of the "Wurlitzer" quote is in John Ranelagh, *The Agency: The Rise and Decline of the CIA* (New York: Touchstone, 1986): 218.

177 *convinced he had just received approval:* Much of the material for this chapter is based on interviews with more than a dozen former executives at U-Turn Media/IMV, hundreds of pages of corporate documents, and discus-sions with current and former military and intelligence officials. Most of the U-Turn/IMV employees would not agree to have their names used because of nondisclosure agreements with the now-defunct company. Michael Fur-long was also interviewed about his information-operations projects for the Pentagon.

179 *fishermen were even asked:* Author interview with Robert Andrews. The Sacred Sword of the Patriots League is discussed further in Richard Schultz, *The Secret War Against Hanoi,* 139–148.

179 *"we all cursed it":* Author interview with Robert Andrews.

180 *ways to communicate:* Early efforts were halting, and in 2004 a report by the Pentagon's Defense Science Board—a panel that advises the Secretary of Defense—concluded that there was a "crisis" in America's efforts to com-municate its messages overseas. The war on terrorism, the report concluded, couldn't be just about dropping bombs on mud huts, jailing terror suspects, and killing people with Hellfire missiles launched by remote control. There needed to be a softer side of the war, an effort to "counter violent extrem-ism" in the parts of the world where the United States was deeply unpopu-lar. Congress gave the Pentagon money to try to solve the problem.

182 *U-Turn was hired to help:* U-Turn Media (PowerPoint presentation to SOCOM).

184 ***"almost every waking minute":*** U-Turn Media (Proposal to SOCOM, May 8, 2006).

184 ***a contract worth just $250,000:*** SOCOM contract H92222-06-6-0026.

186 ***named after a Lebanese commando unit:*** JD Media (Presentation to SOCOM, May 29, 2007).

186 ***get them distributed in the Middle East:*** Michael D. Furlong, e-mail message to SOCOM officials, June 22, 2007.

187 ***the Pentagon's more basic requirement:*** Joseph Heimann and Daniel Silverberg, "An Ever Expanding War: Legal Aspects of Online Strategic Communication," *Parameters* (summer 2009).

188 ***how easy it might be for Russian intelligence:*** Information about the cables from the CIA station in Prague comes from two American intelligence officials.

CHAPTER 11: THE OLD MAN'S RETURN

191 ***the funding for the information program:*** Details about McKiernan's desire for the AfPax contract comes from five current and former military officers in Afghanistan at the time, as well as three private contractors. The timeline for the events chronicled in this chapter comes in large part from a Pentagon investigation into a private spying operation run by Michael Furlong. The investigation's final report, "Inquiry into Possible Questionable Intelligence Activities by DoD Personnel and Contractors" by M. H. Decker, was completed and given to Secretary of Defense Robert Gates on June 25, 2010. The report, hereafter referred to as the "Decker Report," remains classified but a copy was obtained by the author.

192 ***more American troops had died:*** Mark Mazzetti, "Coalition Deaths in Afghanistan Hit a Record High," *The New York Times* (July 2, 2008).

195 ***the CIA's Counterterrorism Center:*** Decker Report, A-2.

195 ***"I had to come up with a euphemism":*** Author interview with Michael Furlong.

196 ***a program the agency thought:*** Decker Report, A-3.

197 ***Jan Obrman's International Media Ventures:*** Ibid.

198 ***classified military-intelligence databases:*** Decker Report, A-7.

198 ***Both fluent in Dari, Pashtu, and Arabic:*** Michael Furlong e-mail.

198 ***"Let's be honest guys":*** Michael Furlong e-mail.

200 ***"Get used to it, world":*** *The War on Democracy,* directed by Christopher Martin and John Pilger, 2007.

200 ***"prying S.O.B.":*** Douglas Waller, *Wild Bill Donovan: The Spymaster Who Created the OSS and Modern American Espionage* (New York: Free Press, 2011): 353.

201 ***operations in Afghanistan and Pakistan:*** Some of the agents in Clarridge's network still work undercover in Pakistan and Afghanistan, occasionally for the U.S. government, and the author has agreed not to reveal the identities or professions of the agents.

202 *"God willing, we will do it":* Intercepted conversation contained in Afghanistan military situation reports released by WikiLeaks.

203 *"moved an operative in" inside Pakistan:* Michael Furlong e-mail.

203 *he would "need top cover":* Ibid.

203 *"huge potential for mistakes":* Decker Report, A-5.

205 *they entered the reports:* Decker Report, A-6.

205 *Taliban fighters in the poppy-growing regions:* Ibid., A-9.

206 *The assassin was his longtime bodyguard:* "Afghan President's Brother, Ahmed Wali Karzai Killed," *BBC News* (July 12, 2011).

207 *missions that the CIA couldn't accomplish:* U.S. Central Command, "Joint Unconventional Warfare Task Force Execute Order," September 30, 2009. The order remains classified, but a copy was obtained by the author.

207 *extremist networks and individual leaders of terror groups:* Ibid.

208 *perhaps the most influential general:* Decker Report, A-6.

208 *lying to his superiors:* Three former military officers and two contractors with direct knowledge of the contents of the memorandum described the memo's contents.

209 *"And I made it happen":* Author interview with Michael Furlong.

210 *"prepare approximately 200 local personnel":* Decker Report, A-9.

CHAPTER 12: THE SCALPEL'S EDGE

213 *"We'll continue saying":* Cable from U.S. embassy in Sana'a to State Department, "General Petraeus Meeting with President Saleh on Security Assistance, AQAP Strikes," January 4, 2010.

214 *posted informants inside mosques:* Michael Slackman, "Would-Be Killer Linked to al Qaeda, Saudis Say," *The New York Times* (August 28, 2009).

214 *"We have a problem":* Cable from U.S. embassy in Riyadh to State Department, "Special Advisor Holbrooke's Meeting With Saudi Assistant Interior Minister Prince Mohammed Bin Nayef," May 17, 2009.

216 *leaving a smoking crater:* "Profile: Al Qaeda 'Bomb Maker' Ibrahim al-Asiri," *BBC* (May 9, 2012).

216 *a Saudi spy network in Yemen:* "Al Qaeda Claims Attempted Assassination of Saudi Prince Nayef," *NEFA Foundation* (August 28, 2009).

216 *"We will reach you soon":* Ibid.

217 *Brennan withdrew his name:* Brennan denounced the CIA prison program after he joined the Obama campaign. However, several CIA officers who served with Brennan in 2002 do not recall him voicing his objections to the program at the time he was serving.

217 *Obama was just as committed:* Cable from U.S. embassy in Riyadh to State Department, "Special Advisor Holbrooke's Meeting with Saudi Assistant Interior Minister Prince Mohammed Bin Nayef," May 17, 2009.

218 *the drone killings in Pakistan:* Interview with two Obama administration officials who attended the meetings at the CIA.

219 *"Once the interrogation was gone":* Author interview with John Rizzo.

220 *the United States could use a "scalpel":* Speech by John Brennan on May 26, 2010, at the Center for Strategic and International Studies in Washington.

220 *"none of the baggage":* Bob Woodward, *Obama's Wars* (New York: Simon & Schuster, 2010): 377.

221 *a military commander for a secret war:* Panetta's reaction to learning about the CIA drone strikes comes from two senior American government officials.

222 *releasing the memos:* Panetta's discussions with senior CIA officials about the release of the interrogation memos comes from interviews with two American officials involved in the discussions.

223 *winning Emanuel over to his side:* The White House discussions, and Emanuel's decision to side with Panetta, come from two participants in the discussions. The debates over the release of the memos are covered extensively in Daniel Klaidman, *Kill or Capture: The War on Terror and the Soul of the Obama Presidency* (New York: Houghton Mifflin Harcourt, 2012).

224 *The cable carried a simple message: Ignore Blair's directive:* The account of the conversation between Blair and Panetta comes from two officials in Panetta's office at the CIA.

225 *covert-action programs usually:* Author interview with Dennis Blair.

225 *"the development of stable":* A full list of the Blair/Gates principles was obtained by the author. The list was first published in the endnotes of *Obama's Wars* by Bob Woodward.

226 *Leon Panetta and Deputy National Security Advisor:* Author interview with Dennis Blair.

226 *a secret war that most believed:* Details of the Jones Memo comes from two former senior Obama administration officials.

227 *the CIA couldn't get legal approval to kill him:* Author interview with former Pakistani government official.

228 *"said more Hail Marys":* Leon Panetta, unpublished interview with *The New York Times.*

228 *"Can you tell me":* Author interview with former senior Obama administration official.

228 *"The CIA gets what it wants":* Daniel Klaidman, *Kill or Capture*, 121.

229 *since he assumed control:* Petraeus had sought advice from Edmund Hull, the former American ambassador to Yemen. Hull had been following the growth of militancy in the country for several years, and was angry that after counterterrorism successes in the years immediately after the September 11 attacks the country seemed to be sliding into chaos. He told Petraeus that if Yemen continued to be ignored it could become another Afghanistan, a safe haven for attacks in other countries; the assassination attempt on Prince bin Nayef's life months later made the prediction seem eerily prescient.

230 *before it could successfully:* Author interview with former American special-operations commander involved in the discussions about military operations in Yemen.

231 *with John Brennan serving:* Ibid.

231 *"Beware of taking the side of America!":* Scott Shane with Mark Mazzetti and Robert Worth, "Secret Assault on Terrorism Widens on Two Continents," *The New York Times* (August 14, 2010).

233 *from $67 million to $105 million:* Cable from U.S. embassy in Sana'a to the State Department, "General Petraeus Meeting with President Saleh on Security Assistance, AQAP Strikes," January 4, 2010. The account of the meeting comes entirely from this cable.

235 *his message was clear:* Text of Blair's remarks at the Willard hotel available at dni.gov/speeches/20100406_5_speech.pdf.

CHAPTER 13: THE SCRAMBLE FOR AFRICA

237 *a violation of a UN arms embargo:* Cable from U.S. embassy to State Department headquarters, "Whither the M/V Faina's Tanks?" October 2, 2008. The cable described the route by which the arms got to Southern Sudan. After the arms arrived in Mombasa, they were sent via rail lines to Uganda, and then on to Southern Sudan.

238 *so the* Faina's *crew:* Harun Maruf interview with Michele Ballarin for *Voice of America* (August 2, 2010).

238 *". . . she is only giving them false hope":* "Ukraine Ship Owners Object to U.S. Woman's Role in Pirate Talks," *Russian News Room*, December 19, 2008.

238 *"become an intermediary":* Cable from U.S. embassy in Ukraine to State Department headquarters, "Faina: Letter from Foreign Minister Ohryzko," February 5, 2009.

238 *"to facilitate the exclusion":* Ibid.

240 *"without fingerprint, footprint or flag":* Gulf Security Group letter to Central Intelligence Agency, August 17, 2007. Copy of letter obtained by author.

240 *a law that prohibits:* Letter from John L. McPherson to Michele Ballarin, August 27, 2007. Copy of letter obtained by author.

241 *at the headquarters of:* The description of Ballarin's meeting at CTTSO comes from a military official involved in counterterrorism programs who attended the meeting.

243 *a more coveted AK-47 could be purchased:* Peter J Pham, "Somali Instability Still Poses Threat Even After Successful Strike on Nabhan," *World Defense Review* (September 17, 2009).

243 *to hound him and go after his money:* Robert Young Pelton, "An American Commando in Exile," *Men's Journal* (December 2010).

244 *a counterpiracy force:* Prince's involvement in the counterpiracy militia in Puntland is documented in two reports by the United Nations Monitoring Group for Somalia and Eritrea.

244 *a new militia would carry out raids:* Information about the Puntland militia comes from three people directly involved in the operations. Separately, the United Nations Monitoring Group did an extensive investigation into

both Saracen and Sterling, and confirmed the two companies' ties to Erik Prince and the UAE.

245 *insisting that each military operation:* JSOC's proposals to strike the al Shabaab camps were confirmed by one retired senior military officer and a former top civilian in the Obama administration. Details about discussions inside the Obama administration over the costs and benefits of striking the camps can be found in Eric Schmitt and Thom Shanker, *Counterstrike: The Untold Story of America's Secret Campaign Against Al Qaeda* (New York: Times Books, 2011). According to the book, most officials believed that hitting the camps wouldn't be worth the possible benefit of killing a small number of senior al Shabaab leaders.

245 *First prize was an AK-47:* "Kids Awarded Guns in Somali Recruitment Game," *Der Spiegel* (September 26, 2011).

246 *"old woman Hillary Clinton":* SITE Intelligence Group, "Shabaab Official Offers Rewards for Information on Obama, Clinton," June 9, 2011.

246 *take him somewhere for interrogation:* Daniel Klaidman, *Kill or Capture: The War on Terror and the Soul of the Obama Presidency* (New York: Houghton Mifflin Harcourt, 2012): 123–124 details the first discussions of the various options presented by Admiral William McRaven. The video teleconference and the options discussed by McRaven were confirmed independently by American government officials.

248 *Somali pirates were currently holding:* The crew of the *Faina* was released just days after the Ukrainian minister sent the letter to Secretary of State Hillary Clinton, but there is no evidence that Ballarin's involvement in the discussions led to the pirates releasing the crew. The pirates ended up pocketing more than $3 million in ransom money from the ship's owners. The interview in which she discussed "unwinding" all of the hostage cases appeared in an article on Military.com on November 25, 2008. It is difficult to discern how much, if any, money Ballarin made from being involved in the negotiations.

248 *failed to deliver:* Author interview with eight different former employees of Ballarin's companies.

249 *"It's not the way forward":* *Voice of America* interview with Michele Ballarin.

249 *All they needed, she said:* The story that follows comes from an author interview with Michele Ballarin. Her story was corroborated by a former American official who knew about her efforts to get the Pentagon to embrace the plan to use Somali hit men to kill the al Shabaab operatives.

251 *"It is forbidden to make graves into shrines":* BBC World Service, "Somali Rage at Grave Destruction," June 8, 2009.

253 *the age's defining struggle of good versus evil:* Author interview with Michele Ballarin.

253 *It was a game of catch-up:* "Hundreds of intelligence analysts" comes from

a former senior American intelligence official with direct knowledge about the movements of analysts within the intelligence community after the beginning of the Arab Spring.

254 *thanking the Libyan spymaster:* Ben Wedeman, "Documents Shed Light on CIA, Gadhafi Spy Ties," CNN.com, September 3, 2011.

255 *"encompass the majority of the Islamic world":* Letter from Osama bin Laden to Atiyah Abd al-Rahman dated April 26, 2011. Text of letter released by Combating Terrorism Center at West Point.

CHAPTER 14: THE UNRAVELING

257 *checking that it had not been:* Description of conditions comes from an American official with knowledge of Davis's circumstances in prison.

258 *named for the gap:* Matthew Teague, "Black Ops and Blood Money," *Men's Journal* (June 1, 2011), and Mark Mazzetti, et al., "American Held in Pakistan Worked with CIA," *The New York Times* (February 21, 2011).

258 *earning upward of:* Information about Davis's CIA salary comes from documents released by Pakistan's Foreign Office after Davis was arrested.

260 *using an allied organization:* Background on the operations of Lashkar-e-Taiba comes from an interview with C. Christine Fair of Georgetown University, an expert on the group.

261 *Pakistan's pro-American ambassador:* The system of American visas for Pakistan was described by an American official in Islamabad with direct knowledge of the process.

261 *even the U.S. embassy in Pakistan:* Ibid.

262 *the hundreds of thousands who had come:* For the best account of the 1979 embassy burning see Steve Coll, *Ghost Wars: The Secret History of the CIA, Afghanistan, and Bin Laden, from the Soviet Invasion to September 10, 2001.*

262 *the new chief did not come to Pakistan:* The CIA station chief in Islamabad remains undercover.

263 *he was skeptical about the long-term value:* The dynamics between the CIA station chief in Islamabad and Ambassador Cameron Munter were described by five American officials. Much of the account of the fights between the two men, and the broader description of the deliberations over the Raymond Davis episode, come from these officials.

264 *"then they are not subject to":* Press conference of President Barack Obama, February 15, 2011.

265 *The United States had just lost its chance:* Details of the meeting between Panetta and Pasha come from two Pakistani officials and from the contents of an internal memorandum of the private intelligence firm Stratfor, made public by WikiLeaks. The memorandum is available at http://wikileaks.org/gifiles/docs/1664671_re-alpha-insight-afghanistan-pakistan-isi-chief-not-for.html.

265 *North Waziristan, South Waziristan, Bajaur:* Classified CIA paper described by two senior American intelligence officials.

267 *"Well, why don't you go in and get them?" Gates asked:* Author interview with a senior military official who attended the briefing.

267 *"I've had enough":* Bush's response to the CIA briefing can be found in Bob Woodward, *Obama's Wars* (New York: Simon & Schuster, 2010): 4–5. The most detailed account of the CIA briefing in July 2008 is in Eric Schmitt and Thom Shanker, *Counterstrike: The Untold Story of America's Secret Campaign Against Al Qaeda* (New York: Times Books, 2011).

269 *Pakistani troops and policemen:* Account of the Mullah Baradar capture comes from five different American and Pakistani intelligence officials.

270 *a personal courier for Osama bin Laden:* Author interview with two American intelligence officials, and from Peter Bergen, *Manhunt: The Ten-Year Search for Bin Laden—from 9/11 to Abbottabad* (New York: Crown, 2012): 122–124.

270 *"I'm back with the people I was with before":* Peter Bergen, *Manhunt,* 123.

271 *it had only small, opaque slits for windows:* Peter Bergen, *Manhunt,* 4.

271 *the telephoto lens was useless:* Author interview with two senior American intelligence officials.

272 *He must not be allowed:* Ahtishamul Haq, "Raymond Davis Case: Wife of Man Killed Commits Suicide," *The Express Tribune* (February 7, 2011).

273 *Davis would be released from jail:* Details about the discussions between Munter and Pasha, and the subsequent narrative of the events leading to Davis's release come from interviews with both American and Pakistani officials.

274 *to offer "forgiveness":* As the talks dragged on, American officials developed a backup plan: appealing the matter to an international arbitration panel in Switzerland. The American officials in Geneva began consulting Swiss lawyers but all the while figuring it was a long shot that a panel in Switzerland would get Ray Davis out of jail.

274 *locked inside an iron cage:* Carlotta Gall and Mark Mazzetti, "Hushed Deal Frees CIA Contractor in Pakistan," *The New York Times* (March 16, 2011).

275 *that he was safe:* Author interview with two American officials.

275 *a fifty-year-old minister:* Sara Burnett, "Charges Upgraded Against Ex-CIA Contractor in Parking-Spot Dispute," *The Denver Post* (October 4, 2011).

276 *"Relax," Maes said, "and quit being stupid":* "CIA Contractor in Court Over Felony Assault Charges," *CBS Denver* (October 4, 2011). As of this book's publication, the legal proceedings in the case had not concluded.

276 *a reduction of terrorist violence:* "Getting Rid of US Saboteurs," *The Nation* (August 11, 2011).

277 *Saeed insisted that night:* Author attended the July 2012 rally in Islamabad.

CHAPTER 15: THE DOCTOR AND THE SHEIKH

279 *an American woman he knew:* Most of the details about Dr. Shakil Afridi's meetings with his CIA handlers come from Afridi's statements to a Pakistani investigative group examining his role in the bin Laden operation. Other details have been filled in by American government officials with knowledge of Afridi's work for the CIA from 2008 to 2011.

280 *sold hospital medicines:* Aryn Baker, "The Murky Past of the Pakistani Doctor Who Helped the CIA," *Time* (June 13, 2012).

281 *Islamabad moved to shutter:* Declan Walsh, "Pakistan May Be Expelling Aid Group's Foreign Staff," *The New York Times* (September 6, 2012).

282 *"I believe it is unreasonable":* John Deutch's statement available at http://intellit.muskingum.edu/cia_folder/ciarelations_folder/ciareldcistmt.html.

282 *the CIA paid him:* Afridi statement to Pakistani investigative group.

283 *when the transmitter:* Ibid.

283 *she agreed to cooperate with Afridi:* Sami Yousafzai, "The Doctor's Grim Reward," *Newsweek* (June 11, 2012).

284 *she should call again in the evening:* Afridi statement to Pakistani investigative group.

285 *dragged it down the stairs:* Mark Bisonette (aka Mark Owen), *No Easy Day: The Firsthand Account of the Mission That Killed Osama Bin Laden* (New York: Dutton): 254.

287 *Panetta kept one hand in his pocket:* Leon Panetta, unpublished interview with *The New York Times*.

288–289 *he immediately ordered:* Peter Bergen, *Manhunt*, 235.

289 *There was a downed American helicopter:* Details about Mullen's conversation with Kayani come from two American officials with direct knowledge of what transpired during the phone call.

290 *a "military-aged male":* The rules governing CIA "signature strikes" were described by four American government officials.

292 *give him the chance:* Author interview with two American government officials.

292 *"No, Hillary," Panetta said:* Details of the fight during the National Security Council meeting come from two participants in the meeting.

293 *an attack against an American base:* Author interview with two American military officials.

294 *a particularly close relationship:* Declan Walsh, "US Bomb Warning to Pakistan Ignored," *The Guardian* (September 22, 2011).

294 *shrapnel killed an eight-year-old:* Ray Rivera and Sangar Rahimi, "Deadly Truck Bomb Hits NATO Outpost in Afghanistan," *The New York Times* (September 11, 2011).

295 *Afridi received an urgent call:* Afridi statement to Pakistani investigative group. Afridi's account has been independently confirmed by an American official with direct knowledge of Afridi's contacts with the CIA after the Abbottabad raid.

296 *the bus driver–cum–drug lord:* Court documents included in a memo from an assistant political agent in Khyber Agency to the senior superintendent of police, JIT, Special Branch, Peshawar. Documents obtained by author.

296 *Dr. Afridi was sentenced:* Ibid.

297 *because of his history:* Agence France Press, "Lashkar-I-Islami Denies Links with Shakil Afridi," May 31, 2012.

CHAPTER 16: FIRE FROM THE SKY

300 *carve out time to do something else:* Author interview with a former senior American official.

301 *"Often I know their background as intimately as I knew my students'":* Harold Koh, speech before the American Bar Association's Standing Committee on Law and National Security, December 2011.

303 *he was picked up multiple times:* Scott Shane and Souad Mekhennet, "From Condemning Terror to Preaching Jihad," *The New York Times* (May 8, 2010).

303 *who both prayed at his mosque:* Ibid.

303 *"the bridge between":* Ibid.

304 *he used Internet chat rooms:* Ibid.

304 *Abdulmutallab had written an essay:* Gregory Johnsen, *The Last Refuge: Yemen, al-Qaeda, and America's War in Arabia* (New York: W. W. Norton, 2012): 257.

305 *Brennan believed that al-Awlaki:* Johnsen, 262.

306 *"dancing in the snake pit":* "U.S. Intelligence on Arab Unrest Draws Criticism," Associated Press (February 6, 2011).

306 *where he spent hours in surgery:* BBC News, "Yemen: Saleh 'Gravely Wounded' in Rocket Attack," June 7, 2011.

306 *in the hope of intercepting e-mail traffic:* Author interview with a senior Pentagon official and a retired American counterterrorism official.

307 *"can't bomb moving targets":* SITE Intelligence Group, "Yemeni Journalist Documents Experiences with AQAP in Abyan," October 21, 2011.

308 *no human being will die:* Johnsen, 276.

309 *they worried that anyone suspected of helping:* Author interview with one current and two former American officials with knowledge of how the CIA handled its advanced warning about *Inspire.*

310 *"I'm going to find my father":* Author interview with Jameel Jaffer and Hina Shamsi, lawyers for the al-Awlaki family.

311 *al-Awlaki was sitting with friends:* Filing in the United States District Court for the District of Columbia in the case of *Nasser Al-Aulaqi et al. v. Leon C. Panetta et al.,* 13.

312 *"blood did not and will not go in vain":* Nasser al-Awlaki's video message can be seen at www.youtube.com/watch?v=9GHP5Rf7dbE.

314 *"You've got an intelligence agency":* Jameson's comments came during an open session of an American Bar Association conference.

314 *"Or whoever is left out there":* President Barack Obama, presidential press conference, December 8, 2011.

315 *The effort to bring clarity:* Scott Shane, "Election Spurred a Move to Codify U.S. Drone Policy," *The New York Times* (November 24, 2012).

315 *they supported the American government:* The poll for Amy Zegart was conducted by YouGov. The author is grateful to Professor Zegart for sharing the polling data.

315 *CIA officials hadn't learned of his death:* Mark Landler and Choe Sang-Hun, "In Kim Jong-Il Death, an Extensive Intelligence Failure," *The New York Times* (December 19, 2011).

316 *were beginning to stream through:* The description of the Benghazi attack comes primarily from a detailed timeline contained in the investigative report of the State Department's Accountability Review Board. Additional details came from interviews with several American officials.

318 *This just is not an intelligence mission:* Author interview with Ross Newland.

320 *it is no longer a stop for tourists:* The author is grateful to Timothy Pratt for his reporting from Indian Springs, Nevada.

BIBLIOGRAPHY

BOOKS

Bergen, Peter L. *The Longest War: The Enduring Conflict Between America and Al-Qaeda*. New York: Free Press 2011.

———. *Manhunt: The Ten-Year Search for Bin Laden—from 9/11 to Abbottabad*. New York: Crown, 2012.

Bissonnette, Matt (aka Mark Owen). *No Easy Day: The Firsthand Account of the Mission That Killed Osama Bin Laden*. New York: Dutton, 2012.

Boucek, Christopher, and Marina Ottaway. *Yemen on the Brink*. Washington, D.C.: Carnegie Endowment for International Peace, 2010.

Bowden, Mark. *Guests of the Ayatollah: The Iran Hostage Crisis: The First Battle in America's War with Militant Islam*. New York: Grove Press, 2006.

Clarke, Richard. *Against All Enemies: Inside America's War on Terror*. New York: Simon & Schuster, 2004.

Clarridge, Duane R., with Digby Diehl. *A Spy for All Seasons: My Life in the CIA*. New York: Scribner, 1997.

Coll, Steve. *Ghost Wars: The Secret History of the CIA, Afghanistan, and Bin Laden, from the Soviet Invasion to September 10, 2001*. New York: Penguin Books, 2004.

Crumpton, Henry A. *The Art of Intelligence: Lessons from a Life in the CIA's Clandestine Service*. New York: Penguin Press, 2012.

Emerson, Steven. *Secret Warriors: Inside the Covert Military Operations of the Reagan Era*. New York: Putnam, 1988.

Gardner, Richard N. *Mission Italy: On the Front Lines of the Cold War*. New York: Rowman & Littlefield Publishers, 2005.

Graham, Bradley. *By His Own Rules: The Ambitions, Successes, and Ultimate Failures of Donald Rumsfeld*. New York: Public Affairs, 2009.

Gunaratna, Rohan, and Khuram Iqbal. *Pakistan: Terrorism Ground Zero*. London: Reaktion Books, 2011.

Hull, Edmund J. *High Value Target: Countering al Qaeda in Yemen*. Washington, D.C.: Potomac Books, 2011.

Hussain, Zahid. *Frontline Pakistan: The Struggle with Militant Islam*. New York: Columbia University Press, 2008.

————. *The Scorpion's Tail: The Relentless Rise of Islamic Militants in Pakistan—and How It Threatens America*. New York: Free Press, 2010.

Johnsen, Gregory D. *The Last Refuge: Yemen, al-Qaeda, and America's War in Arabia*. New York: W. W. Norton & Company, 2012.

Jones, Seth. *Hunting in the Shadows: The Pursuit of al Qa'ida Since 9/11*. New York: W. W. Norton & Company, 2012.

Kean et al. *The 9/11 Commission Report*. Washington, D.C.: U.S. Government Printing Office, 2004.

Klaidman, Daniel. *Kill or Capture: The War on Terror and the Soul of the Obama Presidency*. New York: Houghton Mifflin Harcourt, 2012.

Martin, Matt J., and Charles W. Sasser. *Predator: The Remote-Control Air War over Iraq and Afghanistan: A Pilot's Story*. Minneapolis: Zenith Press, 2010.

Mayer, Jane. *The Dark Side: The Inside Story of How the War on Terror Turned into a War on American Ideals*. New York: Doubleday, 2008.

Musharraf, Pervez. *In the Line of Fire: A Memoir*. New York: Simon & Schuster, 2006.

Naftali, Timothy. *Blind Spot: The Secret History of American Counterterrorism*. New York: Basic Books, 2005.

Nawaz, Shuja. *Crossed Swords: Pakistan, Its Army, and the Wars Within*. Oxford: Oxford University Press, 2008.

Norris, Pat. *Watching Earth from Space: How Surveillance Helps Us—and Harms Us*. New York: Praxis, 2010.

Persico, Joseph. *Casey: The Lives and Secrets of William J. Casey: From the OSS to the CIA*. New York: Penguin, 1995.

Pillar, Paul R. *Intelligence and U.S. Foreign Policy: Iraq, 9/11, and Misguided Reform*. New York: Columbia University Press, 2011.

Priest, Dana, and William M. Arkin. *Top Secret America: The Rise of the New American Security State*. New York: Little, Brown and Company, 2011.

Ranelagh, John. *The Agency: The Rise and Decline of the CIA*. New York: Simon & Schuster, 1986.

Rashid, Ahmed. *Taliban: Militant Islam, Oil and Fundamentalism in Central Asia*. London: Yale University Press, 2001.

————. *Descent into Chaos: The U.S. and the Disaster in Pakistan, Afghanistan, and Central Asia*. New York: Viking, 2008.

Riedel, Bruce. *Deadly Embrace: Pakistan, America, and the Future of the Global Jihad*. Washington, D.C.: Brookings, 2011.

Rodriquez Jr., Jose A., and Bill Harlow. *Hard Measures: How Aggressive CIA Actions After 9/11 Saved American Lives*. New York: Threshold Editions, 2012.

Rohde, David, and Kristen Mulvihill. *A Rope and a Prayer: A Kidnapping from Two Sides*. New York: Viking, 2010.

Rumsfeld, Donald. *Known and Unknown: A Memoir*. New York: Sentinel, 2011.

Sanger, David E. *The Inheritance: The World Obama Confronts and the Challenges to American Power*. New York: Crown, 2009.

————. *Confront and Conceal: Obama's Secret Wars and Surprising Use of American Power*. New York: Crown, 2012.

Scarborough, Rowan. *Rumsfeld's War: The Untold Story of America's Anti-Terrorist Commander*. New York: Regnery, 2004.

Schmidt, John. *The Unraveling: Pakistan in the Age of Jihad*. New York: Farrar, Straus and Giroux, 2011.

Schmitt, Eric, and Thom Shanker. *Counterstrike: The Untold Story of America's Secret Campaign Against Al Qaeda*. New York: Times Books, 2011.

Shultz, Richard. *The Secret War Against Hanoi: The Untold Story of Spies, Saboteurs, and Covert Warriors in North Vietnam*. New York: HarperCollins, 1999.

Singer, Peter W. *Wired for War: The Robotics Revolution and Conflict in the 21st Century*. New York: Penguin Books, 2009.

Smith, Michael. *Killer Elite: The Inside Story of America's Most Secret Special Operations Team*. New York: St. Martin's Press, 2007.

Snider, L. Britt. *The Agency and the Hill: CIA's Relationship with Congress 1946–2004*. Washington, D.C.: Center for the Study of Intelligence, 2008.

Tenet, George. *At the Center of the Storm: My Years at the CIA*. New York: HarperCollins, 2007.

Waller, Douglas. *Wild Bill Donovan: The Spymaster Who Created the OSS and Modern American Espionage*. New York: Free Press, 2011.

Warrick, Joby. *The Triple Agent: The al-Qaeda Mole Who Infiltrated the CIA*. New York: Vintage Books, 2011.

Weiner, Tim. *Legacy of Ashes: The History of the CIA*. New York: Anchor Books, 2007.

Woodward, Bob. *Veil: The Secret Wars of the CIA, 1981–1987*. New York: Simon & Schuster, 1987.

————. *Bush at War*. New York: Simon & Schuster, 2002.

————. *Obama's Wars*. New York: Simon & Schuster, 2011.

Wright, Lawrence. *The Looming Tower: Al-Qaeda and the Road to 9/11*. New York: Random House, 2006.

SELECTED JOURNAL AND MAGAZINE ARTICLES

Baker, Aryn. "The Murky Past of the Pakistani Doctor Who Helped the CIA." *Time* (June 13, 2012).

Bamford, James. "He's in the Backseat!" *The Atlantic* (April 2006).

Chesney, Robert. "Military-Intelligence Convergence and the Law of the Title 10/Title 50 Debate." *Journal of National Security Law and Policy* (2012).

Ciralsky, Adam. "Tycoon, Contractor, Soldier, Spy." *Vanity Fair* (January 2010).

Fair, Christine C., and Seth Jones. "Pakistan's War Within." *Survival* 51, no. 6 (December 2009–January 2010).

Kibbe, Jennifer D. "The Rise of the Shadow Warriors." *Foreign Affairs* (March/April 2004).

Mayer, Jane. "The Predator War." *The New Yorker* (October 26, 2009).

McChrystal, Stanley A. "It Takes a Network." *Foreign Policy* (March/April 2011).

Pelton, Robert Young. "Erik Prince, an American Commando in Exile." *Men's Journal* (November 2010).

Pham, J. Peter. "Somali Instability Still Poses Threat Even After Successful Strike on Nabhan." *World Defense Review* (September 17, 2009).

Richelson, Jeffrey T. "Truth Conquers All Chains: The U.S. Army Intelligence Support Activity, 1981–1989." *International Journal of Intelligence and Counterintelligence* 12, no. 2 (1999).

———. "Task Force 157: The US Navy's Secret Intelligence Service 1966–77." *Intelligence and National Security* 11, no. 1 (January 1996).

Teague, Matthew. "Black Ops and Blood Money." *Men's Journal* (June 1, 2011).

Whittle, Richard. "Predator's Big Safari." Mitchell Institute for Airpower Studies, Paper 7 (August 2011).

Yousafzai, Sami. "The Doctor's Grim Reward." *Newsweek* (June 11, 2012).

Zelikow, Philip. "Codes of Conduct for a Twilight War." *Houston Law Review* (April 2012).

INDEX

Central Intelligence Agency (CIA), (*cont.*)
  Peshawar operations with Munir and ISI, 38–41
  poor communications with Pentagon, 18
  Predator drone program (*See* Predator drones)
  psychological operations of, 175–76
  reliance on foreign intelligence agencies, 26–29
  rifts within CIA over Afghanistan strategy, 32–33
  Rumsfeld critical of, 68–69
  secret war of, 11–17
  Somali warlords backed by, 137–43
  terrorism and, 53–57
  training philosophy of, 25–26
  U.S.C. Title 50 as governing authority, 76, 133, 287
  vaccination campaign spying operation, 279–84
  in Vietnam, 45
Chalabi, Ahmed, 199
Chamberlin, Wendy, 32, 33
Charlie Wilson's War (Grile), 131
Cheney, Dick, 13, 78, 122, 128, 156
  CIA's proposed plan for assassinations presented to, 9–10, 122
  criticizes Obama's ban of coercive interrogations, 218–19
  use of databases for information-mining and, 64–65
Church, Frank, 45–47
Church Committee, 45–46, 47, 88, 120, 282
Churchill, Winston, 6, 36–37
City Mayor (game), 186
Clarke, Richard, 88
  Predator drone program and, 89–93
Clarridge, Duane R., 50–51, 59, 60, 73, 199–211, 323–24, 326
  Bush, H. W.'s pardoning of, 199
  Counterterrorist Center proposal of, 55–57
  covert activities in Central America and, 50–51
  Nicaraguan mining operation and, 52
  private spying operations in Afghanistan of, 201–211
Clinton, Bill, 60, 61, 220
  bin Laden hunt and, 89
  lack of attention paid to intelligence issues by, 58–59

Clinton, Hillary, 238–39, 292
Clinton administration, 223
  lack of leads in hunting bin Laden, 89
CNN, 97, 100
Colby, William, 46
Cold War, 25, 175
Combating Terrorism Technical Support Office (CTTSO), 240–41
Contras, 51, 52–53
Costa Rica, 52
Counterterrorist Center (CTC), 10, 11–15
  creation of, 55–57
  expansion of, 11
  initial success in Afghanistan, 12–13
  "targeting" of foreign nationals, 14–15
covert operations. *See also* specific operations
  AfPax Insider project, 194–99
  of CIA, 43–61
  of Clarridge and Furlong in Afghanistan, 201–11
  legal authority for, 76–77
  of Pentagon, 63–82
Creech Air Force Base, 320–21
Cross Project, 45
Crumpton, Hank, 33, 125, 142–43
CTC. *See* Counterterrorist Center (CTC)
Cuba, 17, 46, 50–51
cycle of intelligence, 230
Czech Republic, 188–90

Daily Telegraph, The, 36
Damadola raid, 134–35
Dante Alighieri, 65
Darkazanli, Mamoun, 10
Datta Khel strike, 291
Davis, Perry, 239, 240–41, 247, 248, 250, 252
Davis, Raymond, 1–4, 257–59, 261–65, 272–76, 279, 290, 291, 327
Dearlove, Richard, 6–7
Defense Department. *See* Department of Defense
Defense Intelligence Agency, 314
defense secretary, legal powers and authority of, 75–77
Deininger, Bill, 247–48
Delta Force, 57, 64, 69, 75, 76, 129, 138, 149–50, 251
Department of Defense, 44. *See also* Pentagon